M000306667

Anglicans and the Roman Catholic Church

Anglicans and the Roman Catholic Church

Reflections on Recent Developments

Edited by Stephen E. Cavanaugh

IGNATIUS PRESS   SAN FRANCISCO

*Decree of the Congregation for the Doctrine of the Faith
on the Pastoral Provision*
© 1980 by Libreria Editrice Vaticana
Anglicanorum coetibus © 2009 by Libreria Editrice Vaticana
Reprinted with permission

Cover design by Riz Boncan Marsella

© 2011 by Ignatius Press, San Francisco
All rights reserved
ISBN 978-1-58617-499-6
Library of Congress Control Number 2010937201
Printed in the United States of America ∞

CONTENTS

PREFACE

Pope Benedict XVI's Anglican initiative embodied in the Apostolic Constitution *Anglicanorum coetibus* has caused some people to wonder, "Where did that come from?" The answer to that question lies in the experience of American and English Anglicans who have been the vanguard of seeking unity with the Holy See while retaining all that is good and noble in Anglicanism. With this volume, I seek to present the thought and experience of these Anglicans who, during the last thirty years, have sought closer communion with the Roman Catholic Church. Several of these essays were originally published in *Anglican Embers*, a journal that has been chronicling the historic developments between Catholic-leaning Anglicans and the Holy See. Some of the authors played a key role in the discussions that ultimately led to Pope Benedict XVI's Apostolic Constitution *Anglicanorum coetibus*. Others contributed to the ground-breaking efforts by recording their own experiences of entering the Roman Catholic Church.

The essays by Father Aidan Nichols, Father John Hunwicke, and David Burt, as well as my own, looked forward to a change in the legal status of the Anglican Use within the Catholic Church that was made possible by the 1980 Pastoral Provision of John Paul II. Because of both the possibilities and the limitations of that provision, much reflection was still needed and these essays pointed the way toward a fuller inclusion of the Anglican heritage within the Roman Church.

While the Pastoral Provision enabled parishes from the Episcopal Church to enter the Catholic Church corporately, retaining some elements of their liturgical heritage, the Pastoral Provision lacked hierarchical, liturgical, social, and spiritual elements needed to preserve the Anglican patrimony in the Catholic Church. Each Anglican Use parish, as one parish among many in its given diocese, had no official relationship with the other Anglican Use parishes. The Book of Divine Worship (BDW), even with all of the elements of Anglican piety and worship that it did preserve, was still a product of its time, the early 1980s, when the English translation of the liturgy in the Roman Rite was still in transition, and some of the rites in the BDW reflect that. With no way to train priests and deacons in the traditions of Anglican liturgy and spirituality, the outlook for preserving this patrimony within the Catholic Church looked as if it would not be able to last beyond the initial generation of Anglicans who entered into full communion. Pope Benedict XVI's Apostolic Constitution *Anglicanorum coetibus* addresses all of these shortcomings and extends this opening to Anglicans seeking communion with the Holy See to the entire world.

Given that there is still much work and prayer to be done in order to bring about the unity that the Lord intends for his Church, I have gathered these important essays in a single volume. It is my hope that Anglicans and Roman Catholics will continue to build upon the foundation that has already been laid.

Stephen E. Cavanaugh
Editor, *Anglican Embers*
December 23, 2010

INTRODUCTION

Father Allan R. G. Hawkins

Ecclesia Anglicana had flourished for perhaps thirteen hundred years before the events of the Reformation created what we now call Anglicanism—a phenomenon that cannot be understood without reference to its ancient spiritual and cultural heritage, even though the separation of the Church of England from the rest of Western Christendom inevitably introduced a schismatic quality to even the best of Anglican thought.

The English Reformation, unlike the parallel movements elsewhere in Europe, was not a single, cataclysmic event, but rather a process that unfolded over more than a century—from Henry VIII's Act of Supremacy of 1534 to the reestablishment of the Church of England with the restoration of the Stuart monarchy in the person of King Charles II in 1660.

A striking feature of this process is the frequency with which the phrase "until further order to be taken", or similar terminology, is to be found in the parliamentary enactments, legal documents, and Orders in Council of the period. In other words, each step of the reform was understood to be *provisional*, of temporary application, until further developments unfolded, until some ultimate denouement be attained.

In every subsequent century, that longed-for denouement has been seen—by at least some—to be the restoration of Catholic unity and peace for the Church. Thus Bishop Lancelot Andrewes, in his *Preces Privatae*, would pray each Sunday: "O let the heart and soul of all believers again become one", and, each Monday, "For the Universal Church, its confirmation and growth. For the Eastern Church, its deliverance and unity. For the Western Church, its restoration and pacification."

On the day of his appointment to Canterbury in 1633, Rome was ready to offer a cardinal's hat to Archbishop William Laud. At the time of the restoration of the monarchy twenty-seven years later, Charles II appears to have sought the formation of a Uniate status for the Church of England. In the eighteenth century, there were some reunion activities—notably the correspondence between Archbishop Wake and certain doctors at the Sorbonne in Paris with regard to the possibility of union between the Anglican and Gallican churches. The nineteenth century brought the Oxford Movement, and all that stemmed from it. The twentieth century saw the Malines Conversations and then the inauguration, by the Archbishop of Canterbury, Michael Ramsey, and Pope Paul VI in 1967 of the Anglican–Roman Catholic International Commission (ARCIC).

Notwithstanding the early achievement of understanding in the long-controversial areas of Eucharist, ministry, and authority, the bright hope that the inauguration of ARCIC originally inspired quickly gave way to the bleak reality of the implications of the pressure for the ordination of women—first to the priesthood and then to the episcopate—in the Church of England and elsewhere in the Anglican Communion. Pope John Paul II and Cardinal Jan Willebrands, then-president of the Council for Promoting Christian Unity, expressed to Archbishop Robert Runcie their profound concern that the course on which Anglicanism was embarked—destroying, as it would, the integrity of its sacramental system—would effectively put an end to the hope of reconciliation. Sometime later,

Cardinal Walter Kasper said that the ordination of women to the episcopate "signified a breaking away from apostolic tradition and a further obstacle for reconciliation between the Catholic Church and the Church of England". Sadly, indeed, Anglicanism chose to proceed on what has proved to be a self-destructive path, and to ignore the imperative of that unity which the Lord wills for his Church "so that the world may believe".

Many Anglicans, however, were unable to abandon that vision and the obedience it demanded. Thus, in 1977, Father James Parker, on behalf of some members of the American Province of the Society of the Holy Cross (*Societas Sanctae Crucis*) presented to the Holy See their petition to be allowed to be ordained to the Catholic priesthood with a dispensation from the law of celibacy, following entry into full communion.

The Society of the Holy Cross had been founded in London in 1855. Its membership is comprised of Anglican bishops and priests who live under a Rule and who desire to bear witness to the Cross of Christ in their vocation and ministry within the Church and their whole lives. The achievement of Catholic unity has long been among its principal objectives.

In the same year, in a parallel initiative, Canon Albert J. duBois, accompanied by two other Episcopal priests, Father W. T. St. John Brown and Father John Barker, traveled to Rome where, with the help of the late Monsignor Richard Schuler, they met with Cardinal Franjo Seper, the prefect of the Congregation for the Doctrine of the Faith (whose English secretary at the time was Monsignor William Levada). They asked for ordination as Catholic priests and the establishment of their parishes with special liturgical customs deriving from the Anglican tradition.

The eventual outcome of these initiatives was the establishment by Pope John Paul II, in the summer of 1980, of a special "Pastoral Provision" which—although rejecting the idea of any kind of "ritual diocese"—made possible the erection, within existing dioceses in the United States, of "personal parishes" for former Episcopalians and Anglicans, who, in full communion with the Holy See, could pray, worship, and celebrate the sacraments within the Anglican-derived ethos of the Book of Divine Worship. William Oddie noted in his book *The Roman Option* that what had been accomplished "was a small step towards the dream of an Anglicanism" which the Malines Conversations of sixty years earlier had foreseen as " 'united not absorbed'; but it was real enough for those who became involved in it." [1]

As Henry Brandreth noted in his *Œcumenical Ideals of the Oxford Movement*, there is scarcely a generation from the time of the Reformation to our own day which has not caught, whether perfectly or imperfectly, the vision of a reunited Christendom. [2]

So it was that a further, very important initiative was undertaken in 1993. In October of that year, Bishop Clarence Pope, then–Episcopal Bishop of Fort Worth, went to Rome with Cardinal Bernard Law, then–Archbishop of Boston and ecclesiastical delegate for the Pastoral Provision, to meet with the Congregation for the Doctrine of the Faith. They took with them a preparatory document, drawn up by two noted Anglican theologians, Doctor Wayne Hankey and Father Jeffrey Steenson. This stated, in part, that

> we believe that a truly historic opportunity now presents itself, namely, for the healing of the great Western schism, in a way which few envisioned. The Anglican Church is

---

[1] William Oddie, *The Roman Option: The Realignment of English Christianity* (London: HarperCollins, 1997), p. 78.

[2] Henry R. T. Brandreth, *Œcumenical Ideals of the Oxford Movement* (London: SPCK, 1947), p. 2.

not the only church of the Reformation to be breaking up, foundering on the rocks of post-modern secularism it has no power to avoid. We now believe there is little hope that the Anglican Communion as presently constituted, will ever be able to move toward corporate reunion with the Catholic Church. The hopes we had placed in the official conversations of the Anglican-Roman Catholic International Commission must now find their fulfilment in some other form.[3]

In the light of subsequent developments, it is of the greatest interest to note that the immediate response was one of generous and full agreement. It was, very evidently, a providential moment; and it was recognized that solutions to the concrete theological, liturgical, and juridical problems must be sought and found. In the light of the underlying agreement in faith this could not be impossible. It was essential to move forward with patience, courage, and tolerance, to define the appropriate juridical structure and to define its details.

And now, at the beginning of the twenty-first century, we welcome the bright promise of the Apostolic Constitution *Anglicanorum coetibus*, the fruit of the patience and courage of Pope Benedict XVI, who has now provided the most generous and pastoral welcome to those who come from the Anglican patrimony. As Bishop Peter Elliott, Auxiliary Bishop of Melbourne, has recently said: "Anglicans can longer speak of 'swimming the Tiber'. Pope Benedict XVI has built a noble bridge. . . . The Tiber crossings of those Anglicans who have gone before us were often difficult and dangerous—and, in any event, it has proven difficult

---

[3] Doctor Wayne Hankey and Father Jeffrey Steenson, "An Approach to the Holy See by Certain Members of the Anglican Church", 4, cited by Oddie, *The Roman Option*, p. 242.

to organize a group swim. Not only is the Holy Father's bridge a noble construction that lifts us high above the perilous waters, it allows us to pass over the deep without breaking ranks." [4]

The word "provisional" can be misleading. As used above, in reference to the stages of the Reformation process in England, it implies a temporary and insubstantial quality. But in the title of the Pastoral Provision of Pope John Paul II for the Anglican Usage of the Roman Rite, it has a very different meaning: it is that which is "provided"—a provision now enlarged and enhanced in the Apostolic Constitution of Benedict XVI. Its purpose is not limited to the perpetuation of a particular liturgy and liturgical style, important though that element of it is. More important, perhaps, is the preservation of a uniquely beautiful spirituality—gentle and pastoral—which, with the lovely cultural tradition that comes with it, is our heritage from *Ecclesia Anglicana* and which we bring home with joy to the Catholic Church. It is this story, this blessed inheritance, that is examined and celebrated in the essays in this book. So, in the words of one of the figures of the Oxford Movement, Isaac Williams, in his 1842 poem *The Baptistery*:

> This union in His Church is God's own gift,
> Not to be seiz'd by man's rude sinful hands,
> But the bright crown of mutual holiness.

The Reverend Allan R. G. Hawkins was ordained as a priest in the Church of England. In 1980, he was named rector of the Episcopal parish of Saint Bartholomew (later renamed

---

[4] Bishop Peter J. Elliott, address given to Forward in Faith Australia at All Saints', Kooyong, Melbourne, on February 13, 2010, as reported by *inter alia*, the Anglo-Catholic blog.

Saint Mary the Virgin) in Arlington, Texas. In 1991, the parish decided to leave the Episcopal Church and to seek full communion in the Roman Catholic Church as a personal parish for the Anglican Use, under terms of the Pastoral Provision of 1980. Members were all received and Saint Mary the Virgin was formally erected as a parish of the Catholic Diocese of Fort Worth on June 12, 1994. Bishop Delaney ordained Father Hawkins to the Catholic priesthood on June 29, 1994, and he has continued as pastor to this day. Father Hawkins is married to Jose and they have two grown children.

HISTORY

Chapter 1

A History of the Pastoral Provision for Roman Catholics in the USA

Father Jack D. Barker

On August 20, 1980, Archbishop of San Francisco John R. Quinn gave the world the first knowledge of the existence of a "Pastoral Provision" that had been approved by Rome through the efforts of the Congregation for the Doctrine of the Faith. The decree of the Congregation was approved by Pope John Paul II on June 20, 1980, and communicated the next month to Archbishop Quinn as the president of the National Conference of Catholic Bishops in a letter from the Congregation's prefect, Cardinal Franjo Seper, dated July 22, 1980 (Appendix B). This decree was for the benefit of Episcopalians seeking full communion with the Catholic Church in the United States. The effect of this decree was to allow a means by which Episcopalians could become Roman Catholic, while at the same time retaining some of their traditions, including liturgy and married priests. In private conversation the night before the press release, Archbishop Quinn, when he had finished reading the decree, said: "I'm not sure what all this means." Such ambiguity would be repeated in the years that followed, resulting in an inconsistent application of the Pastoral Provision.

This momentous decree has been poorly understood and has received mixed responses from both Roman Catholics and Episcopalians. A great deal of attention was given to the idea that some married Episcopal priests could become Roman Catholic priests and retain their wives and the married life. The possible effects of this decree are of far greater historical consequence than merely the issue of married priests. The approval of the Pastoral Provision raised questions concerning its effect on ecumenical relations in the post–Vatican II world, not only between Episcopalians and the Roman Catholic Church, but also between Anglicans in England and the Catholic Church. The advent of this decree also represented another development in the relationship between the Roman Catholic Church in the United States and the Vatican. Depending on one's point of view, this decree may be seen as another event in the one-hundred-year-old history of tension between conservative and progressive elements within the Catholic Church.

To understand the context of the Pastoral Provision, one should return to the nineteenth century. In the closing decades of that century, the "social gospel" was very much a part of Church life both in the Catholic Church on the Continent and among Anglicans in England. This era is the time of Pusey, Keble, and Newman, who were part of the Tractarian[1] or Oxford Movement in England. Several causes contributed to the growth of the Oxford Movement: the progressive decline of church life and the spread of liberalism in theology. Among the more immediate causes were fears that the "Catholic Emancipation Act" of 1829 would lead many Anglicans into the Roman Catholic Church. Keble's sermon on "National Apostasy" and

---

[1] "Tractarian" is the name for the earlier stages of the Oxford Movement within the Church of England, which aimed at restoring the High Church ideals of the seventeenth century. The name derived from the use of tracts or pamphlets written to disseminate Church of England principles "Against Popery and Dissent".

Newman's writings are usually regarded as the beginning of the Movement.

Oxford Movement

A review of the whole process by which Newman ultimately became a Catholic demonstrates that he became increasingly convinced that only one Church could claim historic catholicity, and the Church of England should necessarily be a part of that historic Church. Newman's *Apologia Pro Vita Sua* was his attempt to explain his conversion to a world that little understood why he had "Poped". It is also worth noting that Newman's *Development of Christian Doctrine* and *Grammar of Assent* are classics that anticipated many of the teachings of Vatican II a hundred years later. Newman's early days were spent at Oxford as the Anglican vicar of Saint Mary's Church; it was here that Newman began to write tracts. The development of his thinking is seen in the tracts he began writing, the most notable of which was Tract 90.[2] The storm which this publication provoked brought the series of tracts to a close. By this time, not just Newman, but also many Anglicans had come to hold to a Catholic interpretation of history, doctrine, and Scripture. While this trend of Catholic thought led to Newman's conversion, others remained behind to work "from within" for the conversion of the Church of England to its Catholic roots.

---

[2] Tract 90 was entitled "Remarks on Certain Passages in the Thirty-Nine Articles". This tract was designed to give an explanation of the "Thirty-Nine Articles" of the Church of England from the theological viewpoint of one who holds to Catholic doctrine. These articles were doctrinal formulations accepted by the Church of England to define its dogmatic position in relation to the controversies of the sixteenth century.

Among those who remained Anglican, but who were sympathetic to the "Catholic position" were Edward Bouverie Pusey and John Keble. They were also a part of the Oxford Movement. It was from among these and similarly minded clergy that the Church Union, later the English Church Union, was formed. The English Church Union may then be seen as a child of the Oxford Movement. At the beginning of the twentieth century, this movement spread to the United States, as did the Church Union, which in this country became known as the American Church Union (ACU). These groups experienced rapid growth until the outbreak of the First World War. The intervening Great Depression and Second World War prevented significant further growth of the movement among the clergy. To broaden its base of influence, the American Church Union opened its membership to include the laity during the thirties.

American Roots

After the Second World War, the Reverend Albert Julius duBois, formerly a chaplain in Patton's army, and a rector of the Episcopalian Church of Saint Agnes in Washington, D.C., was elected to be the first full-time executive director of the American Church Union (ACU). Father duBois, a canon of the Episcopal cathedral in Garden City, Long Island, New York, led the American Church Union until his retirement in 1974. The ACU, while not the only organization of Catholic-minded Episcopalians, was the largest and most active in the country, and, in fact, the largest unofficial organization in the Episcopal Church.

As events unfolded in the Episcopal Church, many members of the ACU became increasingly alarmed. Strong forces for change in a liberal Protestant direction predominated in the governing bodies of the Episcopal Church. At the General Conventions[3] of 1970 and 1973, the Protestant Episcopal Church in the United States of America (PECUSA) changed its canons regarding the church's law on divorce, refused to take a firm public stance against abortion, ordained women to the diaconate, and pursued a wide spectrum of changes in its Book of Common Prayer. It was feared that the 1976 General Convention might proceed to the ordination of women to the priesthood and radical Prayer Book[4] revision. Accordingly, Canon duBois was asked to come out of retirement and lead the ACU once again. While the ACU continued with its own executive director, Canon duBois worked closely with the new leadership in fundraising and also founded Episcopalians United (EU). Episcopalians United published a daily newsletter during the General Convention promoting a position of maintaining an option for Catholic faith and practice in the Episcopal Church.

By way of background, it should be noted that Anglicanism has varieties of theological persuasions from liberal to conservative generally tolerated so long as unity of worship is maintained. The Elizabethan settlement had resulted in a church that very much lived *lex orandi, lex credendi.*[5] Without the teaching Magisterium of the Roman Catholic Church, the commonality of worship through the use of various Books of Common Prayer became the earmark of unity in the various Anglican churches throughout the world, in the face of what would otherwise have been certain disunity. This theological diversity was possible as long as there

---

[3] The General Convention is the legal arm and constitutive body of the Episcopal Church in the United States and determines its policies and polity.

[4] The Book of Common Prayer of the Episcopal Church in the United States is both a sign and source of unity of worship for the entire Episcopal Church.

[5] The law of worship is the law of belief.

was a degree of liturgical similarity guaranteed by the use of similar Books of Common Prayer. Liturgical similarity was especially helpful in maintaining a unity that could not be enforced by authoritarian structures, as each province was autonomous.

It had always been the hope of Catholic-minded Anglicans that a full-scale corporate reunion or intercommunion could ultimately take place between the Episcopal Church and the Roman Catholic Church. In short, it was hoped that the Church of England (now including the worldwide Anglican Communion) might once again return to the unity it had experienced prior to the Reformation. Catholic-minded Episcopalians kept in mind the twelve hundred years of Catholic history and teaching in England prior to the break with Rome, and this, therefore, was the basis of their hope for reunion.

General Convention 1976

Such was not to happen. The Episcopal Church proceeded with its agenda of change. The General Convention operated with a simple democratic majority to make irreversible changes to the doctrine, discipline, and worship of the Episcopal Church. The objection of the ACU and of Episcopalians United (and its successor, Anglicans United) to the actions of the General Convention was that these were based on a lack of proper authority and that such moves would set back hopes for reunion with Rome indefinitely. The tide of change could not be held back. The Prayer Book revisions were seen as diluting its doctrinal base, and the ordinations of women were seen as not acceptable to either the Roman Catholic Church or the Orthodox churches and, therefore, would risk setting back ecumenical relations for years; even the position on abortion was altered and weakened. It should be noted that every poll of Episcopalians showed that the majority were opposed to these changes. It was perceived that a Catholicism without Rome and opposed to Rome required too great a compromise of conscience; it was also thought that the new openness and renewal of the Roman Catholic Church since the Second Vatican Council eliminated many of the previously held concerns of Catholic-minded Anglicans. For many, it seemed that continued separation could not be tolerated.

Following the 1976 General Convention of the PECUSA, the daily newspaper of Episcopalians United called for a "Plan of Action", allowing Catholic-minded Episcopalians to find a source of unity outside the official structures of the Episcopal Church in the US. The possibility of some Episcopalians leaving "The Church" created a stir in the House of Bishops and upset some members of the ACU. Many individuals and whole parish groups began to leave the Episcopal Church following that convention. The first entire parish to leave was Saint Mary's in Denver, led by their rector, Father James Mote. For many, Catholic conscience had been stretched beyond what was acceptable and hopes for Catholic reunion were lost. It was unlikely that Rome would move so quickly on what many viewed as radical reinterpretations of ministry and faith. The sense of loss felt by many in the Episcopal Church at that time cannot be underestimated: some died of "broken hearts"; some clergy retired, rather than face an uncertain future. Many were angered by what they felt had been a forced movement on the part of PECUSA away from its traditional role as the "Bridge Church" between Rome and Protestantism. Progressive members of the Episcopal Church were amazed that "High Church" or Catholic-minded members would actually consider breaching the Church's unity, especially in the light of widely held adherence to the "branch theory" among these same Episcopalians, i.e., why leave one part of the Catholic Church for another since each part is incomplete without the other?[6]

A cautionary letter that had been sent to the Episcopal Church by Pope Paul VI well before the convention took place indicated that serious damage could be done to ecumenical relations if PECUSA proceeded with the ordination of women to the priesthood. This letter, however, was withheld from the convention delegates. Following the events of the convention, Rome released the contents of the letter to the press. Many in PECUSA felt betrayed and manipulated.

While still in Minneapolis, the site of the 1976 General Convention, Canon duBois was introduced to sympathetic Roman Catholic clergy. After writing an initial letter to Rome, he was invited to go in person to visit the Holy See. Now the door was open to present both the dilemma and hope for finding a new home for priests and people. Many of the ACU clergy felt that Rome would either not give a positive response, or would take too long to respond to the pastoral need. Given that many of these clergy held to the "branch theory" of Catholicism, Canon duBois was pressured to make contacts with the Polish National Catholic Church and the Antiochian Orthodox Church. Both of these churches had received Episcopalians before and as a result had existing procedures and structures in place for that purpose. Subsequent research substantiated that neither group would foster closer unity with the See of Peter.

---

[6] The "branch theory" of the Church is an Anglican idea that came out of the Oxford Movement. It holds that Rome, Canterbury, Constantinople, and the Apostolic Sees are "branches" of the one Church of Christ; valid branches are churches that maintain apostolic succession of ministry and the faith of the undivided Church. The acceptance of this theology was implicit in the original "Plan of Action".

Diocese of the Holy Trinity

As a consequence, the Diocese of the Holy Trinity was formed out of parishes that had already severed ties with the Episcopal Church. It was the presence of a "corpus" of laity and clergy—Vatican representatives made clear—that gave them a different status for the conversations concerning admission into the full communion of the Catholic Church. Presumably, any individuals or groups of Episcopalians who had not severed ties with the official Episcopal Church would be required to work through the already existing channels in the ecumenical dialogue between the Episcopal Church and the Roman Catholic Church, which operated out of the Secretariat for Christian Unity. Whereas, a "corpus" of those without official ties to the existing Episcopal Church were allowed to deal directly with the Congregation for the Doctrine of the Faith. It should be noted, however, that the leadership of those seeking corporate reunion with Rome maintained cordial relations with the leadership of the Episcopal Church at the national level, meeting on more than one occasion with the Presiding Bishop of the Episcopal Church and a special ad hoc committee of the House of Bishops of the Episcopal Church. The leadership of the Episcopal Church recognized, as a result of these meetings, that those seeking reunion with Rome were doing so as a matter of faith and conscience and that they did not in any way wish to hamper the existing, official, and ongoing ecumenical dialogue.

Pro-Diocese of Saint Augustine of Canterbury (PDSAC)

Many other groups who had varying degrees of dissatisfaction with the Episcopal Church were active at the same

time. The umbrella organization for them was the Fellow-
ship of Concerned Churchmen (FCC). The Diocese of the
Holy Trinity joined the FCC and attended its September
1977 meeting in Saint Louis, Missouri. This meeting in Saint
Louis produced a loose amalgamation of several groups into
the Anglican Church in North America (ACNA), and this
was destined to become a new "Anglican" church in the
United States and Canada. Some of the members of the
Diocese of the Holy Trinity identified with the aims of the
FCC as it moved toward founding the ACNA. Canon duBois
and the Anglicans United (successor to Episcopalians United)
did not. Those in the Diocese of the Holy Trinity who
agreed with the aims of ACNA kept the name "Diocese of
the Holy Trinity" and remained with them. Those who
desired reunion with Rome then formed the Pro-Diocese
of Saint Augustine of Canterbury (PDSAC) to act as the
"corpus" for transitional jurisdiction to full unity with the
Roman Catholic Church. Catholic life requires a bishop as
the center of unity for a diocese. As indicative of the tension between the two factions of the clergy regarding the
role of a bishop, a question was put to the bishop-elect
regarding whether he would be willing to pursue reunion
with Rome. It was the strong negative response to this question that resulted in the splitting of the Diocese of the Holy
Trinity.

Society of the Holy Cross

One of the groups supporting the FCC that was important in
these unfolding events was the American branch of the Society of the Holy Cross (*Societas Sanctae Crucis*, SSC). This group,
the oldest Catholic-minded clerical society in the Church of
England, founded in 1855, was designed to promote a higher

standard for priestly life among the English clergy. In later years, it was openly dedicated to corporate reunion with the Holy See. The society has chapters throughout the Anglican Communion, and its members are governed by a Rule of Life that includes the Daily Prayers of the Church (Liturgy of the Hours), annual retreats, regular confession, and daily Mass. It may be said that such a concept was indeed a by-product of the Oxford Movement among Anglican clergy such as Pusey, Keble, and Lowder, who remained behind when Newman converted. The American branch of the society was led by the Reverend James Parker, of Albany, Georgia, as its provincial, while the master of the society was in England. In the days following the General Convention of 1976, at a provincial meeting of the society held at Saint Anselm's Episcopal Church, Park Ridge, Illinois, the members asked the Provincial to contact the apostolic delegate of the Roman Catholic Church to see if it might be possible for married Episcopal priests to be received into the Catholic Church and still function as priests.

Father Parker was contacted by Bishop Bernard Law of Springfield Cape-Girardeaux, Missouri (later Cardinal Archbishop of Boston), who said he would speak to the apostolic delegate to the United States, Archbishop Jean Jadot, to make it easier to get an appointment. He also referred him to Bishop Raymond Lessard of the Diocese of Savannah, Georgia, for personal contact. It should be noted that both Bishops Law and Lessard were members of the National Conference of Catholic Bishops (NCCB) Ad Hoc Committee, formed to deal with the question of receiving convert married ministers into the Catholic Church.[7] Bishop

---

[7] In 1967, an enquiry from the American bishops regarding a married Lutheran minister received a negative response from Rome. From 1967 to 1975, the question of ordaining convert married ministers was considered

Law was also the only American member of the Vatican
Secretariat for Christian Unity. A meeting took place at
the Archbishop's residence in Washington, D.C., in April
1977. At this meeting were Father James Parker, the provincial of the society; Father Larry Lossing of New Smyrna
Beach, Florida, representing southeast members of the society; and Father Jack D. Barker of Los Angeles, California,
representing the west coast members of the society. The
meeting was to explore what possibilities there might be
for receiving Episcopal priests of this society into the Roman
Catholic Church; the stated goal was to be able to continue to function as Roman Catholic priests, even if married. At the meeting, Archbishop Jadot stated that ultimately
this question would have to be resolved in Rome. The meeting held with Archbishop Jadot was reported to Rome and
to the NCCB. In a chronology of events, it is important to
understand that the SSC group was the first to approach
the American Roman Catholic hierarchy, whereas, the Diocese of the Holy Trinity (later PDSAC) was the first to
approach the authorities in Rome.[8] The work of the NCCB
on this question became specific due to the requests of these
two groups.

The first discussions among the American Roman Catholic bishops specifically relative to receiving married Episcopal clergy took place at the NCCB meeting in May 1977.
The bishops discussed this idea; nevertheless, the authority

inopportune. The issue was raised again at the Administrative Committee of
the Conference of Bishops at its September 1976 meeting, at which time an
"Ad Hoc Committee" was formed to study the question of receiving convert married ministers.

[8] It should be noted that Canon duBois did have a meeting with Archbishop Bernardine of Chicago prior to the 1976 General Convention in which
he informed him of the increasing interest among Catholic-minded Episcopalians
of becoming Roman Catholic.

for the final decision on the Pastoral Provision had to come from Rome. Past requests from the NCCB to ordain married convert clerics had been denied by Rome.[9]

Rome 1977

In the fall of 1977, Canon duBois, ecumenical officer of PDSAC, was to have met with the Sacred Congregation for the Doctrine of the Faith (SCDF). Due to illness, Father W. T. Brown, as deputy ecumenical officer, and Father Jack D. Barker, as president of the Clergy Senate, represented Canon duBois in Rome. While en route, these representatives met in England for extensive conversations with Bishop Howe, the secretary-general of the Anglican Consultative Council (ACC).[10] In addition, meetings were held with the representative of the Archbishop of Canterbury at Lambeth Palace. The talks at Lambeth and with Bishop Howe were to explore the possibility of some parallel jurisdiction for Catholic-minded Episcopalians within the Anglican Communion.

As a consequence of the meetings in England, it became apparent that the Anglican Communion had taken steps away from its commitment to a traditional understanding of the authority of Scripture, tradition, and the recognized councils of Catholic history. The Right Reverend John Maurin Allin, the Presiding Bishop of the Episcopal Church, had indicated in conversations with Father Brown that some sort of parallel jurisdiction might be possible for those Episcopal

[9] See note 7 above.

[10] The Anglican Consultative Council consists of member bishops from all of the provinces of the worldwide Anglican Communion of churches. It is perhaps the most powerful guiding body in Anglicanism, even though it has no direct juridical control over the member provinces.

priests, people, and parishes who had left the jurisdiction of PECUSA. But, after the London meetings, it was concluded that such a parallel jurisdiction was not possible.[11]

Upon arrival of the delegates to Rome, meetings were held with Cardinal Franjo Seper, prefect for the SCDF; other cardinal prefects of Congregations; the apostolic nuncio to Italy; the vicar-general for Vatican City; a representative of the Secretariat for Promoting Christian Unity; and the president of the Works for Religion. The delegates were graciously received in every case.

The principal conversations were held with Cardinal Seper at the offices of the Congregation near Saint Peter's Basilica. The substance of the meetings with Cardinal Seper was a proposal for consideration of what later became the Pastoral Provision, i.e., the possibility of Episcopalians returning to the Catholic Church while retaining something of their Anglican heritage. This proposal was presented to Cardinal Seper at the second meeting held at the Holy Office. The proposal kept in mind as much as possible the faith position of those who were represented, i.e., complete agreement in almost all areas of Catholic faith and morals, with incomplete agreement on the so-called Petrine and Marian dogmas. The proposal was received by the Cardinal with great interest. The restoration of separated Western Christians was an idea very dear to the heart of Cardinal Seper.

Before leaving Rome, confidential letters from the delegation were mailed to Bishop Albert Chambers, the retired Episcopal bishop of Springfield, Illinois, and Father James Mote, bishop-elect for the Diocese of the Holy Trinity. Bishop Chambers was scheduled to be the chief consecrator at the ordination to the episcopate of four Episcopalian

---

[11] The representatives were told that the Anglican Communion could no longer be a proper home for the faith they and their people professed.

priests, including Father Mote, which would inaugurate the new Anglican Church in North America (ACNA) as planned by the FCC. In those letters, both were advised of the results of the Rome meetings and that Rome would see those planned ordinations as a serious obstacle to reunion.

Two weeks after returning from Rome, the delegates spoke at a joint synod of the priests of the Anglican Dioceses[12] of the Holy Trinity and Christ the King, on December 15, 1977. Bishop Chambers presided at this meeting and allowed less than ten minutes for the report on the meetings held in England and Rome. It seemed apparent to all present that the Bishop was not interested. For example, he said, "Your people don't want to be Roman Catholics." This sentiment was echoed by Bishops-elect Mote (of Denver) and Morse (of Oakland). Bishop Chambers continued to plan for the consecrations to take place in January 1978.[13]

Chicago 1978

Bishop Bernard Law invited Fathers Barker and Brown to meet with a canonist in Chicago to explore together the form of an Anglican "common identity" in the Catholic Church. In addition to the above, representatives of SSC

---

[12] Anglican dioceses are those belonging to the new ACNA formed by the FCC; it refers to their heritage, ministry, and use of worship and not to any direct communion with the Anglican Archbishop of Canterbury from whom they have no official recognition at this time.

[13] The reality of such an anti-Catholic stance should not have been surprising. During the nineteenth century, some Anglicans argued that Catholics, who were considering the dogma of the Immaculate Conception, worshipped Mary. In his 1851 lectures, Newman referred to this as an example of how deeply ingrained were the prejudices of the English, including Anglo-Catholics, against Rome.

and the Evangelical Catholic Mission (ECM)[14] were also
invited by Bishop Law. The three groups met with Bishop
Law's canonist at the Hilton Hotel at O'Hare Airport. The
Anglicans present favored the proposal on structure mod-
eled on the military ordinariate, but the small number of
parochial communities, the death of Cardinal Seper, who
had taken a personal interest in this cause, together with
the reluctance on the part of the American Catholic hierarchy mitigated against such a possibility at that time.[15] The
report which came out of that meeting was submitted to
Bishop Kelly (secretary of the NCCB) by Father Bowen,
the canonist. Bishop Kelly, in turn, submitted the report to
the Vatican; the report also served as the basis for discussion
at the executive session of the NCCB that followed in May
1978. It was at this meeting that Bishop Law spoke favor-
ably to the question. It has been reported that the bishops
of the NCCB likewise gave a favorable response. The PDSAC
was informed by Bishop Law that the president of the
NCCB, Archbishop John R. Quinn of San Francisco, would
now be the liaison for the NCCB relative to the Pastoral
Provision.[16]

It was necessary to clarify the desires of those Anglicans
seeking union with the Holy See. Given that the positive

---

[14] The ECM group was composed of about thirty-five Episcopal bishops,
over one hundred priests, and over one thousand laity, led by Father Clarence Pope of Baton Rouge, Louisiana. They were organized as a "loyal oppo-
sition" to the changes in the Episcopal Church. At the Chicago meeting, a
priest representing Father Pope stated that retention of married bishops was
a necessary feature for Anglican-Catholic reunion.

[15] The decree on the Pastoral Provision that later came out leaves open
the possibility of alternate forms of structure to the one that was recom-
mended by the NCCB consequent to the report of this meeting.

[16] PDSAC maintained contact by mail with the SCDF in Rome, as requested
by its prefect, but the deaths of two popes in late 1978 curtailed meaningful
exchange with that Congregation.

conversations held with the SCDF were predicated upon the premise of an existing corpus, an international synod of the pro-diocese was convened in February 1979 at San Antonio, Texas. The conversations in Rome later that year indicated that those seeking reunion needed to be clear about their legitimate patrimony; therefore a symposium of Anglican and Roman scholars was held at the University of Dallas in June of the same year. The features of an Anglican patrimony were the subject of that symposium.

Rome 1979

The same leadership of the Diocese of the Holy Trinity that had been to Rome in 1977 were invited back for another series of meetings in the fall of 1979.[17] A formal meeting took place at the SCDF on October 30, 1979. Representing the SCDF were Cardinal Seper, prefect; Archbishop Jerome Hamer, secretary; Monsignor Bovone, undersecretary; Father William Levada (now the cardinal prefect of the Congregation for the Doctrine of the Faith) as translator and English-speaking secretary to the Cardinal. Representing PDSAC were Fathers duBois, Barker, Brown, and Hamlett. The delegation was told that documentation was complete and that the Holy See was now prepared to receive a petition for reunion. The petition for reunion was prepared and subsequently signed on the altar of the North American Martyrs at the North American College during

---

[17] The 1979 PDSAC delegation to Rome was larger than that in 1977 and international in representation. The working sessions with the Cardinal Prefect were restricted to Fathers Barker, Brown, Tea, Hamlett, and Canon DuBois. At the conclusion of the business of the formal session held on October 30, 1979, the balance of the delegation was invited in to meet the Cardinal and receive his blessing.

a concelebrated Mass on the Solemnity of All Saints, November 1, 1979.[18] Those who signed the petition went to the Church of Saint Gregory, from which Saint Augustine (d. 604) had been sent to England, and offered prayers for the reunion of the Church. The petition was hand-delivered to the residence of the Cardinal Prefect on November 3 by the author (see Appendix A).

Canon duBois died in June 1980 with the dream of corporate reunion yet to be realized, although it should be noted that he was individually received into full communion with the Roman Catholic Church prior to his death. During his illness, private assurances were received from Rome that the petition would be approved.

Announcement

At a private meeting, hosted by Archbishop Quinn at his residence in San Francisco on August 19, 1980, the leadership of the PDSAC was informed that he intended to make a public announcement the following day. This announcement would state that Rome would make Pastoral Provision for former Anglicans, thereby ensuring their identity and the preservation of elements of their worship and would consider for Roman Catholic priesthood even those Anglican priests who were married. The Archbishop read portions of the cover letter addressed to him together with most of the text of the decree sent to him by the Holy See. The PDSAC leaders were not given a copy of the decree at the meeting, nor did they received a letter

---

[18] Each day the pro-diocesan clergy concelebrated Mass together, attended by the laymen representing PDSAC. Altars for these celebrations were provided by the Catholic Church.

addressed to them that the Holy See had forwarded with the decree and had asked to be given to them. The leadership and people celebrated a Mass of thanksgiving in Los Angeles the next evening.

Ecclesiastical Delegate

In March 1981, Bishop Law was appointed as the ecclesiastical delegate to the Holy See for the Pastoral Provision. Bishop Law then met with PDSAC leaders at the chancery offices in Saint Louis, Missouri, on May 12, 1981, to discuss the implementation of Rome's decision. In an effort to provide pastoral leadership for PDSAC, Bishop Law visited Los Angeles from July 14 to 16, 1981. During this visit, he celebrated Masses for two PDSAC parishes, Saint Matthias and Saint Mary of the Angels. Bishop Law preached at the Solemn Mass concelebrated by five priests of the PDSAC on July 14, and, after all the Masses, spoke informally to both clergy and laity. After a meeting between Bishop Law and the Standing Committee of PDSAC, it was anticipated that the two Los Angeles–area parishes would have little difficulty in becoming "personal parishes" of the Pastoral Provision in the Archdiocese of Los Angeles. It was also anticipated at that meeting that some form of national unity would exist for all Pastoral Provision clergy, people, and parishes. Bishop Law indicated a concern for sensitivity toward ecumenical relations with the Episcopal Church as the Pastoral Provision was implemented. At a meeting held July 27 and 28 with Cardinal Seper in Vancouver, Canada, the leadership of PDSAC was assured that ecumenical relations would not hinder the implementation of the Pastoral Provision.

Bishop Law convened a meeting for the Pastoral Provision on October 11 to 14, held at Holy Trinity Seminary, Dallas,

Texas. In attendance were ten priests of the pro-diocese and
several Episcopal clergy from around the country interested
in becoming Roman Catholic priests, among whom were
members of the Society of the Holy Cross. During the conference, three priests of the pro-diocese concelebrated a Votive
Mass of the Chair of Peter, using a proposed Pastoral Provision
liturgy. The delegates at the conference agreed on the pastoral necessity of maintaining a Pastoral Provision liturgy that
allowed for traditional as well as modern English. It was also
agreed that Father John Gurrieri, associate director of the
Bishops' Committee on Liturgy of the NCCB, and Father
Brown should work together on the Pastoral Provision liturgy, which was to include the Eucharist, the Calendar, the
Daily Office (Liturgy of the Hours), Baptism, Confirmation,
Penance, Marriage, Unction, Communion of the Sick,
Viaticum, and rites in connection with the Burial of the Dead.
The completed proposals relative to the liturgy were for-
warded to Father Gurrieri, Cardinal Seper, and Bishop Law
before his November 6 meeting with Cardinal Seper.[19]

Liturgy

Eventually, the Congregation for Divine Worship authorized the Book of Divine Worship (BDW) for interim usage
in 1984, with final approval on February 20, 1987.[20] This

[19] Cardinal Seper had requested the leadership of PDSAC to keep him
directly informed.

[20] The decisions on liturgy made by the Congregation for Divine Worship were based on principles established by the SCDF. Several years earlier,
the SCDF had been involved in the reuniting of separated Anglicans in Amrit-
sar, India. This precedent established that liturgies for reunited brethren were
to contain elements of their liturgy consonant with Catholic faith and in
current use among the official churches of those brethren, together with and
completed by elements of the Roman Rite.

document allowed elements of the 1928 Book of Common Prayer, but the eucharistic liturgy was taken only from the 1979 Book of Common Prayer, with additions of the Roman eucharistic Canons and the ancient Sarum Canon (with the modern English "Words of Institution" from the *Novus Ordo Missae* inserted).

Reception Begins

Reception of former Episcopal priests and their laity into the Pastoral Provision was done in a manner specified by Bishop Law's office. First, application was made to the local Catholic diocese for admission of the clergy and their people if a congregation was involved. The application process involved preparation of dossiers that included information on spouses of the married priests. After approval of the application, oral and written examinations were administered to the candidates by a review board of priests selected by Bishop Law's office. When these procedures were completed and final approval was received from the SCDF, then bishops were free to proceed to ordaining the candidate to the diaconate and then priesthood.[21]

Specific questions concerning procedures and particular cases were submitted by Bishop Law to Rome. One example was that the SCDF determined that former Episcopalian

[21] Ordinations (the sacrament of Holy Orders) in Anglican churches were declared not valid by Pope Leo XIII in the late nineteenth century. Convert ministers from Anglicanism would therefore need to be ordained in order to be received as valid priests of the Catholic Church. The PDSAC representatives were told by the SCDF that the position of the Catholic Church regarding Anglican Orders could be reexamined. However, we were also told that this process would require two or more years to obtain a definitive answer. The PDSAC representatives respectfully declined the offer to re-open the question to avoid further delay for the sake of the people.

clergy being ordained priests in the Roman Catholic Church did not have to be admitted first into the offices of lector, acolyte, or candidate, nor would it be necessary for the time spent in the diaconate to be lengthy if there was a group of faithful dependent on the pastoral care of the person in process. It should be noted that the average time spent as a transitional deacon was one or two months prior to ordination to the priesthood. At the priestly ordination, the ordaining bishop received the laity and canonically erected a parish of the Pastoral Provision. Thus these parochial communities were established as personal parishes of the dioceses in which they were located, which was in keeping with the recommendation of the NCCB.

In an attempt to proceed in a uniform way with the implementation of the Pastoral Provision, each of the diocesan bishops who were scheduled to have Pastoral Provision parishes at that time met with Bishop Law. Present at this meeting, which was held at the home of the Bishop of Reno–Las Vegas, Nevada, on July 4, 1983, were Bishop John Ward, representing Cardinal Manning and the Archdiocese of Los Angeles; Bishop MacFarland for Nevada; Archbishop Patricio Flores for San Antonio; and Bishop Law.

Bishop Ward's presence at this meeting indicated a continuing willingness on the part of the Archdiocese of Los Angeles to consider the implementation of the Pastoral Provision for the two parishes that had made such a request. However, both Bishop Law and the Ecumenical Relations Committee of the Archdiocese of Los Angeles had made it clear that sensitivity to ecumenical relations would be paramount in the carrying out of the Pastoral Provision. It is well to note that the Ecumenical Relations Committee was adamantly opposed to the erection of a Pastoral Provision parish. It has been subsequently demonstrated that this policy has perdured in the Archdiocese of Los Angeles, for no parish of the Pastoral Provision has ever been erected for that area despite the fact that the group of laity there was the largest of any of those in the nation that had been received in other dioceses. In October 1984, Bishop Ward, on behalf of Cardinal Manning, reported to PDSAC clergy in Los Angeles that no parish of the Pastoral Provision would be allowed in the archdiocese and that both clergy and laity would have to be received into the Catholic Church on a strictly individual basis through their local Latin-Rite parish.[22]

Meanwhile, dates were set for the first ordinations and establishment of parishes in various dioceses. They were as follows: August 15, 1983, Father Christopher Phillips and Our Lady of the Atonement in San Antonio, Texas; September 10, 1983, Father Clark A. Tea and Saint Mary the Virgin, Las Vegas, Nevada; February 25, 1984, Father Joseph Frazer and Saint Margaret of Scotland, Austin, Texas; April 7, 1984, Father James Moore and Our Lady of Walsingham, Houston, Texas; and April 13, 1984, Father David Ladkau and Good Shepherd, Columbia, South Carolina.[23]

These Pastoral Provision parishes and a significant number of individual priests, most with families, are now a part of the Roman Catholic Church in the United States. This

---

[22] No reason was given by the archdiocese for its negative decision after such a long period of time, but it has been suggested that ecumenical relations must figure prominently; in addition, the press had branded the clergy leaders as rebels, and the parishes had been involved in civil litigation with the Episcopal Diocese of Los Angeles over real property, a lawsuit which the diocese ultimately lost and which may have been an embarrassment to Catholic officials.

[23] The parishes in Las Vegas and Austin have since closed. New parishes, missions, and chaplaincies have been erected in Corpus Christi, Texas (Saint Anselm of Canterbury, 1992), Arlington, Texas (Saint Mary the Virgin, 1994), Boston, Massachusetts (Saint Athanasius, 1997), Scranton, Pennsylvania (Saint Thomas More, 2005), and Kansas City, Missouri (Our Lady of Hope, 2008).

amazing development has its roots in the history of Anglicanism and Catholicism; its present is in the life of the Church today and yet not widely known; its future remains to unfold as the Church moves into the new millennium. Its meaning for the larger Church is yet to be fully understood. But, it is here, and the decree from Rome leaves it open so long as it serves a need, with a time-frame which is *ad tempus non determinatum.*[24]

Father Jack D. Barker graduated from UCLA in physics and mathematics and worked in the NASA Space Program for several years before ordination in the Episcopal Church. After becoming Catholic, he attended Saint Patrick's Seminary in Menlo Park, California, receiving the M.Div. He has served in several parishes in the Diocese of San Bernardino and is currently pastor of Saint Martha Catholic Parish in Murrieta, California, a parish of over six thousand families.

[24] "The statute or 'pastoral provision' will not be definitive, but rather will be granted 'ad tempus non determinatum'" (Decree of the Sacred Congregation for the Doctrine of the Faith on the Pastoral Provision [July 22, 1980], sec. 4).

Chapter 2

An Example of What It's Like to Come Home to Rome

Father Christopher G. Phillips

Twenty-five years as a time-frame takes a little perspective. As a young Anglican cleric, I was serving in the Church of England as the assistant curate of Saint Stephen's, Southmead, Bristol. After having lived abroad for five years, we decided it was time to return to America. But where to go? I contacted Bishop Belden in Rhode Island, where we had lived before moving to England. He told me about a parish that he thought would be a good match for me. They were looking for a curate. The rector, he told me, was one of the great old priests of the diocese, who, other than having a brief curacy in another parish, had served his whole ministry in this one parish. I got the feeling that I was going to meet someone approaching the age of Methuselah, who had been rector since the age of the Great Flood! When I met Father Olsen, indeed he did seem to be a fairly old man, and he had been at Saint Barnabas for a very long time. However, when he died recently, it dawned on me that when I went to be his curate, Father Olsen was the

This talk was delivered to the Annual Conference of the Anglican Use Society, held at Our Lady of the Atonement Catholic Church, San Antonio, Texas, in June 2008; first published in *Anglican Embers* 2, no. 8: 317–27.

very same age I am now and had been at Saint Barnabas for twenty-five years, the same amount of time I have been at Our Lady of the Atonement in San Antonio, Texas.

Twenty-five years ago, Our Lady of the Atonement was established as a Roman Catholic Anglican Use parish. But what took place twenty-five years ago didn't happen in a vacuum. We were fortunate in San Antonio that the rescript arrived from the Holy See, allowing for my ordination, and the archbishop was ready to proceed immediately. But he didn't wake up one morning and think, "I guess I'll start an Anglican Use parish." No, there were many who had done yeoman work for many years before, preparing the way: people, now departed, who worked within the Episcopal Church, like Canon Albert duBois and Father W. T. Saint John Brown; members of the Roman Catholic hierarchy like Pope Paul VI, Cardinal Franjo Seper, and Pope John Paul II. Of course, the Anglican Use was also encouraged by a certain cardinal, Joseph Ratzinger, now our Holy Father, Pope Benedict XVI. Under his authority as prefect of the Congregation for the Doctrine of the Faith, the Book of Divine Worship was approved (more about that later).

Looking back over this past quarter of a century, perhaps the first question is "Why? Why have many Episcopalians converted to the Catholic Church?" I wish I could point only to the noblest motivations, that we were happily going along as Episcopalians, but then saw the truth and beauty of the Catholic Church, and through pure attraction, just had to make the journey. Maybe it was that way for a few, but for many of us there was another route.

For me, the answer to the question *why?* is that it was because I knew I couldn't stay where I was. I didn't like the idea of moving away from my ministry as an Episcopalian. In fact, where I was wasn't all that bad—1928 Book of

Common Prayer with Anglican Missal additions, very nice people with a fairly Catholic understanding of the faith—but, with the crisis of authority that was becoming more and more evident in the Episcopal Church, with General Convention decisions that represented dramatic changes in doctrine and in the ministry of the church, it was apparent that whatever claim to catholicity I thought there was, was quickly disappearing. For me and others, then, the initial thought of moving was for negative reasons—the need to escape from a disintegrating situation. That's not necessarily a bad thing. Imperfect contrition can develop into perfect contrition, and sometimes it takes a kick in the backside to get moving.

In the mid-1970s, it had become clear to me that with the crisis of authority in Anglicanism, there would be a gradual crumbling of what had been a venerable (although incomplete) expression of the Christian faith. Of course, the Church has always been free to change her discipline, but changing doctrine at the whim of a simple majority vote is antithetical to the will of Christ. When a very small majority of a very small part of the Anglican Communion could make a decision, for instance, about ordination—an issue which strikes at the very foundation of sacramental life—or when a justification for abortion and all sorts of other immoralities was able to be cobbled together, I realized that the Episcopal Church wasn't a safe place to be. For me, it wasn't just the issue of the ordination of women (as impossible as that is, in a Catholic understanding of Holy Orders), nor was it that some were able to wander off into a moral wasteland; rather, it was that the authority to make such decisions was claimed by whichever group could push its agenda the hardest. "What next?" was all I could think. Indeed, what came next was a series of decisions that makes many people question whether the

Episcopal Church is even a Christian denomination any
more.

Of course, there are still many good Episcopalians, and
I can't help but wonder how they're able to continue. When
I see otherwise faithful people remaining where they are,
while their religion falls apart around them, I can't help
but think that maybe some of them have what might be
called "The Vicar of Bray Syndrome". There was a clergyman who managed to hold his position as parish priest in
the village of Bray for more than fifty years, from the days
of Charles II until the time of George I. He was perfectly
comfortable becoming Catholic or Protestant according to
the religion of the reigning monarch. When he was
reproached for his constant changing back and forth, his
classic statement was "Even if I changed my religion, I am
sure I have kept true to my principle; and that is, to live
and die as the vicar of Bray!" It's sad when holding a position becomes more important than holding the truth.

Ultimately, many left the Episcopal Church when they
arrived at the point of saying, "This far, and no further."
That point may have differed from person to person. For
some, it might have been the matter of women's ordination; for others, it was the Prayer Book or some aspect of
moral teaching. There can be any number of "trigger issues",
and people have varying degrees of tolerance for them. However, all of these issues reduce down to one: the matter of
authority. There is but one Church with stable, trustwor-
thy, and godly authority, and that is the Church that was
founded by Christ and built upon the office he gave to
Saint Peter and his successors. For some, the short answer
to "Why?" is that they were looking for a home that didn't
have a constantly shifting foundation. What a joy it is to
wake up every day knowing that what was true yesterday is
still true today, and will be true tomorrow.

Thanks be to God, that the Church to which I was led opened her arms to me with the approval of the Pastoral Provision. With that, there was no excuse to remain outside, and so personal, hard, practical decisions had to be made. As I was faced with making these decisions, I remember reading something from C. S. Lewis in his book *Mere Christianity*:

> We all want progress. But progress means getting nearer to the place you want to be and if you have taken a wrong turning, then to go forward does not get you any nearer. If you are on the wrong road, progress means doing an about-turn and walking back to the right road; and in that case, the man who turns back soonest is the most progressive man. We have all seen this when we do arithmetic. When I have started a sum the wrong way, the sooner I admit this and go back and start over again, the faster I shall get on. There is nothing progressive about being pigheaded and refusing to admit a mistake.[1]

It's hard for anyone to admit that he's got to turn and go in another direction. That kind of decision most often involves some pretty heavy sacrifices. I know that for many of those who have made that decision, there were tough times. My story is only one of many.

On January 17, 1982, my family and I arrived in San Antonio from Rhode Island. We had driven for almost five days, having left New England in the midst of a near blizzard. I had taken our rather decrepit Volkswagen to a mechanic before we left, and when I asked him if we'd make it to Texas his reply was, "Hell, Mister, I don't think you'll make it out of town!" We did, though. We arrived with our (then) three very young children, our dog, and a

[1] C. S. Lewis, *Mere Christianity* (New York: Macmillan Publishing, 1953), p. 36.

hamster, along with whatever supplies we could pack in around them.

On the day we left Rhode Island, I was removed from the clerical ranks of our Episcopal diocese. I was officially deposed by the bishop. My salary had, of course, been terminated. We had lived in parish-owned housing, which we were required to leave immediately. We had been stricken from all diocesan insurance policies, and even my small pension plan had been confiscated. A half dozen people who had been Episcopalians asked if I would come to San Antonio and work with them in building a community that might be able to become a Catholic parish at some time in the future. It seemed to me a long-shot, but we had no other place to go. As we approached San Antonio, it didn't feel like much of a triumphal entry. Of course, God had a plan. It would have been nice at the time to have known what it was, but I suppose he wanted us to learn to walk in faith, which we did.

Looking back, those were some tough days. We had virtually no money. There was only a handful of people even interested in what we were doing. But as difficult as those times were, they were exciting, too. We were doing something worthy, something that hadn't been done before. Big challenges led to little victories, as we worked and waited for our entrance into the Catholic Church.

Every one of the parishes and communities in the Anglican Use has an interesting story. Each person has experienced struggles and triumphs, and each has inspiring stories of God's loving care for him. My own experiences will, perhaps, strike a chord with those who have been through something similar. Even more importantly, I hope my story will encourage those who are at the beginning of their journey within the Catholic faith.

After our San Antonio parish was canonically erected on August 15, 1983, I began to search for a permanent location for us to worship and to grow from the original eighteen members. We were, at that time, meeting at San Francesco di Paola Church, in downtown San Antonio. It's a beautiful little place, built by Italian immigrants, but the location wasn't very well-suited for us. Everyone had to travel quite a distance, and it was difficult to build up a communal life in a place that was fairly remote for all of us. Subsequently, we moved to a convent chapel on the north side of town, but of course, that was temporary, too. So I began to look for some land.

The future growth of San Antonio seemed destined to take place on the northwest side of the city. Several years before, the archdiocese had purchased a small plot of land in that area for the possibility that a territorial parish might be needed there. When I inquired about locating our parish there, the answer was, "Yes, that would be fine. There's not much happening out there anyway, and we probably won't need it for a territorial parish." The short-sightedness of that statement aside, it worked out well for us. To get the property, we were required to pay a rather hefty sum to the archdiocese, which eventually we did.

The first time I saw this land, I knew it was the spot. I had to crawl through the underbrush—literally on my belly—to make any kind of exploration. I had a small medal of Our Lady of the Atonement with me, and I buried it in the earth as I was making my slow progress through the woods and brush, claiming it for our Lady and her parish. Shortly after burying the medal, I came into a small clearing, allowing me to stand up. In the middle of the clearing, a wooden cross was stuck into the ground, and fastened to the rough cross was a small crucifix. I took it as a sign from God that this was the place. This was where our Lord and his Blessed Mother wanted us to be.

At the same time that I had requested the parcel of land, some Dominican priests had approached the archbishop about staffing a chaplaincy for the University of Texas, which is a short distance away. Even though we had asked first, the archbishop thought perhaps a better use for the land would be to give it to the Dominicans. I told the archbishop, "You can't! I've already claimed it for Our Lady of the Atonement." He expressed his regret, but told me his mind was set. I warned him that we'd begin praying, and so we did.

For nine evenings, our parish community gathered to pray the Novena to the Holy Ghost. By the fourth evening, the archbishop contacted me. "I don't know what kind of prayer you've been saying," he said, "but the situation with the Dominicans has fallen through. You can build there." We finished the novena as an act of thanksgiving. We were intensely grateful to God, but not surprised at what he had done. Mind you, I have nothing against the Dominicans, but the Blessed Mother had other plans for the land.

We built a simple wooden shrine to Our Lady of the Atonement on the property where the crucifix had been found and fastened it onto the peak of the shrine's roof. In time, we made plans to celebrate a Mass there and to break ground for the church.

Today there stands the newly completed shrine, a copy of the original wooden one, but now in stone. Within the stone altar is the simple wood altar that stood there originally. The little crucifix is there too, incorporated into the shrine. The entire building is a memorial to our beginnings, and to the ways God guided and protected us as new converts to the Catholic faith.

Looking back twenty-five years calls for a few words about the Book of Divine Worship. The initial request made to Rome included the desire for the Catholic ordination of Anglican clergy, which was granted. It included the request for some sort of parish structure to which the lay converts could belong, which was granted. It also included a request for elements of our Anglican liturgical heritage. This, too, was granted. What form the liturgy would take was anybody's guess at the beginning. There were some who wanted a restored Sarum Rite. Some wanted one of the traditional Anglo-Catholic missals. Some wanted the 1928 Book of Common Prayer with a few Catholic additions. There were others who thought that the most we could hope for would be a couple of traditional prayers thrown into the Mass of Paul VI.

In 1983, a special commission was established by the Congregation for Sacraments and Divine Worship, in conjunction with the Congregation for the Doctrine of the Faith. The task of the commission was to propose a liturgical book to be used by the parishes and congregations being established under the Pastoral Provision. I was privileged to serve on that commission. We met in Rome in the curial offices looking out on Saint Peter's Square. The membership of the commission was mixed. Archbishop (now Cardinal) Virgilio Noe served as chairman, and among the members were various liturgists and theologians. Not everyone had the same agenda. Some of us were working hard to include as much from the Anglican tradition as possible; others wanted to include as little as possible. Some were willing to use the 1928 Prayer Book as the foundational document; others insisted that it had to be the 1979 Prayer Book. There were those who said that if something was not in an approved Episcopalian Prayer Book, then it shouldn't be included. Of particular importance was the Canon of the Mass—the Eucharistic Prayer. Using the 1928 Episcopalian Eucharistic Prayer was never an option; however, the Gregorian Canon had been included in various Anglo-Catholic missals, and it was my request that we be allowed to use that traditional translation, or something close to it, rather than following the general consensus of the commission that we should simply use the newest ICEL (International Commission on English in the Liturgy) translation of the Roman Canon. I was sobered, if not a little frightened, to be the sole voice defending the inclusion of the Gregorian Canon in traditional English, and I was nearly brushed out of the conference room by the professional liturgists there, including Piero Marini, until recently the papal master of ceremonies. I was nevertheless given a chance to make the case, for which I had to speak before the whole commission, and my points did have an impact on the outcome.

There are Anglo-Catholics still in the Episcopal Church or in the Continuing Anglican Movement who find fault with the Book of Divine Worship. Their criticisms are, in some respects, quite legitimate. It isn't a perfect book. There are lots of things about it that I also find dissatisfying. For example, there is a jarring intrusion of ICEL language in the Offertory. There is too much borrowed from the 1979 Prayer Book. The bottom line, however, is this: it may not be as much as was wanted, but it's a whole lot more than was expected. It is easy to overlook how astonishing it is for the Catholic Church to add whole new liturgies—not just the Mass, but also the Daily Offices, Baptism, Marriage, and Burial of the Dead. Given the recent debates by the National Conference of Catholic Bishops about simple words like "ineffable" and "gibbet", it is amazing that Anglican Use Catholics have a whole book full of that kind of language. The Book of Divine Worship is their own living liturgy. There's no reason to think that it will remain frozen as it is; there will be opportunities to develop it and refine it. For now, though, I think it's quite magnificent, and it's nurturing a new generation of Catholics—a generation born and raised in the Anglican Use, a generation of Catholics who know no other kind of liturgical life.

Which brings me to an important point, that is, the future of the parishes of the Anglican Use. The numbers, for now, are small. After twenty-five years, there should be more of us, and there would be, except for a few factors. One is that all but a few Anglican clergy have converted individually and have not brought their people with them. Of course, not every one can bring others with him, and very often it's because the local Catholic bishop isn't open to having a parish of the Anglican Use in his diocese. That brings us to an even more serious problem. It's difficult to convince Catholic bishops in many places that such a parish would be a great addition, rather than a financial drag. They're not accustomed to having such small parishes. When parishes of a couple of thousand families are normal, to establish a parish which begins with only forty or fifty people is simply beyond their experience. Of course, it can be done. As noted earlier, our parish began with only eighteen people, including the children.

What's the solution? In the short term, presenting the case for the Anglican Use more clearly to Catholic bishops is important. For this to be done, the Office of the Ecclesiastical Delegate must be willing to help educate the bishops about the Pastoral Provision and the Liturgy of the Anglican Use. The Pastoral Provision isn't just about getting more priests for the Church, as important as that is. It's also about restoring that unity for which Christ prayed. It's about "gathering up the fragments, that nothing be lost". For every Episcopal priest who enters the Catholic Church, there may be twenty-five or fifty or a hundred or more laity who could be brought into the Church.

At some point in the future, there may well be the possibility of some sort of juridical structure, which would facilitate the establishment of parishes. This possibility was recognized even in the original document outlining the

Pastoral Provision. When speaking of the structure of a common identity, the document states, "The preference expressed by the majority of the Episcopal Conference for the insertion of these reconciled Episcopalians into the diocesan structures under the jurisdiction of the local Ordinaries is recognized. Nevertheless, the possibility of some other type of structure as provided for by canonical dispositions, and as suited to the needs of the group, is not excluded." [2]

What about the Anglican Use parishes and communities that already exist? They need to be strengthened. One way we have done this in our parish was by adding a Catholic school—one of the most rewarding and yet demanding decisions we ever made. Fourteen years ago, we began with kindergarten through third grade with only sixty-six students, and after adding grades over the years, we now offer a classical and Catholic education from pre-kindergarten all the way through high school, with a student body of almost five hundred. Not only does this institution impart a solid and excellent education, but it also is a tremendous evangelistic tool, as families who perhaps have been lukewarm are, through their children, returning to the practice of their faith. The school has done more to spread the experience and knowledge of the Anglican Use liturgy than perhaps any other means. All the students and faculty attend Mass every single day, so even the youngest children are learning and experiencing our traditional prayers and devotional practices. Five hundred children praying the Prayer of Humble Access and singing the Healey Willan setting of the Mass every day is a pretty encouraging thing for the future of the Anglican Use!

---

[2] Decree of the Sacred Congregation for the Doctrine of the Faith on the Pastoral Provision (July 22, 1980), sec. 2, no. 1.

There are great and inspiring things going on in other Anglican Use parishes and communities. There are countless stories of great faith, changed hearts, conversions, and growth. More parishes, however, are needed, which means willing bishops and a supportive structure within the Church are needed as well. There are people scattered throughout the country who are looking for guidance and help in forming the nucleus of an Anglican Use community, and Christ isn't pleased when his sheep are left to scatter.

Father Christopher G. Phillips is the founding pastor of Our Lady of Atonement Catholic Church in San Antonio, which was established on August 15, 1983. From the original handful of faithful people at the beginning, it is presently a parish of about 600 families. In 1994 the parish began the Atonement Academy, which has 550 students enrolled in grades pre-kindergarten through twelfth grade.

Chapter 3

Conversion and Enrichment

Father Peter J. Geldard

A story is told of Ronald Knox (who was a great wit) that after he became a Catholic, he went and stayed as a Catholic priest at a presbytery, which one suspects was very Irish. For friendship's sake, the Irish priest started pouring Knox a glass of Irish whiskey, and as he continued to fill the glass almost to the brim, Knox said, "Slow down; I'm only a convert."

Convert is an appellation that applies to anybody who joins the Catholic Church—although the process of receiving already baptized people into the Catholic Church makes it very clear that the word "convert" in such a case is actually a misnomer. "Convert" should only be applied to people who come into the faith from a totally non-Christian background and shouldn't apply to persons who come via Anglicanism or have otherwise already been validly baptized. If someone can find a single word to describe "the reception of a baptized Christian into full communion with the Catholic Church", Rome would like to know it. Until such a word is found, "convert" must do. The Rite of Reception

From a talk delivered by Father Geldard at the Anglican Use Conference in Washington, D.C., on June 1, 2007. Originally published in *Anglican Embers* 2, no. 4 (December 2007): 127–50.

into Full Communion does say that although "convert" is the wrong word to use in the technical sense, it is the right word in a practical sense.[1] The whole Christian life is conversion, is making bold decisions, is turning to Christ and following Christ, whatever the difficulties and whatever the hurdles. I identify myself as someone who converted first of all to Christianity and to Anglicanism, and then converted to the Catholic Church, and as one whose life, I hope, continues to be one of conversion.

My Life in the Anglican Church

The reason I became an Anglican was in many ways a rather strange one. I was a seventeen-year-old schoolboy from a non-church background, and I was given by my history teacher an essay to write about the Tractarian Movement in the Church of England, something I had never heard about and never fully understood at that stage. He lent me a book, *The Short History of the Oxford Movement* by Canon Ollard. Ollard wrote this book at the beginning of the twentieth century and began it with these words:

> No story in the whole history of the English Church, since Augustine landed in 597, is so splendid as the story of the Oxford Movement. It has every sort of interest. It is exciting, romantic, chivalrous, like the story of a crusade. It has its humor as well as its tragedy, and the actors in it were among the most spiritual men who have ever lived in England. They were men of genius besides; poets like Keble, Newman, Isaac Williams, and Faber; men of letters like Newman and Dean Church; preachers whose sermons are read

[1] *Rite of Receptions of Baptised Christians into Full Communion with the Catholic Church* (London: Catholic Truth Society, 1974).

today; divines and theologians whose fame will last as long
as Christianity endures; so that a more interesting subject
hardly exists in the whole of Church History.[2]

I found these words very exciting, and they aroused my
curiosity. My school was on the south coast of England,
and just down the road was a church that was an heir of
the Tractarian Movement. For the first time, I went to High
Mass there on a Sunday morning. I can remember it very
poignantly because an event happened which surprised me.
It was the early sixties, pre-Vatican II, and it was a very
traditional High Mass. The time came when the Creed was
said, or rather sung, and suddenly we came to the words
incarnatus est, and everyone fell to their knees except myself.
I can remember quite vividly my strange reaction. Whereas
one would expect an adolescent youth to be very embar-
rassed, to feel exposed, I suddenly thought: "These people
know what it is they believe and why, and that is the community which I want to join." So from that moment, slowly
but surely, I decided that was the kind of church that I
wanted to be a part of, a church that knew what it believed
and why, that was prepared to demonstrate its belief in its
worship, and that had behind its belief—though I didn't
fully understand this at the time—the sacramental life which
would sustain me on my pilgrimage of faith.

I don't remember what marks I got on that essay, but I
know the effect it had on me. The teacher gave me his
copy of Ollard's book, which I still have today, and I decided
to read theology at King's College, London. There I was
fortunate to come across teachers of theology who had a
great influence upon me. Eric Mascall was my tutor. Week
by week he advanced me in the knowledge of the catholicity

---

[2] Sidney L. Ollard, *A Short History of the Oxford Movement* (A.R. Mowbray and Co., 1915), pp. 1–2.

of the Church of England and of Anglicanism. There was Father Copleston, who taught me philosophy, who came down from Farm Street. There were also visiting lecturers and preachers. We had a very radical (as we would have thought then), biblical scholar, who used to come across from the States, called Raymond Brown, and we had a very holy man called Michael Ramsey. All these people helped to convince me of the catholicity of the Church of England—a catholicity that recognized that it was not the whole church but was *part* of the Church, and that claimed its sacramental life was linked to that sacramental life of the bigger body, that is, the Church of the Apostles. Through Michael Ramsey and later Robert Runcie, the Archbishop of Canterbury, I picked up the idea that Anglicanism had within itself a *provisionality*; it had within it the idea that, in fact, it was not a permanent church, but that it was on a journey. The real mark and the real hope of Anglicanism was unity with something bigger than itself. It is that concept that so often we lose or have lost in the past.

All of us can be very insular, and not just in little England, but also in the States. When I first visited the States some twenty-five years or more ago, I gave an address at a synod or a diocesan convention and asked them to have pity on me because I was psychologically damaged. I'd been damaged at school because in my school atlas every country filled a page. England filled a page, and the United States filled a page; and no one made it clear that there were different scales. Therefore, I teasingly said, I had thought about bringing my bicycle so I could peddle around it. But seriously, here are some examples of insular thinking.

In a debate about women's ordination, my opponent said, "Well, the reason we should make this change to ordain women is because we should do what the rest of the Church is doing." What, of course, he meant was: "We should do

what the rest of the *Episcopal* Church is doing." I quoted
these words back to him, saying I fully accept the concept
"that we should be doing what the Church does. However, I remind you that the Episcopal Church is not the
whole Church." In 1992, we had that crucial debate in
England about the ordination of women to the priesthood, and it finished at five o'clock in the evening, when
it was announced that *the General Synod* had done something. By the time we got to the nine o'clock news, it
wasn't the General Synod; it was *the Church of England*;
and, by the time we got to the midnight news it wasn't
the Church of England, but *the Church* that had decided
to do something. Bishop Stanley H. Atkins, who fought
hard and long within the Episcopal Church, created that
memorable phrase: "We are but a splinter of a splinter."
This truth is something we need constantly to remind ourselves: how small we are in relation to something that is so
much bigger than ourselves. It's when we recognize that
we are part of something bigger than ourselves that something comes into the equation which even, as a seventeen-
or eighteen-year-old boy, I recognized was lacking.

Ronald Knox and others constantly challenged Anglicans
of their own day by saying: "You use all these arguments
about episcopacy, but an even stronger argument exists about
primacy. Why do you turn a blind eye on that? Why do
you ignore that evidence, if you make such great significance of episcopacy itself?"

As a very cheeky seminarian, I re-reviewed a book by
Archbishop Michael Ramsey, *The Gospel and the Catholic
Church*. He wrote it in 1936, and I still think it is one of his
greatest books; but I challenged him in my review. I wrote
that even as he emphasized the greatness of Christendom,
he also exposed certain faults within it. While I applauded
his radicalness on the recovery of a proper balance between

Church and Scripture, "the Protestant principle and the Catholic substance" (as Søren Kierkegaard used to refer to it), and his emphasis on the episcopacy as being of the *esse* of the Church, I felt he had ducked the question of the Petrine ministry. Was this also of the *esse* of the Church or just the *bene esse*, as he seemed to imply? He came to see me about my review as I was finishing my studies at Canterbury, and I remember turning to him and saying, "Father, on page 64 you ask this question: 'Is the Papacy a legitimate development which grew out of the primacy which Christ conferred on Peter?' Father, we're still waiting for your answer!" That to me is one of *the* questions we need to challenge other Christians about. Is the Petrine ministry also of the *esse* of the Church?

There is a fine sermon on the papacy by Ronald Knox that does not appear in his collected works but can be found in the series *Anglican Cobwebs*. These sermons were given to Anglican converts or people thinking of converting and challenged them to think seriously about certain issues. He asked his hearers whether or not they could ever say the words *Habemus Papam* ("We have a Pope"). He said:

> If you talk to many Anglicans and say, "Do you believe in the Pope?", they will say, "Of course we believe in the Papacy; when England was Catholic in the Middle Ages, there was a Papacy and we believed in it then, and they were right to do so. If we'd been around when Henry VIII was changing the nature of the Church of England and substituting himself for the Papacy, we'd have been one of the martyrs then. And, of course, in the future we will at some time believe in the Papacy."... [But, as Ronald Knox goes on], You cannot say, "*Habemus Papam*." You can say, "*Habuimus Papam*": We did have a Pope in the Middle Ages; or you can say, "*Habuissimus Papam*": We would have had a Pope at the time of the Reformation. You could have said,

even: "*Haberemus Papam*": We would have a Pope now if
only the Pope would take us on our own terms; or "*Habe-
bimus Papam*": We shall have a Pope one day when the impossible happens. But you cannot say now, "*Habemus Papam.*" [3]

The challenge must come back to us to remember the
preface to those words: *Annuntio vobis gaudium magnum* ("I
announce to you an issue of great joy").The Petrine ministry and its primacy is part of the *esse* of the Church and
needs to be recovered by those who haven't got it; and
they need to be reminded that it is the papacy as we have
it now, which is the challenge to us all. The writings of
Hans Urs von Balthasar remind us that we cannot have the
Pope on our own terms. We have the papacy as we have it
through history, as it is in the world today. Even if we want
to ignore the biblical evidence, and the historical evidence,
we can accept it for the pragmatic reason alone that it creates a unity of over a billion Christians throughout the world.
It is all too clear what happens to ecclesial bodies that do
not have such a center of unity.

When I was a seminarian, I was convinced that Anglicanism not only was a part of the wider Church, but also
had a future in the wider Church. Because people like Eric
Mascall and Michael Ramsey said it was so, there was a
time when I believed it to be so. However, all of us have to
face that moment in our own lives when we cannot let
others make decisions for us. We must decide for ourselves
in the light of what we know. Whatever great men may or
may not have done before us, *we* must decide whether a
certain truth is or is not true for us. Mysteriously, God
discloses to people different things at different times. For
me, and for many others like me within the Church of
England, reconciliation with Rome was needed.

[3] Ronald Knox, *Anglican Cobwebs* (London: Sheed and Ward, 1928), p. 55.

In those exciting times, there was actually an effort being made in this direction: the Anglican–Roman Catholic International Commission (ARCIC). There did seem to be the possibility that slowly, but surely, reconciliation of the whole body might be possible. One of the reasons that I visited the States so often (I also went to Australia and Africa, and even obscure parts of the Anglican Communion) is because wherever there were Anglicans, there were bilateral discussions occurring that followed the ARCIC discussions, which I wanted to encourage. I wanted to learn about them, and I wanted to report back to England on them. There seemed a genuine possibility of real unity, so genuine that many times I went to Rome because of it.

There was a major hiccup that I have to recount. They say that at an American dinner party (and this applies to some English ones as well) if the host wants a discussion started when the conversation's gotten a little dull or has gone quiet, he should ask his guests: "What were you doing on Friday, November 22, 1963, at 6:30 central time (when J. F. Kennedy was shot)?" It's one of those poignant moments of history that people can nearly always recount what they were doing at the time when they heard that news.

To me there is also another poignant time, and that was Wednesday, May 13, 1981, when Pope John Paul II was shot. Not long before I had been to Rome and had met John Paul II. Canon William Purdey, who was the ecumenical officer of the Council for Christian Unity, introduced me, and the Pope, in his bearlike way, hugged me and assured me that the work of ARCIC was progressing well. The afternoon he was shot I thought all this work for unity might come to naught. By the grace of God, that was not the case. By the same grace of God, he recovered and a year later came to Canterbury.

While the Pope was recovering, I persuaded my organization, then the English Church Union, that we should give him a "get well" present. One could have a good dinner-party conversation about that: "What do you give a Pope for a 'get well' present?" It's like: "What do you give the Queen for her birthday?" There's a limit to things one can give. Our group had a special stole made. It was a red stole, which had on it the arms of Canterbury and John Paul II's own personal papal arms. On the neck was the dove of the Holy Spirit with the words "May they be one" (*Ut unum sint*). The Holy Father wore this stole the day he visited Canterbury. "May it be soon that the successor of Gregory and the successor of Saint Augustine are soon reconciled", he said. (I didn't know at that point what Cardinal Hume thought of those words, but that's another matter.) The point of this story is at that particular moment in history, there was great hope of unity, a unity which many of us believed would resolve the provisionality of Anglicanism and one of the divisions of Christendom itself.

Women's Ordination and Its Effects on Anglican-Catholic Relationships

That unity of course was not to be. It was not to be, if I dare say first of all, because of a move made by some American Episcopalians. As Canon Purdey said, "The work of ARCIC seemed so clear and so obvious. It was like a tram going down a hill. I could see the buffers at the end. We were going to arrive. And then suddenly our American friends, like a block of concrete suddenly thrown up in its tracks, decided to ordain women to the priesthood." When England made the same decision, the obstacle to unity grew even larger, not because the Church of England is any greater or better than any other part of the Anglican Communion, but for historical reasons. Rome thought, and perhaps still does think, that, in dealing with the Anglican Communion, what happens in England is crucial for the rest. The vote to ordain women in the Church of England, made on November 11, 1982, was very close. The media thought that it wouldn't be passed, and then in the end it was passed by one vote in the House of Laity. When at five o'clock that decision was made, many of us recognized that a certain change had happened, which could never ever be reversed. That night I was interviewed on the BBC 10:30 news by Jeremy Paxton: "Ah, Father Geldard," he said, "so you're very cross today I see. You're cross because the Church of England has moved the goalposts."

"No, Mr. Paxton," I replied, "it's worse than that; they have put them on wheels!"

The next morning I wrote the following for *The Catholic Herald*. It appeared under the headline "We Are Orphans Now".

By 5:00 p.m. on that Wednesday the Church of England had chosen, and in making one decision it had answered many questions. It ignored John Paul II's plea that the Church of England should not proceed any further in creating a further barrier to Christian unity. It clearly turned its back on twenty years of stupendous fruitful progress by ARCIC and affirmed that the immediate ordination of women took priority over the quest for organic visible unity. But more tellingly and fundamentally it proclaimed something about The Church of England herself: a local synod has the right and authority to make change even in the matter of the sacraments, which are common and shared with the wider Catholic Church. What in the past has been affirmed as the purview of only a General or Ecumenical council could

now be decided by the diktat of a doubtfully representative
body of 0.5% of Christendom. In the haunting words of
Newman, "The spell of The Church of England had been
broken." And Tractarianism, which he had started, ceased
that night since the very foundation on which his first tract
was based, "the Apostolic ministry as entrusted to us by
Christ", was overturned. For Catholic traditionalists within
the Church of England who had labored and witnessed hard
not least under the auspices of ARCIC in the belief that
corporate reunion was a realistic and possible achievement,
November 11th was the death knell of all their hopes and
aspirations. How can one continue to claim to celebrate
Catholic sacraments if one's church fails to possess the Catholic priesthood on which they depend? How can The Church
of England be serious about the priority of Christian unity
if it enacts what everyone knows to be a further insupera-
ble barrier to such unity?[4]

The Bishop of London, Graham Leonard, wrote a similar
article for *The London Daily Times*, which appeared on the
same day. He came to the same conclusions and ended with
the plea: "We come and hope that the Church, the Catholic
Church of Rome, will in fact deal with us positively and
hopefully. But we come with no prior requirements and with
no demands; we come merely as supplicants."[5]

A month later, Cardinal Basil Hume asked Graham Leonard, me, and three others to meet at his house in Westminster. In addition to Bishop Leonard and me, there was Father
Christopher Colven, who was master of the Society of the
Holy Cross, SSC (*Societas Sanctae Crucis*); Father John Broad-
hurst, who continued on to be the Anglican Bishop of For-

[4] Father Peter Geldard, "We Are Orphans Now", *The Catholic Herald*,
November 12, 1979, p. 16.
[5] Bishop Graham Leonard, "How to Leave the Church of England", *The
London Daily Times*, November 20, 1992, ed. 1, p. 18.

ward in Faith; and a previous chaplain of Graham Leonard's, David Skeogh.

Besides Cardinal Hume, on the Catholic side (and this shows the seriousness of this meeting and those that followed), were Bishop Alan C. Clark of Norwich, who had been the Roman Catholic Chairman of ARCIC; Bishop Vincent Nichols, an assistant to Cardinal Hume who became Archbishop of Birmingham (and later of Westminster); and then Bishop, but later Cardinal, Cormac Murphy-O'Connor. Also attending was Monsignor Phillip Carroll, who was secretary to the Catholic Bishops' Conference of England and Wales. This group met some six times, and all of us as individuals, in different ways, saw the Cardinal about six times each. Through these meetings, we explored what the possibilities might be.[6]

On one occasion, when all eleven of us were meeting, Cardinal Hume said that he had to go out to take a phone call. Eyebrows were raised as we wondered where this phone call would be coming from. He came back into the room and said, "I've just been talking to someone in Rome, a very senior person in Rome, who asked me to tell you that in our deliberations we should remember Acts Chapter 15, verse 28." There were five bishops of the Catholic Church, the Bishop of London, and many of us who were senior Anglican clergymen, and not one of us knew what Acts 15:28 actually referred to! So a little bell had to be rung, a nun came in, and she was asked to get a Bible. The Bible came back, and we read the crucial words: "Impose no greater burden than is necessary." At that point, Bishop Leonard started to cry. There was a sense that we had reached the possibility that our aspirations could come to fruition.

---

[6] Cf. William Oddie, *The Roman Option* (London: HarperCollins, 1997), chapters 3–7.

What were those aspirations? That we could follow the example of what had happened in America and what in other discussions had taken place in the twentieth century between Rome and various groups of Anglicans, not least the Malines Conversations of the 1920s. Our contact in America was Father James Parker, who was a former Anglican and assistant to Cardinal Law. Many were the phone calls and the very expensive airmail packages that came from him with all the documentation about the Pastoral Provision in the United States and the correspondence that had taken place when American Anglicans first started their own society and organization and relationships. All that came over and was examined in detail by us.

Bishop Leonard himself produced a paper about the possibility of using an Anglican Rite. And this paper, some thirty-six pages of it, we discussed and wrestled with, over about two or three weeks. The possibilities of the financial arrangements were something that I had to deal with. We were very fortunate in one sense: the Church of England had actually produced a financial package to help those people who wanted to leave. Because the vote for women's ordination was so close, and because the decision had to be ratified by the English Parliament, Anglican leaders had been told quite bluntly, I think, that unless there was proper compensation and safeguards for those who were opposed, the legislation could well fail. And so the English Church did produce a package that gave support to clergy who should in fact decide to leave.

One of the most devious contributions I ever made in General Synod was when the financial package was being discussed. One of the proponents of the ordination of women was arguing that this financial package should be available for just three years. I got up and said in a rather plaintive way: "We are told that the ordination of women is so won-

derful, and that when it happens it will have such converting power that many of those that are opposed may want
to come back. Surely you're forcing our hand if you say we
have to do this within three years."

"Oh, we'll make it ten then!" So it was decided that if
anyone immediately left the Church of England he would
get, for ten years, two-thirds salary plus pension enhancement; if a person made that decision sometime within the
following ten years, he would then start the ten-year compensation process.

The compensation plan was clearly a positive thing, and
the Roman hierarchy was very pleased. But there was another
difficulty, similar to one in the States, namely, of course,
that Anglican parishes do not own their own property. Moreover, the Church of England doesn't own its own property
either! In any given little village, even if there are no Christians at all, and there happens to be one Hindu running the
local grocer's shop, he can claim that it is *his* parish church,
and no one can take it away from him. The option of parishes taking not just their priest (who would continue to
be paid by the Church of England) but also their building
was clearly impossible. The idea, therefore, of parishes per
se coming into full communion with the Catholic Church
was not actually workable. What was workable was the possibility that if groups of parishioners left a parish church
and wished to continue with their own priest to serve them,
that they would be accommodated by the Catholic Church
in England. At the end of the day, I brought forty-five of
my parishioners with me, which in the Church of England
is a substantial amount for a little parish church. Father Christopher Colven from Saint Stephen's, Gloucester Row,
after some eighteen months of exploration, brought about
thirty-eight people with him. In both cases, we priests
and the laymen with us did not wish to continue in our

independence; partly because we could see ourselves becoming a group that got smaller and smaller, and partly, of course, because we recognized that most of the people we brought with us were, and I use these words broadly, already Catholics in the English sense, which particularly became apparent when we discussed the liturgy.

Bishop Leonard was talked out of pursuing a Catholic liturgy based on the Book of Common Prayer, not by the Catholic bishops, but by his fellow Anglicans. He implied that if Anglican converts could have their own Prayer Book liturgy, which had been "catholicized", parishes would come in droves. One had to ask, however, "How many of these parishes were at that moment using a Prayer Book liturgy?" Of the people that we represented, how many of us, despite our acknowledgment of the Prayer Book as a source for doctrinal belief, were actually still using the Prayer Book liturgy? In the Catholic Movement (i.e., the Anglo-Catholic Movement, to use that traditional phrase) in England, the bulk of us were already using the *Missa normativa*. Therefore, to suddenly go back to using something we'd abandoned long before not only would be alien to the very people we were bringing, but would almost contradict what already we were doing.

The same applied to the question of whether or not we should have a personal prelature, which was explored in great detail. Here I think geography had to be taken into account. In England, there is an Anglican church on every street corner, and a Roman Catholic church almost next door to it. To create a third jurisdiction would cause confusion, if not contradiction. It is possible in the United States for that problem not to arise, but in England it could hinder the long-term conversion of the country.

In spite of the obstacles, Cardinal Hume was very keen (some would say, too keen) to try to force some deal through.

He took me once—partly, he said because I could charm them (I don't know if I did or not)—to a meeting of some of the Catholic bishops in the north of England. The reason he took me was because Rome had insisted that, if whatever might happen were to happen, it would require the unanimous approval of all the current bishops, and Cardinal Hume was a little concerned that he actually wouldn't get unanimous approval. There was Bishop Tom Holland of Salford, whom he had to acknowledge was being rather sticky and problematical. So I went to the northern gathering of bishops and witnessed Cardinal Hume talk about the options that were available. Some of them have never been publicized, and some of them quite literally took my breath away, as much as everybody else's at that meeting.

Cardinal Hume said, "I am going to apply to Rome that these people should be allowed to be ordained directly to the priesthood *per saltum* and not be required to go through the diaconate. I am going to ask Rome to acknowledge that in certain circumstances they can be allowed to be ordained conditionally." That request was granted. Any Anglican priest, if he wants to, can apply to be ordained conditionally. How long it takes is another matter, but the point is that he can. Hume said he wanted Anglican clergy, including married men, to be used to their full, that is, to be parish priests. He added that he wanted the question of a personal prelature to be acknowledged as a possibility, but that was not a decision for them to make. He then gave them a biblical exposition: "I want you to realize", he said, "that it is possible to be called to the Catholic priesthood long before a man is Catholic. Remember Jeremiah in the wilderness. . . . These men who are coming, therefore, will not require the kind of training others have required in the past. And it must be left to the individual bishops in each diocese as to what training they should or shouldn't receive."

He added that he would ask Rome to give permission for *us* to make the decision as to who can be ordained.

These were very radical proposals, and they caused a reaction. In the end, most of them were accepted. The question of being ordained *per saltum* was rejected because it was assumed it would not be understood by the faithful, and Bishop Holland insisted that married men should not be allowed to be parish priests, but all the other things were accepted and sent to Rome for endorsement. Coming back on the train, Cardinal Hume said (with a little wink in his eye), "We'll get around the 'parish priest' thing within days." And so "we" did. That restriction still technically applied, but formerly Anglican married clergy were allowed to be parish administrators. Hence, there are many married priests who are "parish priests" in reality, but are called "administrators", and, they are doing very well.

After about a fortnight, Cardinal Hume phoned me up and asked me to come see him. He had been headmaster of Ampleforth, one of the very famous Benedictine "public" schools (as we call them in the UK, but they are, in fact, elite private schools), and he said he wanted to tell me how he had gotten on with the "Headmaster" in Rome. I went to see him in Westminster, and he explained that he had flown to Rome the previous week with Bishops Nichols and Murphy-O'Connor. "And first of all," he said,

> we went to see the Headmaster. We went into his office. There he was, a big bear-like man, standing up, beaming. And he called me towards him, put his arms around me, and said: "Basil, Basil! These Anglicans. Be generous. Be generous." We said, at that point, we thought we'd had better go and see the "Deputy Headmaster". So we went downstairs to Cardinal Joseph Ratzinger's room, and it was all very German. His desk was at the end of a big, long kind of corridor. He was writing away; he didn't look up.

We crept in; we sat in the front row like little schoolboys. And then he looked over his glasses, and said, "Cardinal Hume. Be flexible. Be flexible." Peter, the Pope was saying, "Be generous"; Cardinal Ratzinger was saying, "Be flexible"; so we went out and had a Campari!

What was the result? The proponents of the ordination of women (and it's there in the records of the General Synod) very obtusely claimed that 114 priests would leave. How they came to that figure I don't know, but they claimed to know, categorically. They were trying at that time to determine what the compensation would be. I was ridiculed because I publicly said that it was possible that over a ten-year period, 1,000 could leave. By 2007, 580 former Anglicans had been ordained into the Catholic Church, of whom 120 are married. On top of that, I suspect that at least 150 more have resigned but simply decided to remain as laymen. I believe 5 priests went to Orthodoxy, and 7 joined the continuing bodies. Therefore, within the first ten years after the Church of England decided to ordain women, 742 left. Was my 1,000 or their 114 the more accurate figure?

There were, of course, women waiting in the wings, and about a 1,000 women very quickly became ordained; in practical terms, it may have seemed as if nothing much had changed. However, historians look back to the nineteenth century to the Gorham judgment,[7] which brought people like Henry Edward Manning and Frederick William Faber

---

[7] In 1848, Bishop Henry Philpotts of Exeter refused to institute Reverend George C. Gorham as vicar of Brampford Speke because of his Calvinist views about baptismal regeneration. Gorham sued Bishop Philpotts, and the ecclesiastical Court of Arches upheld the Bishop. The Reverend Gorham then appealed to the Privy Council, and in 1850 the Privy Council overturned Bishop Philpotts' decision and ordered Gorham installed. The fact that a secular court was making decisions about church doctrine caused a great scandal and was the occasion for many Church of England clergy abandoning the state church and becoming Catholics.

into the Catholic Church, and see it as one of the turning points in the history of the Church of England. In the wake of the Gorham judgment, 130 priests left the Church of England, and the total number of priests at that time in 1850 was 24,000. In contrast, the 730 recent exits were out of a base of 11,000. I believe, historically, it will be seen as a far greater moment than the Gorham judgment.

The result of the exodus has been predominantly very good. There have been some disappointments, however. Cardinal Hume did ordain some people very quickly, within sixteen days in one case, and there have been, particularly in the Diocese of Westminster, which was his diocese, four or five priests who've fallen by the wayside or have created scandal. I think that is a very small price to pay compared with the total numbers that were involved and the gifts that were brought with them into the Catholic Church. At least one former Anglican has become a bishop. Three have become canons of Westminster Cathedral, which means they hold prestigious positions within that diocese. Others are teaching in seminaries and influencing the Church of the future. All of these men have found a place where they can use their talents and enrich and renew the Catholic Church.

The Gifts Anglican Converts Bring to the Catholic Church

At an ordination in Westminster Cathedral, Cardinal Hume took me aside and led me up a little turret kind of staircase. It reminded me a bit of the temptation of Jesus when Satan said, "Come up here and let me show you my kingdom." We looked out—it was a Maundy Thursday Mass—and there were all the priests of his diocese, and the Cardinal said, rather teasingly, "This is my kingdom." He added, "They are good men, but some of them don't know they've been born. They've been Catholic all their life, whereas yourself, and other people like you, have not been. As we welcome you, we ask you that you use your gifts for the good of the Church."

What are those gifts? I can mention many, but there are *three* in particular which former Anglicans bring into the Catholic Church. The first, as our friend Monsignor Ronald Knox so cleverly demonstrated, is apologetics. Cardinal Hume said to me once: "Peter, I know that everything you believe you had to fight for." Unbeknownst to me, he heard me preach in Southwark Cathedral at the Catholic Renewal Conference. "I saw the way that you defended the Catholic Faith," he said, "in a way that my own friends and flock don't need to. They take it for granted." Ronald Knox, in his writings and in his pamphlets, was the exponent par excellence of that great gift of explaining simply the fundamental truths of the faith. I still have my Francis Hall *Dogmatic Theology* series, and I highly recommend them. They consist of something like twelve volumes, and they are possibly the only titles the American Church Union still publishes. Within them, there are good arguments for so many of the doctrines of the faith, so they are helpful for teaching and converting.

The second great gift that former Anglicans bring to the Catholic Church relates to the liturgy: *Lex orandi, lex credendi* ("The word prayed is the word believed"). I already mentioned how moved I was when I went into an Anglo-Catholic church, and those people genuflected around me. The old aphorisms "The Mass has converting power" and "The Mass is mission" surely still apply today. Their message is symbolized by the statues of Peter and Paul standing outside Saint Peter's in Rome. Saint Peter is pointing to the church, while Saint Paul is pointing in the distance, and

the wags say: "That means we make the liturgy here, but
we enact it over there!" When it comes to worship, some
of us Anglicans were doing it better than our Roman Catholic confréres. We read the rubrics and we kept them. The
most recent rubrical guide to the new Roman Mass is by
Monsignor Peter Elliot, who is now the Auxiliary Bishop
of Melbourne (another former Anglican who has made it
to the purple). He has written his own guide on how worship should be done, and it is one of the gifts Anglicans
have given the Church.

The third gift is pastoral care, one of the great marks of
Anglicanism through history. Perhaps we have excelled as
pastors because our parishes have been fractionally smaller
(we haven't had crowds of people). Our parishioners know
they are a part of a community and a family, and we nurture them, sustain them, and help them on their pilgrimage. This is a great strength we must hold on to. We must
resist the bureaucracy, and the committees, and all that activity that takes us away from pastoring souls. We must reem-
phasize that each and every one is precious and needs to be
protected and developed.

What about the Future?

Enoch Powell, a professor of classics at Sydney University,
Australia, before becoming a member of the English Parliament, once said, "The trouble with the British Commonwealth is, it has nothing in common and no wealth."
I'm not one for saying that the days of the Anglican Communion are over. I am not one, above all, for predicting
that its obituary will be written in a few days' time or even
a few years' time. Look at the Church of Sweden and the
Church of Norway as examples of how churches can carry

on even when the people have totally deserted them. However, one of the things that surely has happened in our lifetime is that the Anglican Communion lost whatever it had in common, as well as its union. There was a time when, of course, in the Communion we had a common Prayer Book and a common ministry, but both of these have gone. The worst, or the best, Anglicanism can claim for itself now is that it is a mere federation of separated bodies. That may seem obvious to us, but it's been a long time for Rome to recognize that. Rome does not wish to be accused in any way of "dividing and conquering" or of "cherry picking". Therefore, Rome will not, in fact, initiate processes within the Anglican Communion which could be interpreted in that way. It *is* recognizing, however (as it is also recognizing in its discussions, by the way, with the Lutherans), that, in fact, both within Anglicanism as a whole, and even within individual provinces, there are no longer any homogeneous bodies. It is possible that in the United States this division will pan out to the point where it will be obvious to everybody and that the time has come when Anglicanism itself, of its own accord, will have to separate. At that time, if a group of Anglicans makes a plea, Rome will listen.

On a visit to London, Cardinal Kasper said he had at long last recognized that possibility. "We cannot act unless there is a crisis," he said, "but if there is a crisis, and people appeal, we are there to listen."

He reminded me of dear old Archbishop Michael Ramsey, that saintly Archbishop of Canterbury, and the words he said on television when Rhodesia was declaring its independence. His words were true biblically, but total nonsense to the unemployed and the workers who must have heard him. "Ah, crisis, crisis", he said. "Remember, 'crisis' in the Greek is spelled with a 'k'. Remember, it means 'God's moment'."

This is God's moment, and God's Church, and we are
God's children. God's moment is not our moment; it is an
engraced moment. When people respond, they respond
because mysteriously God has spoken to them. Nicodemus
came later than others but was not rejected. Within Anglicanism, there will be those moments of crisis, and if at those
moments people ask, Rome will respond. There is no one
plan that fits all. Clearly, the Church will not do anything
that is contradictory, but she is very happy to do things that
are complementary. She will learn from us in England and
see what perhaps works in certain circumstances and not in
others. All good things are possible for the unity of the
Church, and the moment has to come when people must
ask.[8]

There is another moment when the Church might act—
the canonization of John Henry Cardinal Newman. His cause
is progressing, and there is one man in Rome who knows

---

[8] In 2005, I had, rather cryptically, been asked by the apostolic delegate to
do a paper about the possibility of a personal prelature for Anglican converts.
At the time of my talk in 2007, I knew that the Traditional Anglican Communion (TAC), headed by Archbishop John Hepworth of Australia, had talked
to Rome about unity. Later in that same year, the bishops of the TAC met
in Portsmouth, England, and unanimously endorsed approaching Rome about
some way of establishing communion with the Catholic Church, signing a
copy of the *Catechism of the Catholic Church* as a sign of their faith. The
greatest outcome—of which I could but only hint at in 2007, since it has
never happened before in Catholic history—was the publication on November 4, 2009, of the Apostolic Constitution *Anglicanorum coetibus*. This not
only answers, but totally exceeds, the wildest hopes of any of us, who have
prayed for so long, for a worldwide, permanent, structural solution to the
reconciliation of Anglicanism to Roman Catholicism. As I write, it is the
very early days, but my prediction is that from small beginnings—which will
vary from province to province—gradually the process will reach a "critical
mass". At that point, the transition of Anglicans to the Ordinariate will rap-
idly increase, depending on the heterodoxy and heteropraxy of the country/
province concerned. Within two generations of that point, I believe, up to
half of the Anglican Communion worldwide will be reconciled.

more about Newman than all of us put together: Cardinal Ratzinger. He's read his books and has talked at conferences about him; he's been to Newman Symposiums. When (I believe it is "when" rather than "if") Newman is declared a saint, that too could be a crucial moment for the reconciliation of Anglicans to the Holy See. Newman's works, beautiful Victorian English as they are, pose the same questions with which modern Anglicans are wrestling. In his *Difficulties for Anglicans*, which has been reprinted in the States, but which nobody seems to want to reprint in England, are the very questions that confront Anglican converts. They are the questions others have still to ask. When that moment of his canonization comes, there will be a new dawn in the relationship of Anglicanism with Catholicism.[9]

As an Englishman, perhaps I should finish with an English quotation, from one of the most English of all, Robert Browning:

> Grow old along with me!
> The best is yet to be,
> The last of life, for which the first was made:
> Our times are in His hand
> Who saith "A whole I planned,
> Youth shows but half; trust God: see all, nor be afraid!"

The best is yet to be.

Father Peter Geldard was ordained an Anglican priest by Archbishop Michael Ramsey in 1971. He served an eight-year

---

[9] Pope Benedict XVI visited the United Kingdom for a state visit in September 2010. The highlight was his celebration of the Beatification Mass for Blessed John Henry Newman at Cofton Park, Birmingham, on Sunday, September 19, 2010.

curacy in Sheerness, Kent, in the Diocese of Canterbury, which he represented on General Synod for twenty years. In 1978, he was appointed General Secretary of the English Church Union. During that time, he travelled extensively throughout the Anglican Communion, frequently to the United States, where he became well known for his oratory and preaching. He was Chairman of the Catholic Group of General Synod at the time of the ordination of women to the priesthood debate in 1992. In 1994, together with the whole parish council and thirty-five members of his parish congregation in Davington, Kent, he was received into the Catholic Church and was ordained a Catholic priest in 1994. He is the Roman Catholic chaplain and runs the Catholic Society at the University of Kent in Canterbury, England.

JURIDICAL STATUS OF THE ANGLICAN USE

Chapter 4

An Anglican Uniate Rite?

C. David Burt

In the Decree on Ecumenism of the Second Vatican Council, the Catholic Church committed herself to achieve Christian unity, but not unity at all costs. The introduction speaks of the restoration of unity as "one of the principal concerns of the Second Vatican Council". Great excitement ensued following the Council as people began to hope that the bitter divisions among Christians would soon be put to rest. While there is certainly a greater feeling of tolerance today, actual unity seems as far away as ever.

It is certainly true, however, that among Anglicans, whose communion was singled out as having a special place, the hope and drive for unity with the Holy See has remained high. Practically all of the strife in the Anglican Communion—from the Lambeth Conferences, which permitted divorce and artificial birth control, to Bishop Pike, the ordination of women, Bishop Spong, and now the ordination of homosexuals—has been colored by the obvious fact that such innovations in the life of the church make unity with the Catholic Church far more unlikely. This has led to large defections and now seems to be bringing the Anglican Communion as a whole to something that it has somehow avoided

Originally published in *Anglican Embers* 1, no. 5 (February 2005): 121.

throughout its history: a massive and decisive schism.[1] Call
it what you will—realignment or simply a split—the unity
of the Anglican Communion is a thing of the past.

Anglicans of all stripes are "mad as hell" at what is going
on, and even the measured pleading of the Windsor Report
is unlikely to prevent things from taking their course. The
previous schism in the Episcopal Church stemming from
the Congress of Saint Louis in 1977 has disintegrated into
splits within splits. And it must be noted that the original
petitioners for the Pastoral Provision for Anglicans in the
Catholic Church represents one of these splits. Others went
to Orthodoxy, and at last count there were at least three
major continuing Anglican bodies in the United States as
well as some minor ones. Snubbed and smarting due to the
Windsor Report's rewriting of their history in a way as to
render it inconsequential, they are moving ahead to con-
solidate and to form alliances with the Anglicans who are
presently in a state of crisis.[2]

This is what the consecration of David Moyer and David
Chislett as bishops is all about. They are members of Forward in Faith, one of the groups still in official Anglicanism that is trying to "save the day" for traditionalists, and
they have been consecrated by Australian Archbishop Hepworth, of the Traditional Anglican Communion, a continuing church body. Other consecrators were bishops in the
official Anglican Communion, and they have been appointed

[1] For a description of the major Anglican communities in the United States
see William J. Tighe, Ph.D., "Anglican Bodies and Organizations", in *Mere
Comments*, the blog of *Touchstone* magazine, October 22, 2006: http://
merecomments.typepad.com/merecomments/2006/10/anglican_taxono.
html.

[2] See the "Statement from the Metropolitan concerning Church Unity",
July 3, 2007, by Archbishop and Metropolitan Mark Haverland, at the website of the Anglican Catholic Church: http://anglicancatholic.org/met-unity.
html.

as suffragan bishops in the Anglican Diocese of Murray, Australia. Basically, they have their feet in both the "official" Anglican Communion and in the "continuing" church. What this will mean is yet to be seen. Will the Archbishop of Canterbury accept them?

In addition, Archbishop Hepworth has officially asked for unity with the Holy See, and David Moyer and David Chislett have been very vocal in saying that this is what they want too. The Vatican has not told them to go away.[3]

What are they asking for, and what will they get? It seems clear that what they want is an Anglican Rite in the Catholic Church, some kind of "Uniate" status. The Second Vatican Council certainly envisaged such a thing, and possibly if the Anglican Communion had behaved itself in the last thirty or forty years, it would be in full communion with the Catholic Church now. Can you imagine the Pope on one of his trips celebrating Mass in Canterbury Cathedral? We dared to hope for such a thing, but everyone, including the Pope and Cardinal Ratzinger, see that "grave obstacles" have been thrown up, and that such unity is very unlikely now.

The Anglican–Roman Catholic International Commission (ARCIC) official ecumenical dialogue has come out with some remarkable statements of agreement, but the dialogue that once had a sense of hope because of the "special place" the Anglican Communion had in the eyes of the Catholic Church has now been relegated to the back burner

---

[3] The text of the letter from the Traditional Anglican Communion bishops to Pope Benedict XVI of October 5, 2007, may be found on the "Messenger Journal" website of the TAC: http://www.themessenger.com.au/Annoucements/20100127.html#Story2 ("Annoucements" is missing an *n* in the actual URL). The response of the Holy See to this letter and petitions of other Anglican groups can be found in the Apostolic Constitution *Anglicanorum coetibus*, found in Appendix C.

for all intents and purposes. Can Archbishop Hepworth and the Traditional Anglicans who are out of communion with the See of Canterbury pick up on this and become a new Anglican partner with the Roman Catholic Church for talks leading to unity? This seems to be what they are asking, and the Vatican seems interested.

From the point of view of Anglicans in the Pastoral Provision, this is a very hopeful development, although it is not clear what will result from it. Evidently, what is being talked about is not simply extending the Pastoral Provision to them as it is presently constituted. They can't do that anyway, since the Pastoral Provision is limited to the United States. If they are asking for an Anglican Rite, a kind of Uniate status, with their own bishops, what is the precedent for establishing something like this for such a small group? What could be offered to them short of a Rite? Would a personal prelature be a possibility?

One of the shortcomings of the Pastoral Provision from an Anglican Use point of view is that it specifically prohibits the ordination of married men as priests in the future. Only married men already ordained as Anglicans are eligible. What happens when there aren't any more? Could a Rite or a prelature allow the ordination of married men to the priesthood? And could such an arrangement allow the restoration to the priesthood of Catholic priests who have left the priesthood to get married? It is no secret that many priests in the continuing churches are former Catholic priests, including Archbishop Hepworth himself. Archbishop Hepworth, to his credit, has said that if this is a problem, he will step aside.

The fact that there are only a handful of Anglican Use congregations in the United States and none elsewhere should be an indication that the Pastoral Provision as it is presently constituted needs something more. The Anglican Use Society hopes to encourage people to form groups, even without a former Anglican priest, but we don't think that this alone will assure the future of the Anglican Use.

Does the Anglican Use have a future in the Catholic Church, or is its purpose simply to ease the pain and culture shock of Anglicans who convert until they are happy with the Catholic Church as it is, and can be integrated? Are Anglican Use congregations expected to transition to become regular Roman Catholic congregations, much as ethnic parishes have done as the majority of their members have become English speakers? I think that if this is the purpose of the Anglican Use, it is a very cynical purpose indeed, and one that flies in the face of the Second Vatican Council.

Another view is that the purpose of the Anglican Use is to inspire and uplift the Catholic Church in the English-speaking world, and that once the incomparable liturgical style of the Anglican Use becomes more generalized in the Catholic Church, then its mission will have been fulfilled. This is the view of a dreamer, and it should be clear that the last thing most Catholics in the pews want today is Solemn High Mass with surpliced choirs in chancels and all kinds of paraphernalia out of Ritual Notes or the Alcuin Society's manuals. It will never happen.

Well, should the Anglican Use be here to stay or not? I certainly think that it should stay, and all the efforts to publish the Book of Divine Worship and to build beautiful churches suitable for Anglican-style worship should not go to waste.

So what it comes down to is this: we should be very interested in what is going on between the Vatican and Archbishop Hepworth, and we should pray earnestly for the intentions of continuing Anglicans who are seeking unity with the Holy See on somewhat broader terms than those which presently pertain to us. The Pastoral Provision was created to anticipate the exodus from Anglicanism that we are presently seeing. This being the case, the future of the Anglican Use itself may depend to a large extent on the success of Archbishop Hepworth's petition. If they have a sense of urgency in this, we should too.

C. David Burt was born in Boston, Massachusetts, in 1938. Trained at King's College, London, and the Episcopal Theological School in Cambridge, Massachusetts, he was ordained to the Episcopal priesthood. After serving in several Episcopalian parishes, he became involved in the Anglican Catholic Church. When the Pastoral Provision became available, Father Burt and his son were received into the Catholic Church in 1983. Disappointed in his bid to continue his priestly ministry in the Catholic Church, he took up secular work. He was also involved with the formation of the Anglican Use Society, was the first editor of *Anglican Embers*, and collaborated in the editing of the Book of Divine Worship, as well as editing and publishing the Anglican Use Gradual, the Anglican Use Office, and the Anglican Use Sacramentary. He is a member of the Congregation of Saint Athanasius in Boston, where he organized the schola and was the first editor of *Contra Mundum*, the parish newsletter.

Chapter 5

Anglican Uniatism: A Personal View

Father Aidan Nichols, OP

Biographical Introduction

The invitation to speak at the annual conference of the Anglican Use Society in Scranton, Pennsylvania, in spring 2005
was an opportunity to set in order my own thoughts, and
recent experiences, on the important subject that engages
them—important particularly in my own country, England,
but not only there. I was myself christened as an Anglican
and educated at Arnold School, a Broad Church Anglican
school named after that alarmingly dynamic headmaster
Thomas Arnold of Rugby. School religion, represented by
compulsory monthly church service as well as daily morning assemblies, had no effect on me at all. My parents were
only very occasional churchgoers, and my own religiosity as
a boy was basically pagan in character: a feeling for God in
nature, in the sea and the mountains, both of which were
close to where I lived. Any dormant sense of Christianity
was eventually awakened more by Eastern Orthodoxy than
by Anglicanism—through a chance visit to the Russian church
in Geneva, where for the first time I saw an iconostasis and

Originally published in *New Blackfriars* 87 (2006): 337–56. An earlier version of this article appeared in *Anglican Embers: Quarterly Journal of the Anglican Use Society* 1, no. 7 (2005): 171–95, and extracts therefrom in *New Directions*
8, no. 124 (August 2005): 17, and 8, no. 125 (September 2005): 13–14.

had an immediate intuition of the Incarnation. That prompted me, on my own, to start visiting churches in England, and I gravitated toward the Anglo-Catholic ones because, I suppose, they were the closest thing to the incarnationalism glimpsed in Geneva. But lacking any worthwhile religious education—the school curriculum included Bible study but it was quite nondoctrinal and anyway never seemed to get past the Old Testament, and even then, not beyond the Book of Judges—I was ill-prepared to act as a pro-Anglican controversialist when challenged to debate by a very well instructed, fellow student at our piano teacher's. His school put in all sixth formers for a diploma in Catholic apologetics. Eventually, the inevitable happened. I conceded defeat and knocked with considerable trepidation (never having met a Catholic priest and suffering from that residual religion of the English, which is anti-Romanism) on a local presbytery door. My instruction took a year and a half—there was a degree of anxiety, I recall, because I was so young, but I was eventually received in the spring of 1966 when I was 17. In those days, that involved conditional Baptism—in case the clergyman had failed to use the Trinitarian formula, or, as in the christenings of royal princes, one clergyman had pronounced the formula and another poured the water, neither of which was likely to have been my infant lot. It also entailed the profession of a lengthy counter-Reformation creed with much abjuration of errors, most of which had passed me by. That did not prevent my reciting it with considerable gusto.

The Panther and the Hind

My Anglican experience was, obviously, very limited, then. But it was still the church of my Baptism, and where I had learned, however vestigially, what I knew hitherto of the

Scriptures and the sacraments. What I did know quite well—by the time I was a professed and ordained Dominican and sent to Rome to teach at the Roman college of the order, the Angelicum (or, to give it its full name, the Pontifical University of Saint Thomas in the City)—was the history of England. I had read modern history when an undergraduate at Oxford, and in those days—perhaps even now—the syllabus had changed hardly at all since the late Victorian period, when the School of Modern History was established. Though Oxford dated "modern history" as beginning with the conversion of the emperor Constantine, the lion's share of the curriculum was devoted to English history, from the Anglo-Saxon invasion until the Second World War. So when I was asked by the founder of the Angelicum's "ecumenical section" if I could contribute a course on Anglicanism, I at least felt able to offer some lectures with a historical approach to the subject, and these became my book *The Panther and the Hind*, subtitled *A Theological History of Anglicanism*. My feeling for the subject had been reactivated, to some extent, by my years of association with Christ Church, Oxford, my old college, which was also the cathedral of the Anglican diocese. While in Rome, I was able to use the library—excellent for these purposes—of the *Centro Anglicano*, set up after the Second Vatican Council in the Palazzo Doria-Pamphili, where the Anglican representative to the Holy See and his wife were very generous hosts to me. I have always felt slightly guilty at having exploited their hospitality to write a book that is, in a sense, a deconstruction of Anglican claims, or so at least some interpreted it to be, including Doctor Graham Leonard, the last but one predecessor of the Bishop of London, who wrote a foreword for it before leaving the state church to become a Roman Catholic. For those who are unfamiliar with the book, whose publication coincided quite by chance with the 1992 Act of Synod in England permitting the ordination of women to the presbyterate, the basic thesis is that, owing to the nature of its historical origins, the Church of England is really three churches rolled into one. It is at one and the same time a church of a classically Protestant stripe, a church of a recognizably Catholic stripe, and a church of a Latitudinarian—or what would later be called "liberal"—stripe. My conclusion was that, while some Anglicans in the course of the twentieth century claimed to glory in such multiformity, this was making a virtue out of necessity, and a false virtue, not least in the ecumenical arena where the Church of Rome, for instance, might establish a bilateral dialogue to some purpose with one or other of these parties, but hardly with all three at the same time. I ended by envisaging as feasible not the corporate reunion of Rome and Canterbury, which is, surely, a chimera, but a selective union on a basis comparable to that of the Eastern Catholic churches. Such a selective union could, I thought, include the Evangelical emphasis on the primacy of preaching the Atonement as the answer to human sin, and the historic Latitudinarian high respect for rationality as a candle in the house of the Lord, though, naturally, its predominant basis would lie in the Catholic elements of Anglicanism brought to the fore by the Caroline divines, the Restoration High Churchmen and the founders of the Oxford Movement.[1]

The time when the book appeared was not only the period of the controversial Act of Synod, later confirmed by the British Parliament. It was also the epoch of the abortive attempt to arrange a corporate reconciliation for Anglo-Papalists or classical Anglo-Catholics, which, as William Oddie's book

---

[1] Aidan Nichols, OP, *The Panther and the Hind: A Theological History of Anglicanism* (Edinburgh: T and T Clark, 1993), pp. 177–80.

The Roman Option shows, came to grief partly through the intransigence of the majority of the Latin-Rite bishops in England but partly also owing to the ingenious "solution" devised by the then Archbishop of York, John Hapgood, for the problem of those who refused to receive the Act of Synod. The dissenters were declared a distinct and equal "integrity" entitled to appeal, on a parish-by-parish basis, for the alternative episcopal oversight, as offered by the so-called flying bishops, *episcopi volantes*—more properly the "provincial episcopal visitors" in the Provinces of Canterbury and York—and enshrined in the 1993 Episcopal Ministry Act of Synod.[2]

The Significance of New Historical Contributions

Since the time I wrote *The Panther and the Hind*, there have been further relevant developments. The first of these I should like to mention is the revisionist historiography typical of the last fifteen years in England, historiography that has, in one sense, strengthened but, in another sense, seriously weakened the Anglo-Catholic case. The new history writing underlines the way the late medieval Church, on the eve of the Reformation, satisfied the spiritual needs of Englishmen. Here the key figures are the Cambridge historian Eamon Duffy,[3] a Catholic, and his Oxford counterpart

[2] William Oddie, *The Roman Option: Crisis and the Realignment of English-Speaking Christianity* (London: Fount, 1997).

[3] Eamon Duffy, *The Stripping of the Altars: Traditional Religion in England, 1400–1580* (New Haven and London: Yale University Press, 1992); Duffy, *The Voices of Morebath: Reformation and Rebellion in an English Village* (New Haven and London: Yale University Press, 2001). Through the generosity of the author, I briefly had access to the proofs of the first book when reading the proofs of my own—but the impact Duffy's book would make was of course at that juncture unknown.

Christopher Haigh,[4] an Anglican, though these had a harbinger in the Warwick-based J.J. Scarisbrick,[5] also a Catholic. Their studies show that the Protestant aspect of the English Reformation, the dismantlement of the traditional liturgy and its attendant devotions, as well as the furnishings and accoutrements of the parish church, was profoundly antithetical to the historic Christian sensibility of the English people, formed during a thousand years of Catholic influence. That is what modern Anglo-Catholics had always guessed. Such phenomena as, under Henry VIII, the Pilgrimage of Grace became more difficult to dismiss as politically motivated or otherwise unrepresentative against the rising tide of evidence from wills, churchwardens' accounts, devotional manuals, and commonplace books in the local archives now increasingly tapped. Introducing his book *The Stripping of the Altars*, Duffy wrote:

> It is the contention of the ... book that late mediaeval Catholicism exerted an enormously strong, diverse and vigorous hold over the imagination and the loyalty of the people up to the very moment of Reformation. Traditional religion had about it no particular marks of exhaustion or decay, and indeed in a whole host of ways, from the multiplication of vernacular religious books to adaptations within the national and regional cult of the saints was showing itself well able to meet new needs and new conditions.[6]

Of course, this was, for Anglo-Catholics, a two-edged weapon. If popular Catholicism was so serenely successful,

---

[4] Christopher Haigh, *English Reformations: Religion, Politics and Society under the Tudors* (Oxford: Oxford University Press, 1993). See also Haigh, ed., *The English Reformation Revised* (Cambridge: Cambridge University Press, 1987).

[5] J.J. Scarisbrick, *The Reformation and the English People* (London: Blackwell Publishers, 1984).

[6] Duffy, *Stripping of the Altars*, p. 4.

what was the need for a break with Rome in the first place? What was left of the claim that the specifically *papal* Catholicism of the late Middle Ages was crying out—in England, at any rate—for purification?

This shadow hovering over Anglo-Catholic sensibilities—and Graham Leonard would cite (conversationally) Duffy's book, along with my own, as precipitants of his abandonment of the Canterbury communion—became even more ominous when the second movement of revisionist historiography entered the scene. That second movement has as its theme the essentially Protestant nature of the later Reformation in England, and centers on the Oxford Reformation historian and biographer of Cranmer, Diarmaid MacCulloch—who was formerly an Evangelical Anglican, though he now describes himself as a sympathetic observer of Christianity.[7] That second movement is less well known to the educated public, probably because it has no one to rival the television presentation skills of Professor Duffy. In any case, it conforms to the settled assumptions of non-Anglican Catholic Englishmen, unlike the first revisionist movement, which challenges them. Professor MacCulloch speaks of the Church of England from, at any rate, the reign of Edward VI as manifestly a Reformed church on the model of the Continental Reformation. Claims otherwise, driven by a theological urge to emphasize Catholic continuity for the *ecclesia anglicana* across the Reformation divide, are overwhelmingly the creation of the seventeenth and nineteenth centuries. He asks, prudently, "If . . . the

---

[7] Diarmaid MacCulloch, *The Later Reformation in England, 1547–1603* (Basingstoke: Palgrave MacMillan, 1990, 1992); MacCulloch, *Thomas Cranmer: A Life* (New Haven and London: Yale University Press, 1996); MacCulloch, *Tudor Church Militant: Edward VI and the Protestant Reformation* (London: Allen Lane, 1999; 2001); MacCulloch, *Boy King: Edward VI and the Protestant Reformation* (Berkeley: University of California Press, 2002).

debate on continuity is at root a theological one, should historians seek to enter it?" His reply is forthright:

> Certainly, since the case of continuity has always been argued around the historical facts of the English Reformation. Quite apart from the desirability of getting the facts right, one's understanding of the English Reformation should determine the theological conclusions drawn about the nature of Anglicanism; it should materially influence the decisions that Anglicanism makes about such important internal matters as moving toward the ordination of women and priorities in ecumenical ventures with other churches of the Christian West.[8]

What MacCulloch calls the "Anglo-Catholic historiographical victory" in the English universities of the late nineteenth and early twentieth centuries was made possible by the anomalies and compromises of the Elizabethan Settlement, but, as to Cranmer, the subject of MacCulloch's massive biography, "there was nothing of the via media between Catholicism and Protestantism in Cranmer's plans". In Cranmer's conflict with Bishop Hooper, the most radical of the Edwardine bishops, the "point at issue ... was not whether or not the Church of England should retain a Catholic character, but whether or not remnants of the Catholic past could be redirected to Protestant ends, in order to preserve order, decency and hierarchy." As MacCulloch says, "On the issue of ideology versus decency, Cranmer won, and in the construction of a renewed framework for the Church's worship, his work remained permanent."[9]

Although the thinking behind the Prayer Book was consciously aligned with Swiss theology, it remained capable of

---

[8] Diarmaid MacCulloch, "The Myth of the English Reformation", *Journal of British Studies* 30 (1991): 2.

[9] Ibid., p. 7.

being adapted in terms of outward symbolism in a startling variety of directions, as anyone who has done a Cook's tour of Anglican worship will know." [10]

Similar ambiguities continued in Elizabeth's reign, such as the contradiction between the moderate tone of the royal injunctions issued in 1559 and the "almost simultaneous action of royal commissions of senior Protestant clergy that unleashed a ruthless campaign of systematic vandalism in Church furnishings".[11] In an earlier generation, the Tudor historian John Neale proposed that Elizabeth's government wanted little more than an outward break with Rome, but Protestant activists in the House of Commons forced through a much more thoroughgoing set of changes. Research from the 1980s suggests otherwise. The government got the settlement it desired. Hesitations came from the conservative aristocracy—and of course from the Marian bishops. As MacCulloch notes: "Whatever the queen's own views, she quickly resigned herself to the inevitability of a thoroughgoing Protestant settlement in 1559, since the only senior clergy prepared to operate a national church for her were convinced Protestants." [12]

As Calvinist theology became more influential in the 1550s, Calvinist soteriology "became the orthodoxy of the English church from the 1560s to the 1620s". In MacCulloch's view, attempts to argue otherwise have not carried conviction. He points moreover to the anti-sacerdotalism of the Ordinal; the memorialist, or at best receptionist, eucharistic doctrine and consequent dislike of theologies of Real Presence; sabbatarianism; and the iconoclasm which, he remarks, before the Civil War was "murder not manslaughter", meaning: "premeditated and carried out by

[10] Ibid., pp. 7–8.
[11] Ibid., p. 9.
[12] Ibid., p. 10.

lawfully constituted authority, such as churchwardens or
the injunctions of senior clergy, rather than being the result
of some sudden frenzy".[13]

MacCulloch's conclusion is that "Catholic Anglicanism
was [thus] at best waiting in the wings when Elizabeth died:
a synthesis that had not yet been blended from a mixture of
conformist *jure divino* arguments, the Catholic hankerings
of a handful of clergy, the rationalism and traditionalism of
Hooker and a suspicion of systematic Calvinism." [14]

The situation only changed when, under the early Stu-
arts, a diplomatic revolution disposed of English support
for Dutch Protestantism, and Laudian clergy gained the mind
and heart of Charles I. The consequences were dramatic.
As MacCulloch puts it:

> The reaction of the Englishmen who had been nurtured by
> the Elizabethan church was to overthrow the government
> which had allowed such a thing to happen; yet when a
> version of the 1559 religious settlement was restored in 1660,
> never again was the established church to prove compre-
> hensive enough to contain the spectrum of Protestant belief
> that had been possible in the late sixteenth century. From
> this story of confusion and changing direction emerged a
> church that has never subsequently dared define its identity
> decisively as Protestant or Catholic and that has decided in
> the end that this is a virtue rather than a handicap.[15]

Assessing the Catholic "Party" in Anglicanism

Whatever the fairest view of the English Reformation, then,
even MacCulloch admits that a Catholic party emerged

[13] Ibid., p. 12.
[14] Ibid., p. 17.
[15] Ibid., p. 19.

relatively early, certainly less than seventy-five years after Elizabeth's accession. He is inclined to date it to the moment when, on James I's death, the duke of Buckingham asked Archbishop Laud to run his finger down a list of senior clergy and set against their names the letters either "P" or "O", meaning "Puritan" or "Orthodox". By the 1830s, it was certainly impossible to say there was no such party—even if, as Doctor Sheridan Gilley of the University of Durham has argued, it is, as he writes, "tempting to trace [the] troubles of the [present-day] Church of England to the very nineteenth century movement which did most for its revival".[16]

He is referring of course to the Oxford Movement, born as that was in the crisis of the European confessional state at the turn of the eighteenth and nineteenth centuries. In Gilley's words, its leaders were "more than conservatives: they were right-wing radicals who transformed the very tradition they set out to renew".[17]

Hurrell Froude, like the future Tractarian leaders, was a political conservative with a hearty contempt for majorities, and an even stronger contempt for the liberalism and rationalism to which he, like they, traced the radical Utilitarian critiques of the Church as a corrupt institution. With his affection for the theocratic medieval Church, Froude could be called the founder of Anglican Ultramontanism, a harbinger of the Anglo-Papalism of the most extreme or consistent (depending on how one looks at it) Anglo-Catholicism of the twentieth century. More influentially, the rest of the Oxford Movement men did what their High

---

[16] Sheridan Gilley, "The Ecclesiology of the Oxford Movement: A Reconsideration", *Nova* 1, no. 1 (1996): 4.

[17] Ibid., p. 5. The evidence is laid out in Gilley's prosopographical study of Newman in relation to his contemporaries, the distinguishing feature of his biography of the Servant of God, thus Sheridan Gilley, *Newman and His Age* (London: Christian Classics, 1990).

Church predecessors generally had *not* done: they declared that in possessing the apostolic ministry of bishops to guarantee the sacramental and spiritual life, the Church of England was Catholic and not Protestant. The Anglican *via media* was not the "old High Anglican Protestant middle way between popery and radical Protestantism". Rather, Anglicanism, properly understood, was a *via media* between popery and Protestantism itself. In Gilley's words, John Henry Newman "awakened the Church of England from the condition in which it could blithely assume that it was both Protestant and Catholic by asking the question that has plagued it ever since: Is it essentially Catholic *or* Protestant *or* Liberal?" And, as Gilley adds, "The points were connected, for Newman thought that the Protestant doctrine of *sola scriptura* led inevitably to the liberalism which denied the authority of Scripture altogether" [18]—something Gilley declares to be, by the early twenty-first century, a claim New Testament scholars proved daily. But just by calling itself Catholic rather than Protestant, the Oxford Movement awoke folk fears of Rome. By setting out to appropriate the devotional life and discipline of contemporary Catholicism, its followers appeared to be not so much interpreting the Book of Common Prayer as supplanting it. Many informed Protestants came to distrust Newman's appeal to the Fathers, implicit in the new Library of the Fathers, and his appeal to the more Catholic writers of the Anglican tradition, explicit in the new Library of Anglo-Catholic Theology. Though Anglicanism had long been, in Gilley's memorable phrase, an "ecclesiological Noah's Ark", what was novel in the early Victorians was the sharpness of the ensuing self-definition of factions, "partisan and even warring positions". The older, Protestant, High Churchmen were

---

[18] Gilley, "Ecclesiology of the Oxford Movement", p. 5.

marginalized as Anglican Protestantism became an anti-Anglo-Catholic Evangelicalism, and High Churchmanship an anti-Protestant Anglo-Catholicism. A few notable High Anglicans such as W. E. Gladstone retained a strong element of Protestantism in their Anglican Catholicism, but the general tendency of Anglo-Catholicism was toward a repudiation of the Protestant inheritance. The resulting internal divisions weakened the church, leading to the secularization of the University of Oxford in the later nineteenth century, and more widely, new problems in competing with an expanding Nonconformity. Newman's secession to Rome left his remaining disciples under a cloud as secret papists who might even yet secede, though their spiritual and intellectual gifts drew to them many of the best in the Church of England. The Anglo-Catholics, however, could survive and prosper only by flouting constituted authority. Theoretically, they had adopted an exalted theology of the monarchical episcopate owed to Saint Ignatius of Antioch and Saint Cyprian in the early Church. In practice, they defied Protestant and liberal bishops *con bravura*. Secure in the "parsons' freehold", they established "an infallible priest-Pope in every parish, loyal not to his immediate bishop but to Catholic Christendom in some vaguer, wider sense".[19]

So here we have them: on the ascendant from about 1870 to 1940 and then on the decline—and either way, beyond a doubt as to doctrine, worship, and devotion though not ecclesial communion, a displaced portion of Catholic Christendom. But the party system created in the later nineteenth century, with theological colleges teaching diametrically opposed Catholic and Protestant theologies, could in the long term benefit, as Gilley comments,

[19] Ibid., p. 7.

only theological liberalism, for it made the defining character of Anglicanism neither Protestantism nor Catholicism but a liberal comprehensiveness including them both and claiming to be broader, more inclusive, than either.

Appeal to comprehensiveness dilutes both Catholic and Protestant dogma, so that in the end neither Protestants nor Catholics but the theological liberals have proved the victors in the war for the soul of the Church of England.[20]

The question thus arises: What are we to do? Gilley writes:

The decline of Anglo-Catholicism seems to me a serious impoverishment of Christianity. No one who has not known the High Church tradition from the inside can appreciate its seductive fascination. It took all that is best and most beautiful in the Church of England—the King James Bible, the Book of Common Prayer with its wonderful Cranmerian cadences, the ancient cathedrals and parish churches, a tradition of literature and a tradition of learning, and the kindness, gentleness and tolerance of English life, and enriched them with judicious borrowings from the doctrine, devotion and scholarship of the wider Catholic world.

In fact, for Gilley, who himself left the Church of England to become a Catholic at the time of the controversy over the denial of the bodily Resurrection by Bishop David Jenkins of Durham, "it seemed the perfect meeting place between Catholicity and Englishness, without the harshness and philistinism of English Roman Catholicism, which has spent a generation destroying everything that was most beautiful about itself."[21]

---

[20] Ibid.

[21] Ibid., p. 9. This essay is more easily accessible under the same title in *From Oxford to the People*, ed. P. Vaiss (Leominster: Gracewing, 1996), pp. 60–75.

The Question of an Anglican Uniate Church

The question of an Anglican Uniate church is the question of whether all this (or most of it, or, at any rate, a significant part of it) could be preserved in a union, nonetheless, with Rome—not through absorption by the modern Latin-Rite Church in England or elsewhere but in union with the Petrine office, whose continued steadfast guardianship of classical Catholic Christian doctrine in faith and morals remains remarkably unshaken among the squalls of the contemporary world.

The 1992 Synod decision to ordain women to the priesthood induced a crisis in historic Anglo-Catholicism—by which I mean the Anglo-Catholic movement once its modernizing "Affirming Catholicism" element is left out of the count. This put my question on the agenda in an urgent fashion for the first time. And, in one sense, England turned out not the most helpful place to be when thinking through what such a union might involve. Speaking very generally, in England, Anglo-Catholics and Roman Catholics are too close for comfort. Owing to geographical proximity in a relatively small and culturally fairly homogenous country, Roman Catholics think they naturally understand Anglicanism. But they by no means necessarily do. An added problem is the temper of the Latin episcopate in England, at least at the time of the Synod vote. It is the implication of William Oddie's *The Roman Option* that the Latin-Rite bishops were implacably opposed to a Uniate jurisdiction for former Anglicans, Cardinal Basil Hume alone excepted. On my speculative analysis (unlike in the United States of America, in England and Wales, the proceedings of the Catholic Bishops' Conference are shrouded in confidentiality), the larger number of them believed Anglo-Catholics would never become proper Roman Catholics. Anecdotal evidence suggests there was widespread episcopal ignorance of how advanced the Catholicizing spirit is in classically Anglo-Catholic and especially Anglo-Papalist parishes. The remaining bishops, Westminster apart, were equally opposed, one gathers, on quite opposite grounds—namely, that these were aggressive doctrinaire conservatives who would swell the ranks of traditionalist Catholics, already found irksome at their diocesan pastoral meetings or by their letters to the Catholic press. Neither of these negative attitudes was totally without foundation. We can note that so distinguished a former Anglo-Catholic as Graham Leonard now thinks that those "coming over" were saved from impending disaster by such episcopal resistance.

But the upshot was predictable. The pro-Roman leadership of Forward in Faith, the organizational expression of the classical Anglo-Catholics, having ascertained that, where corporate reconciliation is concerned, no help can be expected from the Catholic bishops in England, determined to look to the Vatican directly. It aims in a preliminary move to establish full authority over its own parishes and other institutions through a "third" or "free" province on the territories of the Provinces of Canterbury and York, and this will be "free" not only in the sense of being exempt from the jurisdiction of General Synod, but also in that of being able to establish its own ecumenical agenda, looking away from the Northern European, episcopally ordered Protestant churches and Methodism, to which the eyes of the Synod are now turned, and looking toward Eastern Orthodoxy, and, especially, Rome. One of the reasons Forward in Faith has to tread carefully in the latter respect is the existence in its ranks of "non-papal" Catholics, for whom Eastern Orthodoxy is a reason for not taking the papacy seriously. (This is despite the fact that French Orthodox lay theologian Olivier Clément has recently shown in his study *You Are Peter*—whether or not a given oriental at some particular time chose to affirm or to query the Petrine authority—the topic never left the central agenda in the first millenium.)[22]

Anglicanism has achieved a more or less worldwide diaspora, and its Anglo-Catholic component likewise. So there is a need, even apart from local difficulties in England, to consider these issues on a wider than insular level. At the present time, it is the so-called Traditional Anglican Communion, the largest of the Anglican "Continuing Churches" with most of its strength in the developing world, that is making the running in matters of actually approaching Rome—though this is perhaps more owing to the realistic recognition that an attempt to repair an old schism by a new schism is somewhat contradictory than through enthusiastic rediscovery of the Petrine office as such. They know of course that not all is well in the Roman communion they may be entering, that in some places they may need a special environment not just to preserve an Anglican Catholic ethos but to preserve orthodoxy and orthopraxy until the crisis of postconciliar Catholicism in the West has passed—an eventuality considerably aided and abetted, it can be said, by the election of Pope Benedict XVI. Giving a brief address to their archbishops and others at a meeting in Arlington, Texas, in February 2005, I tried to offer some orientation for possible incomers to the Catholic Church from an Anglican background. I made six points, which I expand somewhat here.

    1. Starting—prophetically enough, as things have turned out—from comments by then-Cardinal Ratzinger, I echoed his view that the great crisis of the present day, underlying the shaking of foundations in all the churches

---

[22] Olivier Clément, *You Are Peter: An Orthodox Theologian's Reflection on the Exercise of the Papal Primacy* (Hyde Park, N.Y.: New City Press, 2000). I owe this point to Father John Hunwicke.

with the exception of those largely cut off from Western influence, such as the Ethiopian Orthodox, is anthropological, that is, to do with the essence of man. Is man simply part of nature, or has he through mind and personhood a spiritual vocation and destiny? Doubt about this is why all of a sudden bioethics has become so central a discipline, in issues like cloning, abortion, euthanasia. For Ratzinger, what is at stake goes far beyond these particular issues, important as they are, and concerns the entire Christian worldview. For Christian orthodoxy, the situation is so serious that a parallel can only be found by going back to the Gnostic crisis of the second century.

2. Secondly, the question *Is man simply part of nature?* inevitably creates huge problems for the idea—the basic credibility—of divine revelation. Is man the kind of creature who has fundamentally spiritual powers of understanding and love that can be elevated by grace into the means of meeting with the self-revealed God?

3. Thirdly, while, on behalf of the Church, philosophers indebted to her are struggling to show the anthropological possibility of revelation, the rest of us who claim the name of Christian must at least bear witness in the world to the essentially coherent nature of the orthodox concept of revelation, namely, that revelation is an utterly comprehensive truth, attested in a unique literature (the Bible), transmitted by a corporate subject, the Bride of Christ, who alone can receive that testimony aright and is equipped for that purpose with apostolic guardians, the bishops, whose task it is to ensure that the doctrinal deposit—which consists of the judgments duly made about revelation's contents—is handed on aright. In our present circumstances, it is

especially important to underline that, owing to this task of guardianship, bishops are primarily teachers, not bureaucrats, much less diplomats out for compromise.

4. Fourthly, there is a consequent need for all Catholic-minded Christians to come together. For the future of catholicity, the greatest potential *rapprochement* is in theory that between Rome and Orthodoxy. But the historical and emotional obstacles to this from the Orthodox side are such that in practice more is to be expected of convergences from the side of the Western communions that split off, directly or indirectly, from the Latin Church in the course of the modern centuries. What this means in terms of hard facts is bodies that have disengaged or are in the course of disengaging from such doctrinally liberalized communions as the Old Catholic Union of Utrecht, the Lutheran state churches in Scandinavia, and the Anglican Communion.

5. Fifthly, while the Latin Church today has considerable internal difficulties that it would be pointless to deny, a comparative survey of the dioceses within it would suggest that there can be successful strategies, usually comprising five pillars: the solid catechetical formation of the laity; enthusiastic encouragement of vocations to the priesthood; a care for liturgical beauty (in a sense, the Church's worship is her heart); missionary outreach; and a spirited defense of the family, which is the main place to nurture a right understanding of man, whose nature and goals the current anthropological crisis has called in question.

6. Finally, I reported that, in England at any rate, many Catholics look to Anglicans for inspiration on the third

and fourth of these pillars. Thanks to a multi-secular experience of vernacular worship, Anglicans know how to do it well. And they also have a drive to home mission linked to a sense of broader responsibility for the wider society. It was pointed out to me afterward that the latter of those is probably a distinctively Church-of-England thing, connected to the role of the crown and to the parish church as center of the larger community, especially in villages. Be that as it may, the Anglican clergy often have a strong sense of the survival of the vestiges of Christendom. At the worst, given the establishment status of the Church of England, this means in England token civic status without either power or respect, but at best it can have real effects at the grass-roots, especially where there is a touch of Evangelical charisma to give it dynamism.

A Vignette: Participation in the "Women in the Episcopate" Committee

I had picked up this last point from my main, recent source of experience of Anglo-Catholics, which came from appointment in 2001 as the representative of the Catholic Bishops' Conference of England and Wales to a committee called the Official Shadow Working Party on Women in the Episcopate, so a report on my experiences there may be relevant. In July 2000, the General Synod of the Church of England voted in favor of a private member's motion to study the possible opening of the episcopate to women, whereupon the House of Bishops established an Official Working Party on the matter with the Bishop of Rochester, an Evangelical of Pakistani origin, as chair. The leadership of Forward in Faith, supported by the Provincial

Episcopal Visitors, sought and gained from the then Archbishop of Canterbury recognition (hence the word "official") of a Shadow Working Party of their own on the same subject, the mandate of which was not to adjudicate the issues in a neutral spirit but to prepare the best possible theological statement of the case for the traditional position as well as to establish a strategy for how to respond in the event of the innovation being made. In the course of my membership of this commission, whose work came to an end in 2004, I certainly learned a great deal about the episcopate, if not necessarily about women! I also learned a lot about how these classical Anglo-Catholics (two bishops, three priests, one layman, and one laywoman) saw the situation.

It transpired that there is little if anything that can be called official teaching on the nature of the episcopate in the Anglican formularies. The best that can be found is some material in the Canons of the Church of England, especially canon 18, which affirms that the bishop is the principal minister in pastoring and teaching, but is otherwise chiefly concerned with a bishop's administrative functions. Though this legislation in a number of respects continues the medieval canons that governed the matter, it also reflects, as one of the provincial episcopal visitors rather brutally put it, the origins of the Anglican episcopate in the Tudor and Stuart civil service. Like all Anglo-Catholics, the members of the Working Party wanted to affirm a richer and more sacerdotal concept of the bishop's role as high priest and bridegroom of the local church, type and sacrament of Jesus Christ, the whole Church's High Priest and Spouse.

Without breaking too many confidences, I can say that the discussion frequently strayed into expressing the wider hurts and anxieties that had followed on the 1992 Synod decision, which the Ecclesiastical Committee of Parliament had subsequently sanctioned as expedient, even if part of the Parliamentary agreement hinged on provision for those who could not accept the introduction of women priests, whose Orders they considered at best dubious and at worst clearly invalid. The participants spoke of a loss of nerve, a disruption of parochial life, collapse of vocations, and damage to mental and physical health amounting to what one termed a "nervous breakdown of Anglo-Catholicism". The knowledge that a vociferous minority in the Synod wished to end the alternative episcopal oversight of parishes and effectively eject those who dissented did not help, nor did the awareness that "tricksy" solutions were being mooted by the Rochester Commission, such as team episcopacy and parallel episcopal jurisdictions, which would include women. One clerical member, contrasting such solutions with the ancient Christian notion that the single bishop as the ministerial principle—in Greek, *archê*—of sacramental life in each local church signifies obedience to the one divine Father there, went so far as to say in a written submission: "A plurality of bishops and thus a plurality of *archai* (polyarchy!) in a Church would make its episcopal ministry an efficacious sign of plurality in the monarchical fatherhood of the first Person of the Holy and Undivided Trinity: in effect, we would be committed to polytheism."

Subsequently, a published survey from an independent monitoring agency, which showed that women priests were more likely to be unorthodox on the Incarnation than were male priests, seemed to vindicate the Working Party's stand that the issues of gender, priesthood, and Christology belong together in a delicate balance that cannot be upset.

Some members were chiefly concerned about the provisionality built into the reform by its recognition of its own experimental character. This meant, they argued, the deliberate institution of avowedly dubious sacraments. I heard predictions that the reduction in seats of the 2006 General Synod would disproportionately reduce the Anglo-Catholic and Evangelical vote. Ideas of "reception", much trumpeted in the debates in Synod and the House of Bishops, were lambasted. Many of those in favor of women priests held that the 1992 decision itself constituted reception, though the notion could also be turned against the innovators. For example, if, as such frequently argued, Junias in the Pauline letters was a woman apostle, or if images on the walls of the Roman catacombs showed women celebrants of the Eucharist, then evidently the Church had subsequently determined not to "receive" these variations in practice.

Realistically, the members of the Working Party knew that few people in the Church beyond were likely to change their minds, so their efforts were directed to leaving behind as impressive a theological document on the subject as they could manage, and, more especially, looking ahead to a new settlement in the form of a free province. Work on this was delegated to a subgroup of canon lawyers who in England, owing to Establishment, are essentially civil lawyers using canon law as an additional tool. It was a task of some complexity, notably in regard to marriage jurisdiction, the law of burial, property law, and pension provision. All of this and more is covered in the final document, containing both the theological report and the legal blueprint: *Consecrated Women?* edited by Jonathan Baker, the Warden of Pusey House, Oxford, and published by Canterbury Press.[23]

I have little doubt that for the leadership of Forward in Faith and the provincial episcopal visitors, at any rate in the Southern Province, the ordination of women into the

---

[23] Jonathan Baker, ed., *Consecrated Women? A Contribution to the Women Bishops' Debate* (Norwich: Canterbury Press, 2004).

episcopate is the hurdle they cannot jump. The key arguments run as follows. When the bishop has ordained women
to the presbyterate, unity may be impaired but the very
impairment illustrates that unity is the norm that could be
restored if the error were removed. If, however, one were
to be ordained bishop who could not possess the character
of a bishop, then the element of unity would be entirely
missing, and an essential note of the Church would be absent.
There would be no local church. Furthermore, irregularly
ordained bishops, in conferring their own irregular Orders
not only on other women but also on men, would disrupt
the male priesthood and diaconate, creating doubt and uncertainty of a kind in practical terms impossible to resolve about
the wider sacrament of Holy Orders. Such bishops, once
welcomed into the provincial college of bishops, would place
its competence in doubt, not least in the matter of its com-
missioning any future episcopal visitors for traditionalist
groups.

Invited to address the 2002 Forward in Faith National
Assembly in London, I included the following passage. The
stand of the classical Anglo-Catholics on the issue of the
ordained ministry

> would not make complete sense unless it formed part of a
> wider movement to recover and maintain the Great Tradi-
> tion, the *Paradosis* of apostolic Christendom, in its fullness,
> in matters of faith and morals as a whole. The unity of
> Catholic Christendom is the unity of a face. In a face no
> one feature can be changed without altering the cast of all
> the rest. Contemporary orthodox-minded Roman Catho-
> lics look with admiration at those Anglican divines who, in
> various historical periods, sought to restore the authentic
> portrait of the Church and the faith of the Church. One
> thinks for example of Thomas Ken and John Keble as well
> as, closer to our own day, Gregory Dix and Eric Mascall.

These are separated doctors in whom the Church of Rome can recognize the overwhelming preponderance of the apostolic patrimony she has received. Your task is now not only the negative one of defending their work, but also the positive one of completing it. The Decree on Ecumenism of the Second Vatican Council makes this clear. The purpose of the Ecumenical Movement is not to arrive at a lowest-common-denominator Christianity. It is to restore the integrity of Christendom on the basis of the total revelation given to the Church by Christ and daily rendered a living reality by the Holy Spirit.

Inevitably, I had to refer to the delicacy of this project. Through the instrumentality of ARCIC, the Anglican–Roman Catholic International Commission, the Catholic Church has been engaged for the last forty years in a bilateral dialogue with the Anglican Communion as a whole. At one time, great expectations were placed on this dialogue. It was thought at Rome to be the one dialogue that might actually lead to organic reunion. One has the impression that bishops and archbishops were selected by the Holy See for the Church in England by the criterion, in part, of how warmly they would collaborate in that process. That is true most obviously of the present Archbishop of Westminster, Cardinal Cormac Murphy-O'Connor, who was for a time the Catholic co-chairman of those negotiations. Many English Anglicans and a few English Catholics knew that owing to the comprehensiveness of Anglicanism it was never going to work, but until recently it was—and in some quarters no doubt still is—politically incorrect to say so. Certainly, it is true that on any showing the Church of England will remain for any British Christian of whatever type an important part of the landscape to which some relation must be worked out. That is not to say that the hind can embrace the panther as a whole. The problem now is not only historic comprehensiveness or increasingly anarchic moral inclusivity, but it is also the arrangements made recently for ministerial exchange with Continental Lutherans and, mediately, the Reformed. I hope what I said was not so coded that it failed to strike home at all. It went like this:

> We know how delicate in practice is the ecumenical path we tread. There is in England a wider Anglicanism with less of a common mind than yours and yet a crucial national role to play in sustaining what remains of a Christian culture in this land. We can think of this as the Anglican Thames, sweeping down to the Westminster of Parliament, to Whitehall and beyond, out to the North Sea and the entrances to the Baltic and the Rhine where the national churches of the Lutheran Reformation have their homes. The ecumenical conversations between this Anglicanism and the Catholic Church will inevitably be long and arduous.

"But then", I went on,

> there is also another Anglicanism, more restricted in size but at the same time more compact and coherent in doctrinal outlook and sacramental practice. Perhaps, for those of you who know Oxfordshire, this is not the Thames but the Thame, a river without ocean-going pretensions, with clearer water, more at home in its historic landscape, which is still the country Alfred and Saint Edmund of Abingdon would have recognized, not to mention Doctor Pusey. This is the Anglicanism that looks to pre-Reformation Christendom, to the apostolic see of the West and, further afield, to those of the East. It is an Anglicanism that has already received much from the Latin Catholic inheritance, liturgically and otherwise. It is an Anglicanism too that has often nurtured the hope of restoring union with the patriarchal Church of the West from which it was sundered.... With this other Anglicanism, the ecumenical road is, by any reasonable assessment, shorter and more secure.

Naturally, this particular way of putting things was tailor-made for people in England, but the general issue—how to deal simultaneously both with a wider communion, with which one wants at any rate peaceable and friendly relations, and a narrower body within that communion, with which one seeks actual ecclesial unity—could crop up almost anywhere.

Conclusion

In my conclusion, I ask, how might the way to union with such smaller bodies—the way of Uniatism, in a word—be "shorter and more secure"? What are its chances of success, and what the pitfalls on its way? Speaking from a Roman Catholic standpoint, this question falls in one sense outside our responsibility to answer. It is up to bodies like the Polish National Catholic Church, emerging from the Union of Utrecht, the Nordic Catholic Church, emerging from the Lutheran Church of Norway, the Continuing Churches of the wider Anglicanism and the free Province of Saint Augustine of Canterbury—which Forward in Faith may or may not succeed in establishing—to decide what it is they ask of Rome, whether by "Rome" we mean the Catholic Church generally or the Holy See. We can, however, take steps to prepare for a response from our own side.

  1. Firstly, it should hardly need to be said that groups seeking Catholic communion while retaining a distinctive ecclesial life must manifest that desire for communion by a willingness to find in and as the Word of God the doctrine of the Catholic Church in its entirety—everything taught by Peter. If you want the communion of Peter, you must have Peter's faith. This is a *sine qua non*, and needs to be recognized as such.

2. Secondly, if we take the model of the Eastern Catholic churches, which is the only model for churches united but not absorbed that we have, we need to say that petitioning groups must be able to specify what it is about their distinctive patrimony that they wish to safeguard through having what used to be called a "ritual Church" of their own and in the present Codes of Canon Law is termed a Church *sui juris*, which I think should be translated "by its own right" rather than "with its own law". Anglican Catholics need to specify what it is theologically, liturgically, spiritually, that it would be both legitimate and desirable to retain in communion with Rome. This is a particular difficulty for English Anglo-Papalists, who are already, what one well-known representative of their number described to me as, "Roman-Rite Anglicans". The Book of Divine Worship produced for the Anglican Use parishes in the United States is a start here—though it may not be easy to commend it to the leadership of Forward in Faith UK, whose view of anything connected with the Prayer Book tends to be "We can't go back to that." Archbishop John Hepworth, the Primate of the Traditional Anglican Communion, has called it, at least in private, a basis for a definitive book. One reason for regarding it as not yet definitive are the criticisms put forward by well-informed, orthodox-minded, Latin-Rite Catholics who point to the desirability of some further fine-tuning of the Cranmerian texts it includes.[24] At the meeting I attended in Arlington, Texas, the Reverend David Moyer (who, controversially, was ordained

---

[24] See R. I. Williams, *The Book of Divine Worship: A Catholic Critique* (Bangor is y Coed, 2004), for details. I disagree with Mr. Williams inasmuch as he objects to any use of Cranmerian paraphrases or compositions on principle; I would defend it on the patristic principle of "despoiling the Egyptians".

a suffragan bishop in the Australian Diocese of the Murray by bishops of the Traditional Anglican Communion in a ceremony in his own embattled parish church in Philadelphia) spoke of the need for at least one theological college that would cultivate a distinctively Anglican Catholic ethos as well as for a married presbyterate and episcopate. I doubt myself that Rome would permit a married episcopate, except possibly by way of dispensation for a single sacramental generation, but the theological college would certainly be indispensable. There must be some way of transmitting a tradition with a small "t" within the Tradition with a capital "T". One cannot be forever living from hand to mouth. That is already a problem even now for the Anglican Use parishes of the Pastoral Provision, since despite the word "provision", no provision has been made for a future supply of pastors willing and able to lead their parishes on the basis of the Anglican Use. As I see it, such a college would take for its textbooks not only Roman Catholic works of impeccable orthodoxy but also *within that framework* Anglican "classics", any deficiencies in whose doctrinal understanding would be catered for in advance through contextualization by Catholic works.

3. All this would have to be presented prudently to the wider Catholic public. It can certainly be pointed out that the Second Vatican Council goes out of its way, in the Decree on Ecumenism, to give a special place to Anglicanism among the ecclesial communities that emerged from the Church crisis of the sixteenth century, and assurances that whatever is valid in the patrimony of Anglican worship, thought, and spirituality could be preserved in Catholic unity have been

forthcoming, if in very general terms, from postconciliar popes. Places to look would be, for instance, the speeches of Paul VI at the canonization of the Forty Martyrs of England and Wales and of John Paul II on his visit to Canterbury Cathedral.

Saint Thomas Aquinas, when speaking of the variety of religious orders in the Church, liked to cite the psalm which, in its Latin version, describes the Church as *circumdata varietate*, surrounded by variety. The pains and purgatories of the postconciliar period have taught us to treat "variety" with some caution, since pluralism comes in two forms, the legitimate and the anarchic. But an Anglican Uniate body, defined with discernment and sensitivity, could, I believe, join the ranks of the Churches *sui juris* which give Catholicism an indispensable dimension of its plenary or holistic quality.

John Aidan Nichols, OP, was born in Lytham Saint Anne's, England, in 1948, and educated at Arnold School and Christ Church, Oxford. He entered the Order of Preachers in 1970 and after ordination served as a university chaplain in Edinburgh and Cambridge, as well as teaching in a variety of Church institutions in England, Rome, and the United States. He was John Paul II memorial lecturer in Roman Catholic theology at the University of Oxford from 2006 to 2008. He is currently a member of the divinity faculty of the University of Cambridge and subprior of Blackfriars, Cambridge. He has written some forty books on different aspects of theology, including ecumenics.

Chapter 6

Whither the Anglican Use?

Stephen E. Cavanaugh

Among those in which Catholic traditions and institutions in part continue to exist, the Anglican Communion occupies a special place.[1]

The Pastoral Provision for the Anglican Use is in many ways the first fruits of the ecumenical movement in the Catholic Church. Through this provision, a real corporate reintegration of children of Reformation communities with the See of Peter has come about, which respects those aspects of Catholic tradition that have been preserved and fostered even in separation from the Catholic communion.

The great proponent of liturgical renewal, Father Louis Bouyer, Lutheran convert and Catholic priest, recognized these preserved and recovered traditions, writing:

> In the Church of England were found also some of the men who first perceived that the way to a true liturgical renewal lay neither in Protestantism nor in the Baroque

Originally published in *Anglican Embers* 1, no. 9 (March 2006): 236–42.

[1] Second Vatican Council, Decree on Ecumenism, *Unitatis redintegratio*, in *Vatican Collection*, vol. 1, *Vatican Council II: The Conciliar and Post Conciliar Documents*, ed. Austin Flannery (Collegeville, Minn.: Liturgical Press, 1975), p. 463.

mentality. And here also were some of the first men to see more or less clearly where the true way should lie.

We need not be afraid to acknowledge this fact, for the worst of heretics may sometimes have some very useful truths to tell us.... Nor were these men we have just mentioned, the Caroline Divines, the worst of heretics—far from it! ...

What was admirable about their work, and what had such a measure of success that it has endured even until our days ... is a Divine Office which is not a devotion of specialists but a truly public Office of the whole Christian people. This Office has some defects ... but, in spite of these defects, we must admit frankly that the Offices of Morning Prayer and Evensong ... are not only one of the most impressive, but also one of the purest forms of Christian common prayer to be found anywhere in the world.[2]

The Pastoral Provision and the Book of Divine Worship, which has been authorized for the use of the communities established under the provision, enshrine this tradition and make it available to the wider Catholic community. But, as those of us who are part of the Anglican Use congregations well know, ours is not a long-term solution. What will happen when our priest retires or dies? What if the next bishop of our diocese is hostile to the Pastoral Provision? Is there anything we can do to ensure that this Use, faithful to the Catholic heritage of English Christians, can be maintained? How can this Pastoral Provision, which we have experienced as a generous and merciful gesture on the part of the Church, be better enabled to serve as a bridge for those children of the English Reformation who wish to return to Catholic communion?

[2] Louis Bouyer, *Liturgical Piety* (Notre Dame, Ind.: University of Notre Dame Press, 1955), pp. 44, 47.

A glance at the recent history of two different groups in the Catholic Church will reveal that the best hope for the continuation of this Use is the erection of a *sui juris* church; that is, a church with its own law under an archbishop, himself under the jurisdiction of the Bishop of Rome, which can maintain its liturgical and devotional traditions in full communion with the Church Catholic.[3]

The Polish Catholics in America

By the end of the nineteenth century, the hierarchy in the United States was largely Irish. But increasingly, large numbers of the faithful were recent immigrants from Poland, the Ukraine, Italy, and the Baltic states. The Polish, in particular, chafed under the rule of the Irish bishops, who seemingly turned a deaf ear to their pleas for respect for their customs and traditions. The 1880s and 1890s saw an increasing number of defections from the Church, until finally, at the dawn of the twentieth century, the Polish National

---

[3] The Apostolic Constitution *Anglicanorum coetibus* does not establish a *sui juris* church; however, the ordinaries of the soon-to-be established personal ordinariates will be directly under the jurisdiction of the Bishop of Rome, and some particular canon law has already been created for the ordinariates in the apostolic constitution and the complementary norms published with it. Among the most important particular laws for the personal ordinariates are (1) the establishment of governing councils, partly elected by the clergy of the ordinariates, which must be consulted by the ordinary in specific cases; (2) the right of the governing councils to submit a *terna* (slate of three names) of candidates for ordinary when a new ordinary is to be appointed; (3) the requirement of pastoral councils at the ordinariate and parish level; (4) the right to establish houses of formation for clergy candidates; and (5) the right to establish ordinariate parishes where needed, after hearing the opinion of the ordinary of the diocese where the parish is to be established. Together with the rest of the apostolic constitution and complementary norms, these canons should allow the ordinariates to flourish.

Catholic Church (PNCC) was formed.[4] Father Francis Hodur, a priest from Scranton, Pennsylvania, was elected bishop of the new church, and in 1907 he traveled to the Netherlands to be consecrated bishop by the Jansenist Bishop of Utrecht. With this consecration, undeniably authentic apostolic succession was secured, and the new Polish denomination began organizing itself. One year later, the first Roman Catholic Polish priest, Father Paul Rhode, was selected as an auxiliary bishop for Chicago and consecrated as the first Polish bishop for the United States.

While its numbers are small, the PNCC has many congregations in areas with large Polish communities, such as western Massachusetts, northeastern Pennsylvania, and Chicago. While we must lament the rupture of ecclesial communion represented by the PNCC, we can see in this sorry chapter in the life of the Church in the US a good example of what was meant by the Fathers of the Second Vatican Council when they wrote: "But in subsequent centuries much more serious dissensions made their appearance and quite large communities came to be separated from full communion with the Catholic Church—for which, often enough, men of both sides were to blame." [5]

The breakdown of communion was not primarily doctrinal, but cultural misunderstanding and suspicion. The immigrant Polish Catholics brought to their new American homeland tensions and divisions that had arisen in their dismembered homeland (Poland having disappeared from the map of Europe after the Napoleonic wars) and that were characterized as making a decision about whether one was "a Catholic Pole or a Polish Catholic".[6] This conflict between

[4] Joseph John Parot, *Polish Catholics in Chicago: 1850–1920* (DeKalb, Ill.: Northern Illinois University Press, 1981), p. 155.

[5] *Unitatis redintegratio*, p. 455.

[6] Parot, *Polish Catholics in Chicago*, p. 29.

the nationalist and clerical parties had no central leadership that could bridge the two parties' differences, and the nationalist element had no desire to trade the Russian, Austrian, or Prussian overlords they left in Europe for an Irish one in America. The Irish hierarchy in the United States, in its turn, had no real understanding of Polish Catholic culture, and some prelates harbored prejudicial attitudes toward the Polish Catholics.[7] Many Poles, feeling slighted and impatient to receive recognition despite their impressive work in creating a large network of parishes, schools, orphanages, and hospitals (Saint Stanislaus Kostka parish in Chicago was, by 1900, likely the largest Catholic parish in the world)[8] left the communion of the Church to organize the PNCC. Greater sensitivity to the cultural and religious aspirations of the Poles, along with an earlier appointment of a Polish bishop, might have kept the schism from ever forming.

Eastern Catholics in America

The Eastern Catholic churches (also known, less correctly, as the Eastern Rite Catholics) although they are *sui juris* churches, have been subject to "latinization" or the modification of Eastern liturgies and customs and modes of thought by the adoption of foreign, i.e., Latin Catholic, practices since the sixteenth century. But in the United States, one of the most significant latinizations occurred as a result of the Latin bishops reacting negatively to the married clergy of Eastern Catholics, who arrived during the great waves of immigration at the beginning of the twentieth century. In October 1890, the Sacred Congregation for the

[7] Ibid., pp. 133–34.
[8] Ibid., p. 74.

Propagation of the Faith responded to the American hierarchy's requests by ordering all married Eastern priests to leave America. This resulted in huge protests from clergy and people, because most of the Eastern Catholic clergy were married.[9] Two years later, this order was rescinded, but while married priests were now allowed to stay, their wives and children were ordered to return to their original countries. Yet another series of protests ensued. One Byzantine Catholic priest, Alexis Toth, after poor treatment by Archbishop John Ireland, left the Catholic communion, placing himself under the authority of the Russian Orthodox Archbishop of San Francisco, and led thousands of Ruthenians out of the Catholic Church and into the Russian Orthodox Church.

Despite papal teaching that the "diversity of liturgical form and discipline of the Eastern Churches is approved in law ... [and] it has redounded tremendously to the glory and usefulness of the Church",[10] this pattern of treating Eastern Catholics with suspicion and without regard to their rights continued. According to one history of the Melkites and Maronites in the US, Latin bishops in the US "rarely, if ever, understood or sought to understand the mentality, customs and traditions of their Eastern subjects, who were consistently treated as foreigners and 'fake' Catholics".[11]

In the 1920s, the Latin Church bishops again petitioned Rome, which declared in *Cum Data Fuerit* that the secular clergy of the Ruthenian Rite who desired to immigrate to the United States must be celibate, and that married men were no longer to be ordained to the priesthood in the

---

[9] Daniel P. Grigassy, "The Eastern Catholic Churches in America", *Contemporary Review* vol 284, no. 1659 (April 2004): 193–99.

[10] Pope Leo XIII, *Orientalium Dignitas*, November 30, 1894.

[11] Phillip M. and Joseph M. Kayal, *The Syrian-Lebanese in America: A Study in Religion and Assimilation* (New York: Twayne Publishers, 1975), pp. 153–54.

United States. This caused another series of violent distur-
bances within the Eastern Catholic churches of the United
States, as loyalty to the Holy See and loyalty to traditions
sanctioned for hundreds of years (and established in canon
law!) were pitted against each other.[12] Ultimately, many thousands of Byzantine Catholics left the Catholic Church and
formed the American Carpatho-Rusyn Orthodox Church.[13]

Not only were thousands of souls lost to the Catholic
Church due to Latin mistrust and misunderstanding of the
Eastern Catholics, but the ecumenical implications have been
disastrous. As Eastern Orthodox Christians contemplate
reunion, they can only regard with horror a fate they must
believe would be theirs. Despite the terms of treaties like
those in the Union of Brest-Litvosk and Uzhorod, which
established the Ukranian Catholic and Ruthenian Catholic
churches, the Eastern Catholics have repeatedly been treated
shabbily by their overwhelmingly more numerous Latin
brethren.

Finding a Path Forward

In their common declaration, Pope Paul VI and Archbishop of Canterbury Donald Coggan stated: "Many in both
communions are asking themselves whether they have a common faith sufficient to be translated into communion of
life, worship and mission. Only the communions themselves through their pastoral authorities can give the answer.
When the moment comes to do so, may the answer shine
through in spirit and truth, not obscured by the enmities,

---

[12] Grigassy, "Eastern Catholic Churches", p. 193; Joan L. Roccasalvo, *The
Eastern Catholic Churches: An Introduction to Their Worship and Spirituality* (Collegeville, Minn.: Liturgical Press, 1992), p. 55.

[13] Grigassy, "Eastern Catholic Churches", p. 193.

the prejudices and the suspicions of the past."[14] In addition to those Anglicans who have already come into communion with the Catholic Church via the Pastoral Provision, other Anglicans stand at the door and knock, awaiting entry[15] as Anglicans who share the Catholic faith.

The experience of Polish Catholics and Eastern Catholics at the turn of the twentieth century in the United States has several lessons for Anglican Catholics: (1) The cultural differences between Anglican and the majority Roman-Rite Latin Catholics will need to be patiently explained to our Latin bishops and demonstrated to be fully Catholic even if different from customs of the wider Latin Church. (2) The ability of the Pastoral Provision to serve as a bridge to communion for Catholic-minded Anglicans, in both the Anglican Continuum and the Anglican Communion, is weak precisely because the status of Anglican Use Catholics depends not on right, but on positive law, which can be changed at will. In order to make a true home for Anglican Catholics within the Church, and not a way station, the Church needs to create a structure that will respect the legitimate traditions and rituals of Anglican Catholicism, unlike what occurred with some of the Eastern Catholics, for, like the Eastern Catholics, Anglicans know that "Romanism and Catholicism are not synonymous and that Catholicism must remain open to every form of organization compatible with a unity of faith".[16] (3) We need bishops who will be not only ambassadors to and advocates for Anglican Catholics,

---

[14] Pope Paul VI and the Archbishop of Canterbury, Donald Coggan, *Common Declaration* (April 29, 1977), in *Vatican Council II*, vol. 2, *More Post Conciliar Documents*, ed. Austin Flannery (Collegeville, Minn.: Liturgical Press, 1982), p. 185.

[15] David Chislett, *Letter* (February 10, 2006): http://www.themessenger.com.au/news.html.

[16] Kayal, *Syrian-Lebanese in America*, p. 37.

but also leaders within the community; as this need was belatedly recognized for the Polish Catholics, with Bishop Rhode acting as a center and a bond of communion, so Anglican Catholic bishops will serve as bonds between individual Anglican Catholics and with the Church Catholic.

This goal of a *sui juris* church, which will succor and sustain the patrimony of Anglican Catholicism, is in the hands of Divine Providence and the pastors of the Church. We must hope that it will be a further fruit of the ecumenical movement, a work of the Spirit in reconciling the dispersed children of God, that they may be one.

Steve Cavanaugh is a communicant at Saint Athanasius in Chestnut Hill, Massachusetts. He is the editor of *Anglican Embers* and the parish newsletter "Contra Mundum". Mr. Cavanaugh has taught in private, public, and parochial schools, and he is presently the managing editor for a major pharmaceutical journal. He and his wife have three children and live in Brockton, Massachusetts.

Chapter 7

Facing Realities, Looking at Options

Bishop Peter J. Elliott

The False Options

We are called to a hope based on realism, and the timely warnings of Cardinal Cormac Murphy-O'Connor and Cardinal Walter Kasper,[1] should remind all concerned Anglicans

Paper given at Forward in Faith Meeting, All Saints, East Saint Kilda, Melbourne, Australia, February 11, 2006. Originally published in *Anglican Embers* 2, no. 1 (March 2007): 33–39.

[1] Cardinal Walter Kasper addressed the General Synod of the Church of England on June 5, 2006, in a talk entitled "Mission of Bishops in the Mystery of the Church", which can be found on the Vatican website (http://www.vatican.va/roman_curia/pontifical_councils/chrstuni/card-kasper-docs/rc_pc_chrstuni_doc_20060605_kasper-bishops_en.html). In that address, Cardinal Kasper noted: "The episcopal office is thus an office of unity in a two-fold sense. Bishops are the sign and the instrument of unity within the individual local church, just as they are between both the contemporary local churches and those of all times within the universal Church", sec. 2, para. 11.

It is one of the heartening experiences of ecumenical dialogue that we have been able to establish that this understanding of the Church as koinonia, and with it the "koinonial" understanding of the episcopal office, is not just a particular Catholic tradition, but an understanding we share with the Anglican Communion. It can be found in the ARCIC conversations from the very beginning.

Should we not therefore also be in a position to say together: the decision for the ordination of women to the episcopal office can only be made with an overwhelming consensus and must not in any way involve a conflict between the majority and the minority. It would be desirable that this decision would be made with the consensus of the ancient churches of the East and West. If

of certain realities. But facing reality means first shooting down fantasies that have emerged in recent decades, what I call the *false options*, and this requires abandoning that recurring Anglo-Catholic tendency to grasp at dreams.

First of all, let us dismiss the concept of "flying bishops" and an "alternative jurisdiction" with "limited communion".[2] An independent jurisdiction within the Anglican Communion is a theological and canonical absurdity. At best, this merely describes a pro tem arrangement for the sake of distressed, Catholic-minded clergy and laity in a time

---

on the contrary the consecration of a bishop becomes the cause of a schism or blocks the way to full unity, then what occurs is something intrinsically contradictory. It should then not take place, or should be postponed, until a broader consensus can be reached.

Cardinal Cormac Murphy-O'Connor's warning that the ordination of women as bishops would result in ecumenical relationships stalling on a plateau was reported in the pages of the *Telegraph* on February 7, 2006. See Jonathan Petre, "Cardinal's Warning on Women Bishops", February 7, 2006: http://www.telegraph.co.uk/news/worldnews/middleeast/israel/1509865/Cardinals-warning-on-women-bishops.html.

[2] "Flying bishop" is a popular name for a "provincial episcopal visitor"; these are suffragan bishops appointed by the Archbishops of Canterbury or York to minister to parishes that cannot in conscience accept the ministry of women ordained to the priesthood. Three provincial episcopal visitors have been established: the Bishops of Richborough and Ebbsfleet for the Province of Canterbury and the Bishop of Beverly for the Province of York. Dioceses are also allowed to establish episcopal visitors, and the Diocese of London has established the Bishop of Fullham to this role, which has been extended to the Dioceses of Southwark and Rochester. An *alternative jurisdiction* would be a third province in England or a second province in the United States, which would be completely separate juridically from the existing provinces. There has been little support for alternative jurisdictions in England, although there is some hope that the nascent Anglican Church of North America, founded in 2009 and headed by Archbishop Robert Duncan of Pittsburgh, might be accepted as a second Anglican province in the United States. The idea of *limited communion* could involve everything from denial of shared Holy Communion to limitations on pulpit exchange and sharing; it has been proposed as a means of correction by the majority of the Anglican Communion applied to the US Episcopal Church.

of transition and decision, and many of our friends in England regard it as such. At worst, it is a recipe for bitterness, delusion, and division. It raises "hope against hope", another way of sliding back into fantasies and dreams.

So let me say at the outset, that I believe there is *nothing* to be said for attempting some kind of independent jurisdiction within an Anglican Communion that ordains women bishops, or condones this practice. Some people will strive to persuade you to "hang on" and find an oasis. That simply ends up as a retreat into congregationalism.

Those who would persuade you that this "flying bishop" structure has some future are usually the *Affirming Catholics* or well-disposed liberals. I wonder about their motives. I respect their right as liberal Christians, with or without Catholic opinions, to hold their own views, but I suspect that any effort on their part to secure "flying bishops" as a viable option may be mainly a salve to their own consciences. They can assure themselves that they have "looked after the extremists" and can present this to the public as "concern". They may be quite sincere about this, but as they lack a Catholic mind on the essential nature of the Church and Holy Orders, one cannot take their proposals seriously, even if they are well meant.

The question of Anglicans becoming Eastern Orthodox is an interesting option. I respect those Anglicans who have done this, their trail blazed by the remarkable Archbishop Kallistos Ware, who was an influence during my Oxford years. But this is a difficult journey. It involves a total cultural "makeover", and few of us are capable of that, especially in mid-life or sunset years. So I would dismiss this as, if not a false option, at least a burdensome and unnecessary one.

What then remains, apart from trying, and this will be futile in Australia, to seal yourself up in a parish or small group? *There is only one real option—what you call "Rome" and what I call "home"; what some of you still call "Auntie", but many millions call "Mother".*

Looking at the Roman Option

The Roman option takes three forms, which I will explore.

1. The reconciliation of individuals with the Church.

That has been going on for over four centuries, and the statistics are higher in certain eras than many Anglicans imagine. However, focusing on clergy, at his first meeting with "interested" Anglican clergy in Westminster, Cardinal Basil Hume made it clear that *Apostolicae curae*[3] still stands, that there can be no bargaining about Holy Orders. Whatever scholarly arguments may be raised about Anglican Orders (and the question is admittedly more complex than it was in 1896), the fact that women are deemed to be priests by most Anglicans—and that within a few years some of these will be deemed to be bishops—has made the question of Anglican Orders academic, even irrelevant. In some instances, as in the case of Monsignor Graham Leonard, former Bishop of London, conditional ordination would be feasible, but that is a detail. Anglican clergy who are reconciled to Rome,

---

[3] In his Encyclical *Apostolicae curae* (1896), Pope Leo XIII declared Anglican Orders to be null and void due to the "new rite for conferring Holy Orders ... publicly introduced under Edward VI" by which "the true Sacrament of Order as instituted by Christ lapsed, and with it the hierarchical succession" (no. 3; cf. no. 36). Recognizing that the issue had been raised anew by recent research, Leo XIII had ordered a commission to examine it again; however, it found the Anglican ordination rite to have defects of both form and intention (nos. 3–5, 33). Following the declaration, Leo expressed his concern, love, and support of his Anglican brethren (nos. 37–39).

who seek Orders, and succeed in their petition, are ordained absolutely.

2. The "corporate reunion" model of an "Anglican Rite".

This is apparently what is being sought by the Traditional Anglican Communion (TAC). I am not privy to negotiations, and Archbishop Hepworth would know more about this. In no way do I wish to "put him on the spot", because there seems to be much hope around that this might be possible. But a "corporate reunion" model logically applies only to an existing body, like the TAC, hence to clergy and laity who have chosen to join that body in the past and any clergy and laity who choose to join that body with a view to benefiting from a corporate reunion arrangement. However, there is a third option, which involves smaller groups.

3. The reconciliation of a parish or group.

Ever since the Caldey affair,[4] nearly a century ago, there has been reticence among Catholic bishops about groups of persons being reconciled together. But, putting to one side cases like the parish of Bethnal Green, the reconciliation of an Anglican parish, so that it retains its identity, is already an accomplished fact in the United States, in several instances. Moreover, this has included a recognition of some Anglican liturgical usages, what is popularly termed an "Anglican Rite", although it seems more "Sarum" than Anglican

---

[4] In the early twentieth century, a group of Anglicans founded a monastic community on Caldey Island off the coast of Wales. These monks were received into the Catholic Church in 1913, although the order later sold the property on Caldey Island in 1925 due to financial difficulties. The monastery is currently the home to a Cistercian order. See the Monks of Caldey Island website home page: http://www.caldey-island.co.uk/monks.htm.

to this liturgist! Strictly speaking, this concession involves a specific indult. A "rite" spelt with a small "r", should not be confused with the formal establishment of a Rite in terms of a structure, involving a distinct hierarchy and ecclesial autonomy, as in the case of the existing Catholic Eastern Rite churches.

Possibilities and Problems

Looking at the options and returning to option 2. *Would it be possible for those involved in a larger act of corporate reunion to become a distinct Rite in the Church, i.e., a Catholic Western Rite Church?*

The cautious answer I offer is Italianate—a no, but with a carefully qualified yes or maybe—in that order. If you mean Anglicans becoming a Rite within the universal Church, having a distinct hierarchy structured like the Ukrainians or Maronites, I would say no. There is no precedent for a body of Christians from the Reformation era forming a new Rite in the universal Church. Moreover, the history of Eastern Rites is complex. Some, like the Maronites, can argue that they never left Roman communion and jurisdiction. However, the other communities returned to full communion as fully constituted *churches* and are recognized as such within the universal Church.

I used the expression "a body of Christians from the Reformation era". At present, as our most recent Roman directives indicate, strictly speaking, we cannot apply the term "church" to any Anglican body, within the current Anglican Communion or derived recently from it. That is one of the "hard sayings" I have to add today, a touch of unpalatable realism. But let me hasten to pour some oil into any wound I may have caused and add that qualified yes or maybe, which of course only suggests a speculative possibility. Could some special structure be formed within the Catholic Church that would maintain the human cherished connections, the good pastoral care, gracious spirituality, noble heritage, and culture of all that is best in Anglicanism?

With his profound understanding of ecclesiology, our Holy Father, Pope Benedict XVI, will, I believe, do all that is possible to assist those Anglican Catholics who seek peace and unity in the universal Church at this time.[5] We may hope and pray that he will make it possible for option 3 to continue, for smaller groups, and for option 2 to develop in terms of some existing hierarchical structure being reconstituted within the Church. Being the Supreme Pontiff and ultimate lawmaker, with full and immediate jurisdiction, he can modify my initial no.

Furthermore, there is a new canonical precedent for a body that is not a full Rite, but which has its own bishop within the wider Church. This is the *personal prelature*. At present, there is only one, the Prelature of the Holy Cross, Opus Dei. The Prelate of Opus Dei is a bishop without territorial jurisdiction, but he has spiritual jurisdiction over the members of "The Work". This may well provide a model for coherent pastoral care and the spiritual flourishing of Anglicans who have been formally reconciled to the universal Church but who want to retain a corporate identity.

Some will say, "But that Roman 'personal prelate' sounds much the same as one of our Anglican 'flying bishops'." That may seem to be so, but look very carefully at the context. The personal prelature is a distinct structure that has arisen within the Catholic Church, in no way contrary to

---

[5] With *Anglicanorum coetibus*, Pope Benedict XVI has not only made possible the reconciliation of smaller groups of Anglicans (as was possible in the United States under the Pastoral Provision), albeit on a worldwide scale, but also larger groups, such as the Traditional Anglican Communion.

her doctrines and canonical polity. A "flying bishop", on the other hand, is an attempt to keep a kind of Catholic prelate operating within a wider ecclesial community that has in fact abandoned him, a body now without any serious claim to apostolic succession because it ordains women. The "flying bishop" is an anomaly. He contradicts the very *raison d'etre* of the structure within which he is expected to operate—and that will become clearer when there are Anglican women bishops in Australia and England.

Other Local Considerations

What is not widely appreciated beyond these shores is the distinct make-up and structure of the Anglican Church in Australia, very different from the Provinces of Canterbury and York. This is why you need to anticipate and watch what the Diocese of Sydney, and its affiliated dioceses, will do in the event of approval for and the consecration of women bishops. Will Sydney break away? But surely that is already happening. The Diocese of Sydney and its affiliates already constitute a distinct body, and Evangelical parish "plantings" are happening in various guises beyond the geographical confines of Sydney. Moreover, do not be surprised if some existing Evangelical parishes take legal steps to separate from the local diocese and unite themselves to Sydney or to a bishop derived from Sydney, when the women bishops appear on the scene.[6]

[6] The Anglican Diocese of Sydney has both planted churches in the territory of other Australian Anglican dioceses and established protocols for affiliating already existing Evangelical churches with the diocese in its Affiliated Churches Ordinance. As of 2008, six churches had affiliated with Sydney. See Robert Wicks, "Affiliated Churches: A Report from the Standing Committee", August 29, 2008, Sydney Diocesan Secretariat website: http://www.sds.asn.au/Site/103901.asp?a=a&ph=cp.

Therefore let us end this fatuous talk of maintaining "limited communion", etc. Sydney rightly reminds you that you are either in communion or not in communion. And if you want an even clearer statement of that reality, talk to the Eastern Orthodox about the meaning of apostolic communion and read the Second Vatican Council's Constitution on the Church, *Lumen gentium*.

The Ministry of Former Anglican Clergy

What then can Catholics of the Roman Rite offer Anglican clergy who seek reconciliation with the See of Peter? In practical terms, celibates of stable life can be incorporated easily into the Catholic *presbyterium*, or fellowship of diocesan clergy.

In the case of married clergy, we are discovering that they can be incorporated into the particular church, the diocese, even if there are difficulties. At present, the Congregation for the Doctrine of the Faith places statistical limits on how many married priests can work in each diocese. That restricts what bishops may want to do, but the policy may change with the new circumstances that are unfolding. I hope that wider pastoral options will emerge, such as former Anglican married priests working in parishes, and already we see this well established in Perth and Adelaide, and beginning in Melbourne.

One practical warning is needed here, and again I must be blunt. There is a wide cultural difference between a Catholic parish and an Anglican parish, not merely because most Catholic parishes are multi-ethnic, etc., but also because they are usually big and busy. Sixty people were at Mass this morning, on a Saturday, in my small "quiet parish" (well, it was the Memorial of Our Lady of Lourdes!), but approximately 340 will come to the Sunday Masses. So, Anglican clergy who are not prepared to work hard, should not contemplate seeking priestly ministry within the Catholic Church in Australia. Having grown up in a vicarage, I can assure you that the quiet pace of a good vicarage and focused ministry to a small group of wonderfully committed people is an option not usually available in Australian Catholic parishes.

Words of Welcome

Let me conclude simply by welcoming Anglicans, by *daring* to welcome them, not with blaring triumphalism or earnest convert challenges, rather by quoting a wise parish priest I know. He is currently based in Birmingham. Like me, he worked for some years in the Roman Curia, but in a different department. This man of deep ecumenical commitment and experience put the realistic option in this human way: "Brothers and Sisters, the door is open, the table is set and the kettle is on."

At the time of original writing, *Bishop Peter Elliott* was parish priest of Saint Mary the Immaculate Conception, East Malvern; the Director of the John Paul II Institute for Marriage and Family, Melbourne; and Episcopal Vicar for Religious Education, Archdiocese of Melbourne. He worked in the Roman Curia as an Official of the Pontifical Council for the Family, 1987–1997. He was appointed as an Auditor at the 2005 World Synod of Bishops on the Eucharist. Bishop Elliott is well known for his liturgical manuals, *Ceremonies of the Modern Roman Rite* and *Ceremonies of the*

Liturgical Year. Bishop Elliott was consecrated bishop on June 15, 2007, and is Auxiliary Bishop of Melbourne, Australia. He has been a Consulter to the Congregation for Divine Worship and the Discipline of the Sacraments. He is a member of the International Council for Catechesis of the Congregation for the Clergy. In 2009 the Australian Catholic Bishops Conference appointed him Episcopal Delegate for the establishment of a Personal Ordinariate in Australia. His late father, the Reverend Leslie Llewelyn Elliott, was President of the Australian Church Union, 1958–1961, approximately.

ANGLICAN DIFFICULTIES

Chapter 8

Unity's Winding Path

Father John Hunwicke, SSC

The Catholic clergy spent their time in sacraments and prayer,
Perusing Scripture, offering outdated pastoral care,
But we, the Ecumenicals, had planned our route before,
Through Lima and through acronyms and through Reports
   galore;
"Porvoo!" we sang in drunken joy, with "Meissen!" our
   refrain,
The night we went to Reuilly by way of Fetter Lane.[1]

(after G. K. Chesterton, with apologies)

This article originally appeared on the *Trueshare* website: http://trushare.com/ 0138NOV06/16B%20Hunwicke.htm (November 2006) and is used with the permission of the author. Published in *Anglican Embers* 1, no. 12 (December 2006): 336–40.

[1] "Lima" is a reference to the *Baptism, Eucharist and Ministry* report (Faith and Order Paper No. 111) from the Faith and Order commission of the World Council of Churches, published after meetings in Lima, Peru, in 1982. See http://www.oikoumene.org/resources/documents/wcc-commissions/ faith-and-order-commission/i-unity-the-church-and-its-mission/baptism-eucharist-and-ministry-faith-and-order-paper-no-111-the-lima-text/baptism-eucharist-and-ministry.html#c10470. "Porvoo" refers to the agreement to share pulpits and establish intercommunion between the Anglican churches of England, Wales, Scotland, Ireland, and the Lutheran churches of Sweden, Norway, Finland, Lithuania, Estonia, and Iceland. This agreement was finalized in 1996 and is named after the Finnish city where the representatives of these churches celebrated a Eucharist together. See http://www. porvoochurches.org/whatis/outputo1.php. "Meissen" was the city in which a 1988 agreement of mutual recognition of ordained ministries and mutual faith between the Church of England and the Evangelical (Lutheran) churches

No one is sure which of the aforementioned momentous ecumenical documents explains the full Catholic authenticity of German Lutherans or French Calvinists or the Moravians or the Scandinavians. People have better things to do with their time! References to them can be found in Rochester[2] and above all in *An Anglican-Methodist Covenant,*[3] which cannot assert that Methodist ministers really are priests, because the Church of England had already committed itself in these documents to accepting that its own Orders were not essentially different from those of non-episcopal Reformation denominations.

Like bearers of a horrible mutation of avian flu, those distant chickens have now come home to roost. To put the final icing on the cake, women bishops will soon mean that we have nothing, just nothing, to look forward to but a bleak future of "unity" with liberal Protestantism and feminism. And this is happening just at the moment when Rome and Orthodoxy are in a striking phase of

---

of Germany took place; see *The Meissen Common Statement* (1988), accessible at http://www.cofe.anglican.org/info/ccu/europe/ecumbackground. "Reuilly" refers to the *Reuilly Common Statement,* an intercommunion agreement between the British Anglican churches and the Lutheran and Reformed churches of France; see "Reuilly Factsheet", accessible at http://www.cofe.anglican.org/info/ccu/europe/ecumbackground/reuilly. Finally, "Fetter Lane" refers to the intercommunion, faith-sharing, and pulpit-sharing agreement between the British Anglican and Moravian churches, which was agreed to in 1995; see "The Fetter Lane Declaration", at http://www.cofe.anglican.org/info/ccu/england/moravian/fetterlane.

[2] "Women Bishops in the Church of England?" is a report issued by a committee chaired by Bishop Michael Nazir-Ali of Rochester, England, which was issued in November 2004 and is known as the "Rochester Report"; see http://www.cofe.anglican.org/news/pr4504.html.

[3] The *Anglican-Methodist Covenant* reports on the formal talks between the Church of England and the Methodist church of Great Britain. The report urges mutual recognition of ministries with the ultimate goal of reuniting these two churches. It was published on December 12, 2001; see http://www.cofe.anglican.org/news/an_anglican-methodist_covenant.html.

rapprochement. So, is a new and even greater chasm to open between us and the ancient communions of East and West at the precise time when that schism of the first millennium has the best chance in a thousand years of being mended? No wonder Cardinal Walter Kasper starkly asked the English college of bishops, "Where and on what side does the Anglican Communion stand, where will it stand in the future? Which orientation does it claim as its own?"[4]

Pope Benedict

It is now clear that Benedict XVI is making Christian unity the great aim of his "brief pontificate". We hear of a visit to the Ecumenical Patriarch; reports of a major and extended visit to Rome by the Patriarch of Moscow; of a major Roman Catholic–Orthodox document; of overtures to some of the more orthodox separated fragments of Latin Christianity. There surely can be no doubt that Cardinal Kasper's visit to England [in 2006] should be seen in this context. Rome is in effect saying, "Do you want to join the game? After all, we thought you did, back in the sixties when together we set up ARCIC [the Anglican–Roman Catholic International Commission]. Have you really now abandoned the old Anglican dream of unity with us and with the ancient churches of the East? Does the Lord allow you to do that?"

There are persistent rumors of a Vatican committee set up to take a careful look at those parts of the fracturing Anglican faith community that are Catholic-minded and

---

[4] Cardinal Walter Kasper, "Mission of Bishops in the Mystery of the Church," www.vatican.va/roman_curia/pontifical_councils/chrstuni/card-kasper-docs/rc_pc_chrstuni_doc_20060605_kasper-bishops_en.html.

Catholic-converging. After all, Benedict XVI is the Joseph Ratzinger who spoke so sympathetically about Anglicans in the early 1990s; who sent a telegram of solidarity to a traditionalist Anglican gathering in America;[5] who encouraged the Anglican Usage of the Roman Rite (Anglican parishes in America united with Rome and continuing to use what is in effect an Anglican Book of Common Prayer). In the past, some Catholic Anglicans have been keener on unity with Rome, while others have looked further east. This is now a seriously dated disagreement. What lies ahead is East and West uniting, while Anglicans sink into a morass of women bishops, gay marriage, and liberal Methodists; doubtful sacraments; and clergy who make light of the doctrines of the Creed. Meanwhile, all Cardinal Kasper got from his journey to England was unreconstructed archiepiscopal abuse of Rome in our Synod, and a silly "paper" by two bishops saying that Junia is the answer to everything.[6]

Worth examining is an ecumenical report of 1982, which has not been mentioned in Rochester or Guildford or the Anglican-Methodist "Covenant". Porvoo, Reuilly, Meissen, and the rest don't include it in the close-meshed apparatus of footnotes by which they cite and adduce each other so as to build up their incestuously self-validating magisterium of pan-Protestant ecumenical theology. I am referring

---

[5] Joseph Cardinal Ratzinger, Letter to the "A Place to Stand" Gathering. See http://www.american-anglican.org/letter-from-joseph-cardinal-ratzinger-to-the-a-place-to-stand-gathering.

[6] "Junia" is the person referred to in Saint Paul's letter to the Romans (16:7): "Greet Andronicus and Junias, my kinsmen and my fellow prisoners; they are men of note among the apostles, and they were in Christ before me." Junias (or Junia) is thought to possibly be a female name, and some have proposed that this phrase names the woman Junia as one of the apostles. This is used as "evidence" to promote the ordination of women to the priesthood. The interpretation is a bit tendentious and relies on a complete absence of corroborating evidence (as well as a fairly large body of evidence contra).

to a slender document called *The Mystery of the Church and of the Eucharist in the Light of the Mystery of the Holy Trinity* (also known as *Church Eucharist Trinity, CET*). It was produced by the thirteen main Orthodox churches and the Roman Catholic Church. Its authors included very big hitters: then-Cardinal Joseph Ratzinger; John Zizioulas, the famous Greek theologian who is now Metropolitan of Pergamon and chairman of the current Roman Catholic–Orthodox discussions; Louis Bouyer; Jean Tillard; and Jan Willebrands.

A Serious Ecumenical Report

CET emphatically asserts: "The bishop receives the gift of episcopal grace ... in the sacrament of consecration effected by bishops who themselves have received this gift, thanks to the existence of an uninterrupted series of episcopal ordinations [Porvoo, please note], beginning from the holy apostles. ... [He] receives the ministerial grace of Christ by the Spirit in the prayer of the assembly and by the laying on of hands ... of the neighboring bishops, witnesses of the faith of their own churches." [7] Indeed, *CET* repeatedly uses the phrase "sacrament of consecration". Protestantizing ecumenical apparatchiks, who treat episcopacy as a matter of organization ("furniture which can be shifted around", as they sometimes call it) are talking about something totally different from what the Orthodox–Roman Catholic dialogue is describing.

[7] Joint Commission for Theological Dialogue between the Roman Catholic Church and the Orthodox Church, *The Mystery of the Church and of the Eucharist in the Light of the Mystery of the Holy Trinity* (also known as *Church Eucharist Trinity*; *CET* hereinafter), Second Plenary Meeting, Munich (June 30–July 6, 1982), sec. 2, nos. 3 and 4.

As Cardinal Kasper warned, the Anglican Communion is "moving a considerable distance closer to the side of the Protestant churches.... It would indeed continue to have bishops ... but as with bishops within some Protestant churches, the older churches of East and West would recognise therein much less of what they understand to be the character and ministry of the bishop in the sense understood by the early church and continuing through the ages." [8]

As for the authors of Rochester and Guildford, with their concern for the minutiae and niceties of episcopal jurisdiction, they are wrong-footed by the *CET* assertion that "the union of the community with [the bishop] is first of all of the order of *mysterion* and not primordially of the juridical order" (sec. 2, no. 3).

Cardinal Kasper's paper given to the English bishops, explaining what episcopacy is all about, can be summarized in his words: "The episcopal office is thus an office of unity." [9] *CET* likewise cogently declares: "The eucharistic unity of the local church implies communion between him who presides and the people to whom he delivers the word of salvation and the eucharistic gifts.... The bishop cannot be separated from his church any more than the church can be separated from its bishop.... He is the minister of unity" (sec. 2, no. 3). This leaves no space for the sort of organizational tricks attempted by Anglican committees, whereby a confused answer is given to the question "Who is my bishop?" There is no way of getting round this question or fudging it.

An authentic particular church has one bishop who is *the* bishop (even if he may have coadjutors who function as extensions of his episcope). *CET* starkly says, "Mention of

[8] Walter Cardinal Kasper, "Mission of Bishops in the Mystery of the Church", June 5, 2006, sec. 3, para. 10.
[9] Ibid., sec. 2, para. 11.

him in the anaphora is essential" (sec. 2, no. 4). Mentioning the bishop in the Eucharistic Prayer, as Orthodox and Catholics do, is not so much an expression of prayer for him as of full, unimpaired unity with him. We need a structure in which for each of us there is "the bishop", and it is perfectly clear who he is, so that we have no difficulty mentioning him by name.

Relevant to the Crisis

Another area in which *CET* is relevant to the current crisis in Anglicanism is its conviction that "mutual recognition between this local church and the other churches is also of capital importance.... It ... implies unity of witness and calls for the exercise of fraternal correction in humility" (sec. 3, no. 3b). Fraternal correction, surely, is exactly what Cardinal Kasper, in the name of Christ, came to offer us. These words of *CET* echo the 1999 ARCIC agreement, which proposed that Anglicans should "receive" the papal ministry. Where has that got to in our synodical processes?

In conclusion, there is an important teaching of *CET* on what "the Church" is. There is the "universal Church"; there is the "local church". The local church is not a denomination or a national or regional body. It is "the local church which celebrates the eucharist gathered around its bishop", and "the eucharistic celebration makes present the Trinitarian mystery of the church" (sec. 3, no. 1; sec. 1, no. 6). Therefore, "the local church ... is not a section of the body of Christ" (sec. 3, no. 1). On the contrary, "the universal church manifests itself in the synaxis of the local church.... The one and only church is made present in [the bishop's] local church.... The universal and local are necessarily simultaneous" (sec. 3, nos. 3, 4, 2). Readers will here recognize the "eucharistic ecclesiology" that has characterized the writings of John Zizioulas, and the documents *Communionis notio* and *Dominus Jesus* of Cardinal Ratzinger, now Bishop of Rome and Successor of Saint Peter.

In his enthronement sermon at Exeter, Bishop Michael Langrish memorably called ecumenism "a journey without exits" and added, "There can be no easy walking away from those with whom we are put together in Christ." Let us pray that we are not now on a slip road taking us away from the main motorway.

Father John Hunwicke, SSC, was formerly the Head of Theology at Lancing College, Sussex, and is currently the priest-in-charge of Saint Thomas the Martyr Church in Oxford.

Chapter 9

The Priesthood and Women

Linda Poindexter

I was raised in Indiana, in a Christian environment. We were members of a very Protestant brotherhood, called the "Disciples of Christ". This church had a very distinctive feature. It had a celebration of Holy Communion as a part of every service. As in many Protestant churches, the sermon still seemed to occupy center stage, along with the pastoral prayer offered by the minister (both were very long for us children!). The Holy Communion was not the sacrament as Catholics understand it but a memorial of the Last Supper. It did, however, hold up its centrality in our lives.

The particular church we attended had another, really unusual feature. The front and sides of the small chapel had several reproductions of the great paintings of the Blessed Virgin Mary. It was known as the Madonna Chapel. For a Protestant church in the American Midwest, this is very different. I discovered later that this had been the project of an early pastor's wife, who must have been a closet Catholic or an art lover!

I believe that these early influences were more formative than I had realized. In hindsight, I have come to believe that

From a talk given at the Anglican Use Conference on June 1, 2007. Originally published in *Anglican Embers* 2, no. 6 (May 2006): 230–49.

my whole spiritual life has been a quest to draw closer to our Lord in his Body and Blood and to his Blessed Mother.

Marriage and Reception into the Episcopal Church

John and I were married in 1958. John gave me my "miniature" of his class ring at the Ring Dance on June 1, 1957. It is an old US Naval Academy tradition for the midshipmen to receive their class rings at the end of their second class (junior) year, and often, fortunate young women are given their engagement rings at the same time. We have always thought of our meeting as an example of God's Providence. We are both from Indiana; at the time we met, John was a midshipman at the US Naval Academy in Annapolis, Maryland, and my family lived about forty miles away in Chevy Chase, Maryland, but we met in Burlington, Vermont. I was a freshman at the University of Vermont, and John came there with the Navy debating team. I was assigned to time his debates. We always tell people that I gave him a little extra time. Our five sons are probably tired of hearing that story. They are all married and have given us fourteen grandchildren. Just imagine—what if we had been Catholic since the beginning of our marriage. People used to ask us if we were Catholic, because at that time everybody was supposed to have 1.3 children, and I would answer, "No, we're careless Episcopalians."

We joined the Episcopal Church not long after our marriage and raised our family in that faith community, very happily. We grew to love the liturgy, which was the service used at the Naval Academy chapel. Regardless of the brand of the chaplain, we had Morning Prayer according to the 1928 Book of Common Prayer. That was the primary reason for our becoming Episcopalian. We did love that liturgy. It was home for us, too, wherever John's naval career moved us.

Vocation as an Episcopalian Priest

When our boys were becoming independent, three of them off to college, in about 1980, I began to believe that God was calling me to the priesthood in the Episcopal Church. That was four years after women were first legally ordained in the Episcopal Church. That surprised me; I had always been active in the church, but I had not expected to feel that particular call. But I pursued it, which wasn't easy. There were too many people at that particular time who had the same idea, and it was difficult to get through the diocesan process and become a postulant, and go to seminary, which I did, back in the Washington area.

The seminary chaplain, the Reverend Churchill Gibbons, told us, "Episcopalians don't think that they are accountable, and when they find out that they're accountable, they think that they're ordainable." I was an Episcopal priest for thirteen years. I liked the work: I loved leading the liturgy and counseling with people, but I did not love the constant tension between the parish and the family. More and more, I came to see why the celibate priesthood wasn't such a bad idea, because my heart and mind were with the family when I was at the parish, and with the parish when I was home with the family. Since our boys were grown up, grandchildren started to come, and, as anyone can tell you, that takes a lot of grandmother time.

Well, for many years I was happy in the Episcopal Church. I had admired and envied the Catholics I knew when I was growing up. I really believed that great three-branch theory— you remember, that the Catholic Church has three branches, Roman, Anglican, and Eastern—I thought that was very convenient. I also believed in the Real Presence of Christ in the Eucharist, as do many, many Episcopalians.

Naturally, I did not believe that the priesthood was restricted to men, which many Anglo-Catholics do, and that of course is what made life so comfortable in the Episcopal Church. I could move down the cafeteria line and choose what I wished to believe. Years ago, there was a poster, which I think was put out by the church, that showed a picture of Jesus with the caption "He came to take away your sins, not your mind." At the time, I thought that was pretty clever, but now I think that it's a major putdown of Catholics and Evangelicals alike.

Difficulties with Changing Episcopalian Doctrine

At the time of *Roe v. Wade*, I considered myself essentially anti-abortion but pro-choice. That's a really mindless position, and it didn't take long before the Lord and several good friends of his changed my mind. As a result, I became more and more unhappy with the Episcopal Church's essentially pro-choice position. I also believed that those churches that blessed homosexual unions and in other ways supported the idea that the practice of homosexuality was part of God's plan were leading people into grave sin and were exposing them to both physical and spiritual sickness. Needless to say, my views on abortion and homosexuality did not win me too many friends in the Episcopal Diocese of Washington. But I was tolerated because I had always been there, and because they figured I would "grow" and come along.

I also belonged to NOEL (National Organization of Episcopalians for Life), and at the last General Convention I had any connection with, we were trying to pass an amendment that condemned partial-birth abortion. The best we could get through was the statement "We're gravely concerned about it." What a ghastly image we created of people standing around stroking their chins while they watch a baby being murdered, saying, "This really is a concern."

Those who objected to abortion were often told that we weren't keeping up with the times, that, after all, the Anglican Communion even opposed birth control in the old days, back in the 1930s. Of course, they implied that birth control was a very good thing. Increasingly, the Episcopal Church was taking its teaching from the secular society around it. Many will say that the Catholic Church must do likewise, if it is to survive in the United States. I think it was Father Richard John Neuhaus who pointed out that the example of the Episcopal Church going along with society is the last one to follow, as its membership declined from only three million people in 1960 to a robust two million people by 1980.

Of course, along with the social issues, what really upset me was the Church's toleration of heretical teaching. Episcopalian Bishop John Shelby Spong has managed to deny just about every tenet of the Creed. A good friend of mine, a dean of an Episcopal seminary, said the Bishop was trying to rise to the level of heresy, but he wasn't smart enough. However, Spong's statements sound like heresy, and what distressed me was that he was not rebuked by anybody, except for a few of those right-wing, dangerous, conservative, orthodox types.

Investigating the Catholic Church

Finally, I noticed that making up one's own mind was getting out of hand, and I could no longer think or say that the Episcopal Church was Catholic. I began then to think seriously about the Catholic Church. I was still in the "stay-and-fight" mode, or the "stay-and-do-what-you-can-for-people-and-pretend-that-the-larger-church-does-not-exist" mode, which I'm convinced is how many, many Episcopalians now survive—by pretending that only their little church exists, and that it believes the right things, and ignoring the rest of it.

During this time, I prayed often in thanksgiving for Pope John Paul II and for the Roman Catholic Church for upholding eternal truths and upholding the sanctity of life. In the mid-90s, I was the assistant at All Saints on Chevy Chase Circle. It was a troubled parish, haunted by visions of past glory, when there had been nine hundred kids in the Sunday school, and struggling to grow again, though rife with conflicts. It was absolutely impossible to walk into that church and pray quietly because, as the younger generation would say, "The vibes were bad." It was unsettling to be there because of the troubled spirit.

One day I walked around Chevy Chase Circle to the nearby Catholic church, and I entered for some quiet prayer time and an escape from my working environment. I was very surprised to walk in and feel a complete sense of being at home—a sense of the presence of the Lord. I didn't think about it at the time, because I thought we had the presence of the Lord over at All Saints, in the ambry, but I was in the presence of the Lord. That church is fittingly named the Shrine of the Blessed Sacrament; I began to go there more and more often for prayer, so I could get away. Addictions are dangerous: next, I found myself sneaking over for daily Mass when I could, removing my clerical collar, or hiding it under a scarf, so as not to be noticed. Since I was an Episcopalian, and I believed in the Real Presence, I felt entitled to make my own rules and receive Communion while I was there. (Obedience to Church teaching was not a blessing I had as yet been granted.)

At that time I loved the rules of the Church when they were things I agreed with, and I tended to explain away those things I did not. Cardinal Newman was very helpful in opening my eyes about this. Of course, the first thing I did, as many others have done, was run out and buy the *Apologia*. Among other gems, I discovered his thinking on the teaching authority of the Church and her infallibility:

> Supposing then it to be the Will of the Creator to interfere in human affairs, and to make provisions for retaining in the world a knowledge of Himself, so definite and distinct as to be proof against the energy of human scepticism, in such a case,—I am far from saying that there was no other way,—but there is nothing to surprise the mind, if He should think fit to introduce a power into the world, invested with the prerogative of infallibility in religious matters. Such a provision would be a direct, immediate, active, and prompt means of withstanding the difficulty; it would be an instrument suited to the need; and, when I find that this is the very claim of the Catholic Church, not only do I feel no difficulty in admitting the idea, but there is a fitness in it, which recommends it to my mind. And thus I am brought to speak of the Church's infallibility, as a provision, adapted by the mercy of the Creator, to preserve religion in the world, and to restrain that freedom of thought, which of course in itself is one of the greatest of our natural gifts, and to rescue it from its own suicidal excesses.[1]

That was the best thing I had ever read about infallibility. Up until then I was thinking, "Catholics have to accept all the rules of the Church; I don't know if I can get into that or not." Of course, it remained for me to apply that acceptance to my own cherished ideas; it's very easy to accept

[1] John Henry Cardinal Newman, *Apologia pro Vita Sua* (London, New York and Bombay: Longmans, Green, and Co., 1904), pp. 152–53.

the authority of the Church when it comes to dealing with issues with which you agree. Having the humility to accept the truth about something that you haven't already decided in your own mind is more difficult.

Reception into the Catholic Church

After leaving that parish, I accepted one more call to enter ministry, somewhat unwillingly because I had begun to go to daily Mass and was thinking seriously of conversion. I thought I should give the Episcopal Church one more chance, to make sure. It was a good ministry for a year and a half, and I think we all did good work together; but, as soon as I got out of there, I hurried back to daily Mass and fell rather gratefully into the arms of Mother Church. I was received into the Church the following Easter in 1999. I was happy to have the confidence that the Holy Father and the Church had the authority to proclaim the truth, and that I didn't have to make up my mind about everything. A lot of people think that first a person must agree with everything that the Church teaches before he can become Catholic, but this idea misses an important point. By the way, there is an interesting webpage on BeliefNet,[2] which asks several questions and matches a person's answers to a corresponding church. It saves a person all this tiresome business of having to believe something that he doesn't already believe. I was glad that I matched up pretty well with the Catholic faith, and even with Saint Augustine. That really did a lot for my ego.

But back to this point about one's willingness to trust in order to believe. *Introduction to Christianity* by Cardinal

[2] See http://www.beliefnet.com/Entertainment/Quizzes/BeliefOMatic.aspx

Joseph Ratzinger (now Pope Benedict XVI) discusses the nature of belief, what it really means to say "I believe". He wrote: "To believe as a Christian means, in fact, entrusting myself to the meaning that upholds me and the world, taking it as the firm ground on which I can stand fearlessly. To believe as a Christian means understanding our existence as a response to the Word, the Logos, that upholds and maintains all things. It means affirming that the meaning we do not make, but can only receive, is already granted to us so that we have only to take it and entrust ourselves to it." [3] That seems to me to capture the whole difference between the Catholic Church and the Episcopal Church that I knew, because we had been accustomed to making our own belief. Thinking, studying, praying, what have you, but still, making our own. To encounter the three-legged stool of the Catholic Church—Scripture, Tradition, and the Magisterium—was revelatory, and I found it very freeing.

John didn't come into the Church with me, but he was received two years later, in August of 2001. The timing was a gift of Providence, because just a month later was 9/11, and John became very, very busy and had no time to think about such issues, as he worked toward securing our country. It was very good for him to have that strength and that backing provided by the Church.

People usually ask me how I could possibly give up my life as a priest, and if I miss it terribly. I was so strongly convinced that the Catholic Church was the true faith, the Church that Jesus established, and my true home, that it was not hard to relinquish my past, and I have never missed it. After all, it took me sixty years to get there. (People

---

[3] Joseph Cardinal Ratzinger, *Introduction to Christianity* (San Francisco: Ignatius Press, 2004), p. 73.

who knew me better said I had converted so I wouldn't
have to get up and go to work every morning.) Oddly
enough, when I had felt first called to the priesthood in
the Episcopal Church, I had never met a woman priest,
nor was I anxious to. Emotionally and intuitively, I wanted
a priest to be male, but I attributed that to my own particular psychological needs, without questioning the right-
ness of ordaining women. There are probably times when I
should pay more attention to my intuition. In my own sense
of call to ordination, I believed it was a part of wanting and
seeking to grow closer to Christ in the Eucharist.

I must also add that I never felt at home at the altar. I
liked leading liturgy, because I used to do a lot of dramatic work when I was a kid; good liturgy is good
drama. Also, it was a great privilege to give the Body and
Blood of Christ, at least I considered it such at the time,
to the people at communion, but it felt wrong to be the
one who said the words. I dismissed this feeling as a
manifestation of the common psychological phenomenon
of feeling like an impostor. Interestingly enough, my friend
Jennifer Ferrara, an author and convert who was a former
Lutheran pastor, has said the same thing: she also never
felt quite right at the altar. I never felt like an impostor
when I was functioning as a teacher, a counselor, an admin-
istrator, or any of those things. Of course, it didn't help
that most of the women priests that I knew at the time
were quite liberal, pro-choice, and militantly feminist.
That didn't help my own image, and I didn't have much
company.

People also ask me about women's ordination in the Catholic Church—well, first they ask me, why I changed my mind,
or, why I turned my back on things that I once believed. I
don't think I turned my back on any of the important things,
those things that I've always believed; and I don't know

that I changed my mind, at least not about Protestant churches.

At the 1997 General Convention in which they discussed revoking the conscience clause in the Episcopal Church,[4] there were actually forty or forty-five orthodox women priests who signed a letter to the convention, asking them not to do that, asking them to keep things the way they were. Our letter, of course, was not persuasive; it was read, but nobody paid much attention to it. I later heard from some classmates from my seminary days, and one said I had betrayed the cause of womanhood—I had turned my back on them. I was rather astonished, because I had no recollection of taking vows of fidelity to feminist doctrine. When I'm accused of having changed my mind about female ordination, I reply that I have not; I have no problem with Protestants ordaining women. As I understand it, within Protestant communions, and really in the Episcopal Church as well, ordination is for the performing of certain functions. Didn't we learn in the Episcopal Church that there are only two sacraments, Baptism and the Eucharist, and all the rest are just sacramental acts, including ordination? At any rate, we seminarians were constantly told we were being ordained to perform functions. Nobody talked about us being symbolic or representing Christ, in the way the Catholic Church teaches. Of course, it's hard to find any written doctrine of the Episcopal Church. That was one of the frustrating things: people would say, "What does the church believe?" And I'd say, "Which one? This one or the one downtown?"

[4] Jeffrey Steenson and Bob Libby, "Ordination of Women Made Mandatory", *Living Church* 215, no. 5 (Aug. 3, 1997): 10–11; see http://www.episcopalarchives.org/cgi-bin/the_livingchurch/TLCarticle.pl?volume=215&issue=5&article_id=3.

Considering the Ordination of Women

In the late 1970s, back before I felt I should be ordained, I said I'd have a great deal of trouble being part of a church that didn't ordain women, meaning I was happy to be part of the Episcopal Church after they had decided to do so. That was my response to the atmosphere of the time; I thought that seemed natural and right, that the long domination of males in leadership roles was coming to an end, and that women would take their rightful places. It was considered quite a move when the Episcopal Diocese of Washington decreed in the 1960s that vestries had to have two women members. Nobody elected any more. I really can't imagine how they found enough men to fill up the vestries in those days.

I was looking at the issue of women's ordination from the standpoint of the natural rights of women. My consciousness had been significantly raised by the feminism of the times, a feminism that seemed at times extreme to me, but was justified by a long period of repression. It did seem extreme to me when people on the street would ask a woman why she wasn't working in an office, why in the world was she just raising children—and diddling away at home and being useless. That kind of feminism bothered me. Nevertheless, I thought it was right for women to begin to take bigger places in society, including the priesthood. I didn't significantly alter the viewpoint of natural rights for many years, and that's the framework through which I saw these issues.

At the time, I enthusiastically and joyfully came into communion with the Catholic Church—I had reached a willingness to accept as true and governing those things which the Catholic Church believed and taught, even though I didn't understand them. Ten years ago, I would have said that the Church moved slowly to make changes, and that was all right. I used to say that, sooner or later, there would be married priests—and I was right. Of course, the former Episcopalian priests of the Pastoral Provision weren't exactly what I meant at the time. I also thought that at some time in the future, not in my lifetime, or perhaps even in that of younger people, there would be women priests. I looked on it as a slow progression.

Even when I was an Episcopal priest, I said that if the ordination of women were of God, it would be accepted someday by all three of the branches of the Catholic Church (as noted earlier, I was really fond of that three-branch theory). I also used to say if it were not of God, it would die off and fade away. However, in the years since I converted, I have come to appreciate the theological thinking behind a male-only priesthood. I think that many lifelong Catholics are in the same boat I was. Back in 1993, Michael Novak wrote in a *First Things* article about the pressing need to do theology around the ordination issues. He said that in the past people accepted what was, with perhaps a subconscious understanding that that was what should be, but nobody had outlined the reasons for what was.

When the question about the rights of women to be ordained arose, all the logical arguments seemed to be with those who sought change, not with the defenders of the status quo, because, frankly, nobody had done the homework. This question was being viewed through the prism of natural rights, which could be neither conferred nor withheld by man.

Then-Cardinal Ratzinger discussed this very thing in a commentary on *Inter Insigniores*, the Vatican decree of 1976 restricting the priesthood to men, and he shed a rather interesting historical light on the question of rights. He contrasted the rights in the American Declaration of

Independence, the rights that are given to people in creation, which are endowed by our Creator, with the rights
set forth in Declaration of the Rights of Man of the French
Revolution, which did not mention God or creation. In
fact, he wrote, there appears in the Declaration of the Rights
of Man a new form of human rights, the full significance
of which became evident only in the course of time, and
which is supplanting the Christian form more and more.
According to the Declaration of the Rights of Man, rights
appear as a merely human institution: man lays down what
is to be valid as right. Behind man there is no Creative
Will, and he has reality completely at his disposal. Human
rationality is the source of right, which is formed by the
will of the majority and is progressively improved.

In the view of Protestants who ordain women, and in
the view of those Catholics who would ordain women
priests, the priesthood is an institution that derives from
the Church, which she must regulate according to the point
of view of equal opportunities. If this were so, and there
were a possibility that the priesthood could be conferred
and freely regulated by the Church, then the prohibition of
priestly office to women would be a clear case of prejudice.
But the Catholic Church regards the priesthood as a sacrament, something she cannot change at will. The priesthood is not an opportunity that she can assign on her own
authority. It is not an opportunity or right, but is to be
seen as a vocation, which no one can claim as a right, and
which cannot be simply bestowed by the Church whichever way she pleases. The conflict arises from applying the
Enlightenment terms of natural and rational rights to the
supernatural understanding of creation and rights, which
asserts that our true rights are derived from our place in
creation. God made us equal in his eyes and in dignity, but
it doesn't imply that everything in life is going to be equal.

God didn't make all the peoples of the world his special and chosen people; he picked the Jewish people as those who would know him first and bring him to the world. No other people were given that opportunity. The question of the ordination of women is so often stated in all negative terms, showing all the reasons that women are inadequate for the priesthood. I would hope to offer some positive thoughts, too, for consideration.

God created man. He could have created us without sex, exactly alike in all respects, but he didn't. He created us male and female, in his image. He didn't choose to make us exactly alike; we have different qualities, different appearance, different bodies, which do rather drastically different things. I very seldom hear men complain that they can't have babies. Male and female are two different and wondrous ways of being human, of being the image of God. John Paul II in his beautiful Apostolic Letter *On the Dignity and Vocation of Women* speaks of the beauty of the creation of man and woman, particularly speaking of the older story in Genesis, the second one, which speaks of woman being taken from man, from the rib. Recently, one of our retired priests who occasionally says Mass on Sundays for us, Father Peter Reynierse, a former Episcopal priest, was giving a slightly different version of the creation story; he spoke of man, and of man being alone, and of man needing a companion, and the Lord God looked at him and realized he needed a companion. He needed someone to love, someone to relate to, and so God created dog. And dog looked at man with adoring eyes, and licked man's hand, and thought that everything that man did was wonderful, and followed him everywhere, and worshipped at his feet, and slept with him, and consequently man became extremely puffed up, filled with pride, thought that he must be like God because of the worship of dog.

So God created cat, and man soon learned of his true place in creation.

Father Reynierse's story was correct about one thing, at least: men don't exist in isolation; they are created, male and female, to live in community. From the very beginning, God gives us the nuptial imagery, we are created for life, in communio, and created to be fruitful and multiply. John Paul says that every individual is made in the image of God, insofar as he is a relational and free creature, capable of knowing God and loving him. Man cannot exist alone; he can exist only as a unity of the two, and therefore in relation to another human person. Being a person in the image and likeness of God thus also involves existing in relationship, in relation to the other "I". From the beginning, man and woman are called to exist not only side by side, but to exist mutually, one for the other. To be human means being called to interpersonal communion. The whole history of mankind unfolds within the context of this call, being for the other, in interpersonal union. The relationship between man and woman became a contest when sin intervened, and Eve was told that her desire will be for her husband and he would dominate her. It is important to recognize that God did not originally intend man to dominate. Male domination is not the way God instituted creation, but the way that sin deformed it, and there is no denying that women have been dominated, abused, ill-used often, and in the ultimate deformity, radical feminism seeks to remedy that historical abuse by denigrating all the beauty that God created in femininity, and by turning women into poor imitations of men. Existing for the other becomes existing for the self, and (heaven help us) self-fulfillment. Thus anything that is open to males should be open to females, and the Church is seen as dishonoring women and closing the door on their advancement, or put a little more softly, on their ability to serve Christ, to love and honor him. In honoring the priesthood and admiring it, have we forgotten to honor, admire, and seek the ways of loving Christ and serving him that are not related to ordination? After all, I think some 99.5 percent of men will not be ordained either. Have we made the same mistake that Churchill Gibson referred to when he spoke about those Episcopalians who believe that ordination is the only way to express accountability? To express a desire to love God and serve in his Church?

Why has the Church said, infallibly, that only men will be ordained? First, the priesthood is a sacrament: the priest represents Christ and acts *in persona Christi*. The priest is a symbol of Christ within that sacrament, and symbols are not arbitrary and interchangeable. My friend Taylor Marshall reminded me that even in pagan religions, priestesses did not serve and represent male gods, but goddesses. The old and the new pagans understand the power of symbols. While God is neither male nor female (the divine generation is both), our Lord Jesus Christ came to us as a man, and so far I haven't heard any feminists deny that. While God created all mankind equal in his eyes, with equal dignity and worth, he didn't give the same gifts and the same calling to all of us.

As previously mentioned, God called a particular people to be his own. Again, we notice the nuptial imagery— Israel is the bride of the Lord, frequently, the unfaithful bride. Israel is the spouse called to live in relationship to God. When God chose to dwell among his people in a more intimate way, he did not choose to come into human life as an angel, as he could have, without gender. Instead the Word became fully human, while yet fully divine, born as a male person born of a female person. The Incarnation does not seem to me insignificant or accidental, but God's plan of salvation. Continuing the imagery and language of the nuptial relationship present since creation, Jesus speaks of himself as the Bridegroom. He calls forth and establishes his Bride. The Bride is the Church, which is built upon a rock, and that rock is a man, Peter.

Jesus chooses the apostles, who will be his representatives, and they are all men. Now some will tell you that Jesus was choosing men because of the culture of his time and the lowly place of women. Are they accusing Jesus of sexism or political correctness? Jesus never acted either way; he interacted with women all his earthly life in a way that was counter to the prevailing customs of that time. He gave them great honor. So the argument that only the culture prevented the calling of women to be apostles does not hold water. Consider a few instances: how about some of the firsts that women hold in the Scriptures? It was a woman, Mary, who first learned of the coming of the Messiah; the first to learn that Mary was carrying the divine and human child was Elizabeth (although I suppose that John in the womb was first); the first miracle at the wedding at Cana, which was instigated by a woman. The first to view the empty tomb were women. Mary Magdalen was the first to see the risen Lord. Perhaps, though I'm on shakier ground here scripturally, the first to be told, by Jesus, of his being the Messiah is the Samaritan woman, who had no standing at all, for she was a female, a semi-Gentile, and a sinner. Then there is that conversation with Martha, after Lazarus has died— one of the most important in the Gospel. Jesus tells her, "I am the Resurrection and the Life" (Jn 11:25). Oddly enough it is Martha, not Mary, even though she had chosen the better part, the listening and meditation, while Martha was serving, who has this stunning conversation with the Lord.

How have those stories, those enormously important conversations with women, come to be in sacred Scripture? I can imagine that those women were asked to tell over and over again, through their earthly life, about their conversation with Jesus. They were probably asked to tell it for the benefit of catechumens, of the newly baptized entering the Church, and of the children being raised up. The apostles went forth, making converts, celebrating the Eucharist, while the women, all those faithful followers of Jesus, helped Christians to grow in their faith, nurturing them, caring for them and for the needs of the apostles. Does this, perhaps, suggest that women are chosen and extremely well-suited to the extremely important role of education and catechesis? Think about all those times when the women were there with Jesus, on almost every occasion, including Pentecost, to receive the gift of the Holy Spirit. There are two occasions when there were only men, the Transfiguration and the Last Supper, that were particular moments for the men, for the apostles, for their strengthening, for their vocation— but there were many moments for the women.

Jesus never belittled the ways of women, their caring and loving. Rather, he used his encounters with women as teaching moments, such as when a woman anointed his feet, or when another poured oil over his head before his Passion. Jesus used those occasions to show the men around him how they should be. If God had chosen to be incarnate as a woman, the message of servanthood and humility, of taking the lower seat, would hardly have been surprising; that is what women did. It is almost as if Jesus were trying to teach the men how to behave as the women did without losing their manliness. He was teaching them to become servants, not the rulers and the masters. Have we not, at times, been guilty, of confusing the ordained ministry with ruling and privilege, rather than understanding it as servanthood? As Cardinal Ratzinger stated, the priesthood is not a position of privilege; we must convince people, in actual fact, that the priesthood, in its empirical form, must correspond to its theological idea and must continually be purified of any appearance of being a privilege.

Peter Kreeft has a vivid answer to the strident demands on the Church to ordain women:

> The most egregious error of all is the demand to be priest-esses for empowerment. I can think of no term that more perfectly proves the speaker's utter incomprehension of what she says than that. It is like wanting to manage the Boston Red Sox because of a thirst for success. [Here you see, is the problem of making a time-sensitive reference; he made that comment in 1993.] Priests are not power brokers or managers, they are sewers—like Christ, they drain off the world's sins. They are spiritual garbage men—like Christ, they clean up our spiritual garbage. They wash feet, dirty, smelly souls—ours. The Pope, priest of priests, is the servant of the servants of God. This is not a clever PR slogan—this is his real job description.[5]

When we're thinking of the reasons the Church cannot ordain women, we must consider the constant Tradition of the Church from the time of the apostles. Women were not called to the priesthood, although they were active and working throughout the early Church.

The least important reason, and I only mention it in passing, that I have heard put forth for denying ordination of women is the practical one. It would divide the Church and give rise to disorder, and, perhaps, to something even worse than the sad spectacle of the Lefebvrist movement. But that implies an approach that would have the Church

---

[5] Alice von Hildebrand and Peter Kreeft, *Women and the Priesthood* (Steubenville, Ohio: Franciscan University Press, 1994). An audio file of Kreeft's four chapters in this book is available on his website: http://www.peterkreeft.com/audio/09_priestesses.htm.

denying something that is right for reasons of peace and quiet; I do not believe she does that.

Women's Ministry in the Catholic Church

Leaving aside the radical feminists—the dissenters who would reform the Church to bring her in line with society and think ordination is intended to be a power trip and a step up the spiritual ladder—what do we say to women who love Jesus with all their hearts, and want to serve him in their lives? Some of those women feel that they are called to be priests, to be the one who says those words that makes Christ's true Body and Blood present for the faithful. I can certainly understand their longing to draw close to Christ, to be close to the Body and Blood in the Eucharist. First, we have to say to them that those who wish to be closest to Christ must do the very tough job of emulating him, of offering themselves, not for what they want to do, but for what God calls them to do. It is hard to be open to a call in one direction when we yearn to go in another, but that way of humility and self-offering is the way of Christ, and the way, ultimately, of fulfillment.

Possibly, we all need to meditate on and honor the particular gifts of women. It is difficult to speak of some of those gifts without appearing to be a reverse sexist, that is, to deny that men have similar gifts; that is not my intention. It is a commonplace to recognize the particular piety and devotion of women. Somehow they seem to be the ones who keep society on an even keel with their relationship to the sacred. By nature, by creation, women are more receptive, and, says Alice von Hildebrand, receptivity is the key to holiness. Women are primarily relational beings. They are images of immanence and of the Church, which is prepared to receive Christ's love. Men, by contrast, are more representative of transcendent love. Their relationship to creation is often one of detachment and distance, of fatherhood. Edith Stein always said that all women need to accept their maternal nature if they are to accept their vocation specifically as women. All women, married or celibate, are mothers, all the time. The same can be said of men and of fatherhood. John Paul II reminds us that celibacy is not a rejection of marriage, but a form of marriage. It is a nuptial giving of oneself for the purpose of giving, in a particular way, the nuptial love of the Redeemer.

I spoke with some of the women who work in our parish about this subject and their thoughts. Some of them are parish staff; some are volunteers. None of them have felt the yearning to be a priest, but they all shared a desire to serve Christ and his Church, and they all feel their desire is being fulfilled. One staff member, who does business work among other things, said that she thought that the special gift of women was praying. She said they are the pray-ers, who remember the names and particular needs of many people, and offer prayers daily for them. It is an extension of that gift of mothering, which all women have, whether they've given birth biologically or not.

We have a new school in our parish, and the principal, who is also head of our nursery school, tells me that women are everywhere in the Church. They are the ones running things, the schools and hospitals, for example. Each woman's gift and calling is not only administrative, although she is very good at that, but she's the one in close touch with many young families, with the cares and concerns that those parents have. Her opportunities to minister to them are many, and varied, and she finds great satisfaction in them. She says that the face of the Church is a female one. Walk into the Church for Mass and the greeter and information giver

is a woman. Walk into the school or the Christian Education center, and the director is a woman. In hospitals, most
of the people who deal directly with patients and their families are women, many of them religious. In many ways, it
is women who are called to welcome people into Christ's
body, the Church, and help them to be a part of that body.

Our director of religious education was for over twenty
years with IBM. The company offered people an attractive
buy-out to induce people to retire somewhat early, and while
she was considering it, a friend asked her what she would
do if she accepted the buy-out. She answered she would
offer herself to the service of the Church. She tells me she
has no idea where those words came from, but, in fact,
they were prophetic. She has gone from being a volunteer
teacher in the catechetics program to running a program
that educates over one thousand children and young people. Her joy, she said, is to pass on the authentic and orthodox teaching of the Church, to help people love the Church
as she does, and to see the Church's teaching as the way to
living joyful Christian and Catholic lives. A very good friend
of mine, who is very active in the Church, is a widow who
has found that her life is filled with the work she does; she
does a tremendous amount and does it well. She sees her
particular role as one of support for the priests, of freeing
them of some of the details of parish life so that they have
more time for the work of priests, liturgical and pastoral.
There are many other women in our parish who lead prayer
and meditation groups, and help people find Christ. There
are women who work as counselors in a Christian context.
Then there are all of us who serve on committees and do
lots of the little and not so little jobs that need doing.

As I'm fond of saying, I used to work for the Church for
money, now I do it for free—or more accurately, for joy. I
served my time on the parish council, which wasn't quite

as bad as being on a vestry, and then I volunteered for the vacant position of scheduling the extraordinary ministers of Holy Communion. It's about sixty-five people every weekend. I thought of that, actually, as a mortification of the flesh, or as an extended Lenten discipline, but I can't really claim it as that. It's been more interesting and challenging than I expected (and as a bonus I've learned a lot about using Excel). I also find that I come in contact with a wide group of parishioners, and that did surprise me. But at any rate, it is a rather surprising joy—it is, after all, a part of bringing Christ's Body and Blood to people.

There is the huge number of women who find their vocations in what is euphemistically called the working world—as if those of us who made a full-time job of caring for home and family weren't working. There's no shortage of chances to witness to Christ in that world, by doing excellent work and offering it, by focusing on the needs of others rather than on self-aggrandizement, and by being a good friend. I have not even mentioned those blessed women whose vocation lies in being brides of Christ, within religious communities. I've often said I was glad that wasn't my calling, but when I see the happiness and peace on the faces of young women as they go through the stages of entrance I wonder why I say that. They look very happy and very fulfilled.

When first I thought of entering the Catholic Church, I half-believed all that talk of its being a male-dominated place, but I believed so strongly that it was the Church of Jesus Christ, that I was willing to take my chances with its being that way. I found, from the beginning, that it is the Catholic Church which is friendliest to women, which gives particular honor and deference to that which is feminine. I truly believe that there is a fulfilling call for any woman within this Church, that more and more the Church finds ways to value the gifts and contributions of women. After all, when I mentioned the firsts belonging to women, I left out the most important: first in holiness in all mankind is our Blessed Mother, Mary.

Linda Poindexter entered the Roman Catholic Church at Easter 1999; prior to that she was an Episcopal priest for thirteen years; she is a graduate of Virginia Theological Seminary. She is married to Vice Admiral John Poindexter, USN, ret., and the mother of five and grandmother of fourteen. She is active in their parish, Saint Raphael's of Rockville, Maryland, coordinating the RCIA and the extraordinary ministers of Holy Communion.

LITURGY

Chapter 10

The Monastic Quality of Anglicanism: Implications for Understanding the Anglican Patrimony

Brother John-Bede Pauley, OSB

Viewed from the perspective of many Catholics, Anglicanism might be summarized in the following way. The Church of England resulted not from theological principles but because of an absolute monarch's desire for a divorce. As the establishment of the Church of England arose from political concerns, so too, the summary continues, did the shaping of its theological identity. The strong claims of both Catholic and Protestant beliefs in Reformation England led to the "Elizabethan Settlement", a politically astute, if theologically nebulous, compromise between the two theological perspectives. This theological identity means that if the Anglican tradition has anything to contribute to the Catholic Church—especially in English-speaking countries—it is not in its theology but in its aesthetic sense. Examples might include sixteenth- and seventeenth-century English translations of liturgical and Scriptural texts (translations that, if

Following publication in *Anglican Embers* volume 1, number 5 (with additional material added in volume 1, number 9), the research in this chapter was revised and published as "The Implication of Monastic Qualities on the Pastoral Provision for the 'Anglican Use'", *Antiphon* 10, no. 3 (2007): 261–76.

now regarded as archaic, nonetheless set an example of what
can be accomplished in vernacular liturgies), choral Evensong, the preservation and renewal of certain ecclesiastical
architectural styles, the literary/theological writings of an
array of writers from John Donne though Ronald S. Thomas,
and so on.

Though merely a summary, and therefore vulnerable to
the charge of inaccurate generalization, this thumbnail sketch
makes valid and accurate points, the significance of
Anglicanism's aesthetic contributions being chief among
them. Anglicanism's striking successes in the aesthetic sphere
are relevant to the following discussion because those very
successes often unfortunately have deflected deeper reflection on the theological perspective that gives the Anglican
tradition its distinctive character. What I hope to accom-
plish in the following essay, then, is to set aside the aesthetic claims of Anglicanism in order to explore some of
the ways in which Anglican identity is the expression of a
monastically influenced theology of prayer and worship. For
this reason, the following essay will not wander into the
glories of such Anglican contributions as Tallis' or Stan-
ford's choral anthems, the preservation of the English per-
pendicular, or even the novels of Anthony Trollope or
Barbara Pym. There will be, however, a nod to the beauty
of the prose of the Book of Common Prayer (BCP).[1]

Another strategy for focusing my analysis will be to look
primarily at the first two centuries of Anglicanism's existence.

---

[1] An exploration of the role of aesthetics in worship, whether specifically
Anglican or not, would take us beyond the scope of this essay. Several works
on this topic might aid the interested reader: Jeremy Begbie, *Voicing Creation's
Praise: Towards a Theology of the Arts* (Edinburgh: Clark, 1991); Albert Black-
well, *The Sacred in Music* (Louisville, Ky.: Westminster John Knox, 1999);
Frank Burch Brown, *Religious Aesthetics: A Theological Study of Making Meaning*
(Princeton N.J.: Princeton University Press, 1989).

Dealing with that period alone will be precarious enough. The establishment of the Church of England under the Tudor and Stuart dynasties was, to put it mildly, confusing. Indeed, one author has even identified Anglicanism, then and now, as a "mood" that makes a virtue of uncertainty.[2] But even in the midst of this confusion, Anglicanism's first two centuries, from the liturgical choices and the masterful prose Thomas Cranmer, Archbishop of Canterbury, inscribed into the first version of the BCP in 1549[3] through the theological reflections of the Caroline divines,[4] reveal a consistent

[2] Diarmaid MacCulloch, "The Church of England 1533–1603", in *Anglicanism and the Western Christian Tradition: Continuity, Change and the Search for Communion*, ed. Stephen Platten (Norwich: Canterbury, 2003), p. 18.

[3] The first Book of Common Prayer (hereinafter, BCP) was issued in 1549, under Edward VI. It was largely the work of Thomas Cranmer, Archbishop of Canterbury from 1533 to 1556. Cranmer essentially translated selected passages from the Breviary and the missal with additions from other sources. The BCP of 1549 has been revised in succeeding centuries and in different provinces of what we now know as the international Anglican Communion. Nonetheless, "the overall character of the Book of Common Prayer as shaped by Cranmer remained, and to a large extent shapes Anglican devotion to the present day", according to Gordon Jeanes ("Cranmer and Common Prayer", in *The Oxford Guide to The Book of Common Prayer: A Worldwide Survey*, ed. Charles Hefling and Cynthia Shattuck [New York: Oxford University Press, 2006], p. 21). See also, William Sydnor, *The Story of the Real Prayer Book, 1549–1979* (Wilton, Conn.: Morehouse, 1989).

[4] The term "Caroline divines" basically refers to leading seventeenth-century Anglican writers and clergy. See William Haugaard, "From the Reformation to the Eighteenth Century", in *The Study of Anglicanism*, ed. Stephen Sykes, John Booty, and Jonathan Knight, rev. ed. (1988; Minneapolis: Fortress, 1998), p. 24. It does not include the theological perspective of Oliver Cromwell's Puritan Commonwealth in the middle of the seventeenth century. Indeed, the suppression of the Church of England under Cromwell was instrumental in crystallizing certain pre–civil war religious traditions and theological writings of the Caroline divines into a much clearer notion of the Church of England. On this, see Judith Maltby, "Suffering and Surviving: The Civil Wars, the Commonwealth and the Formation of 'Anglicanism'", in *Anglicanism and the Western Christian Tradition*, p. 143. This development, which the post-Commonwealth Caroline divines took up again, guided this

theological thread that proved foundational in establishing Anglicanism's identity. This theological thread is unique in the story of sixteenth- and seventeenth-century Protestantism, for it placed a significant emphasis on the authority of early Church councils and the Latin and Greek Fathers, more so than most Continental Protestant theologians.[5] In other words, the theology of Cranmer, Jewel, Hooker, and the Caroline divines expressed, in many ways, a continued appreciation of patristic theology even while much of the Christian West had already embraced Scholastic theology.[6]

Patristic theology, in contrast to Scholastic theology, is also the perspective of the monastic way of doing theology.[7] It comes as no surprise, then, to find in Anglicanism's foundational years a greater openness to the monastic perspective than the dissolution of the monasteries under Henry VIII would lead us to expect. Monastic theology and liturgical expression were inscribed into, and thus preserved in, the BCP and in the influential writings of the Caroline divines.

The claim that Cranmer preserved, in the BCP, a perspective both Patristic and monastic seems intuitively wrong

---

idea through their era into what was eventually to lead to the nineteenth-century concept of "Anglicanism" as a theological position more than a merely national connotation (see Haugaard, "From the Reformation", p. 3; Paul Avis, "What is 'Anglicanism'?" in *Study of Anglicanism*, p. 461).

[5] Haugaard, "From the Reformation", p. 24; Henry Chadwick, "Tradition, Fathers and Councils", in *Study of Anglicanism*, p. 105. On the Carolines' synthesis of patristic sources with fourteenth-century English and other spiritualities, see Martin Thornton, *English Spirituality: An Outline of Ascetical Theology according to the English Pastoral Tradition* (Cambridge, Mass.: Cowley, 1986), pp. 231–43.

[6] For a discussion of the two milieus of Christian reflection in the Middle Ages, which I will call "monastic" and "Scholastic", see Jean Leclercq, *The Love of Learning and the Desire for God*, trans. Catharine Misrahi (New York: Fordham University Press, 1982), pp. 191–235.

[7] Ibid., p. 191.

since Cranmer was involved in, and seems to have supported, the dissolution of monasticism in England. Regardless of what Cranmer truly thought about the dissolution—a question perhaps impossible to answer since the project was essentially that of Henry VIII, an absolute monarch who brooked no disagreement[8]—Cranmer's religious views were not as revolutionary as those that took hold in Continental Protestantism. Monasticism's deep roots in England had helped form Cranmer's theology more positively, it seems, than the spirituality of the Augustinian Canons had impacted Martin Luther's theology. Regardless of how conscious Cranmer himself was of this monastic influence, one of his aims was to ensure that what was essentially a monastic approach to theology and liturgy was made as fully available as possible to the entire nation. From Cranmer's perspective, the dissolution of the monasteries would have favored this goal since it implicitly claimed that an essentially sound approach to theology, that being the patristic/monastic approach, should no longer be regarded as solely the preserve of monks and nuns.

It is worth noting that pre–Conquest England has been labeled "the land of the Benedictines". Monasticism's contribution to the establishment of important and numerous cathedrals and schools in England was unique in European history. These historical monastic roots have formed English spiritual theology from the days of Saint Augustine of Canterbury—the sixth-century missionary monk who established England's first archiepiscopal see—to the present.[9] Since, moreover, England is not a nation known for casually

---

[8] Gordon Jeanes, "Cranmer and Common Prayer", in *The Oxford Guide to the Book of Common Prayer: A Worldwide Survey*, ed., Charles C. Hefling and Cynthia L. Shattuck, 21–38 (New York; Oxford: Oxford University Press, 2006), 21.

[9] Thornton, *English Spirituality*, p. 46.

tossing aside its traditions and institutions, it might be sufficient to posit that the historical importance of Benedictine cathedral foundations and schools explains why monastic qualities remained in Anglicanism, the many upheavals of the English Reformation notwithstanding. But the Caroline divines probed deeper than that. By grounding themselves in the Church Fathers, the Carolines rediscovered, whether they were aware of it or not, the very sources of monastic theology and liturgical expression.

I will begin this essay by exploring aspects of monastic theology and liturgical expression in Anglicanism's foundational years and in the BCP. I will then take a more reflective turn in order to relate these observations to the Pastoral Provision for the "Anglican Use",[10] Rome's generous response to Episcopalians—Anglicans dwelling in the United States—who have converted to Catholicism, and to what the Anglican theological perspective might mean for the future of the Anglican Use within the Catholic Church. I will also present my own reflection on why the Pastoral Provision is a hopeful sign for ecumenism.

This chapter was first published as an article well before the Apostolic Constitution *Anglicanorum coetibus* was promulgated on November 4, 2009. Much of what is discussed here contributes to the discussions that arise from *Anglicanorum coetibus'* use of the term "Anglican patrimony" and from considerations of *Anglicanorum coetibus'* implications for ecumenism. This chapter, however, retains its focus on the Pastoral Provision of 1980 that addressed the situation of

---

[10] The term "Anglican Use" is not approved usage; see William H. Stetson, "The Pastoral Provision", *Anglican Embers* 1, no. 10 (2006): 265. The correct term might be "common-identity parishes". Since, however, this term does not describe what that common identity is, and having acknowledged that the term "Anglican Use" must be used loosely, this essay will continue to use the term "Anglican Use" as a sort of short-hand identifier.

converts from the Episcopal Church in the United States of America. It does so because though Anglo-Catholics in America and those in England share the same patrimony, there are also differences of perspective that, once broached, would lead to another chapter in its own right.

The Monastic Quality of the Anglican Liturgical Tradition

Although the landscape of Caroline England included recently razed monastic foundations, one has to wonder just how anti-monastic Caroline England really was. Even though it did encounter some suspicion and was not to survive the death of founder Nicholas Ferrar, the semi-monastic community at Little Gidding was peacefully tolerated and even admired by prominent writers and theologians.[11] John Bramhall, seventeenth-century Archbishop of Armagh, admitted that covetousness was a "great oar in the boat" of the Reform "and that sundry of the principal actors had a greater aim at the goods of the Church than at the good of the Church. . . . I do not see why monasteries might not agree well enough with reformed devotion."[12] Another Caroline divine, Herbert Thorndike, is less reticent: "It is certainly a blot on the Reformation when we profess that we are without monastic life."[13]

The BCP continued the basic monastic pattern of the Eucharist and the Divine Office, in the form of "Matins" (which basically combined the Offices of Vigils and Lauds) and "Evensong" (drawing from the offices of Vespers and

---

[11] Stephen Neill, *Anglicanism* (Harmondsworth, UK: Penguin, 1958), p. 148. Cromwell's soldiers dispersed the community in 1646.

[12] John Bramhall, *Works*, vol. 1 (Oxford: Parker, 1844), pp. 118–20.

[13] Herbert Thorndike, *Works*, vol. 5 (Oxford: Parker, 1842), p. 571.

Compline) as the principal public forms of worship.[14] The Caroline divines usually spoke of "the liturgy" in the singular, albeit in the composite sense of Eucharist and Office. This notion of the liturgy has to do not with a service but, as with monasticism, an integrated system of gatherings for common prayer.[15] Anglicanism has been unique in this respect. Continental Catholicism developed a devotional pattern centered on the Eucharist, with extra-liturgical devotions such as the Rosary and Benediction filling the spiritual needs of most of the laity. The Office was considered in most places the business of the clergy and religious, and the fact that in its full canonical form it could be recited only in Latin meant that it tended to disappear from popular use except in some form of a "Little Office".[16] Continental Protestantism, which celebrated the Eucharist infrequently, developed a truncated form of the Eucharist (Lutheranism) or a more informal worship service, retaining some elements of the Office.[17]

Daily celebration of Matins and Evensong in the non-parochial churches of the Church of England, such as schools, colleges, the Chapel Royal, and cathedrals, is fully documented from the late seventeenth century onward.[18] Statistics indicate that the daily celebration of the hours in many parishes continued as well, even though there seems to have been an eighteenth-century slump in religious practice in England in general, followed by a significant nineteenth-century restoration owing, at least in part, to

[14] Celebrations of the Eucharist occurred less frequently, however, than some of the Caroline divines desired (Thornton, *English Spirituality*, p. 278).

[15] Ibid., p. 262.

[16] Thomas Mudge, "Monastic Spirituality in Anglicanism", *Review for Religious* 37 (1978): 507.

[17] Ibid., p. 508.

[18] George Guiver, *Company of Voices: Daily Prayer and the People of God* (New York: Pueblo, 1988), p. 116.

the Oxford Movement.[19] Anglicans, then, have generally
been a people of the Divine Office. This, of itself, does
much to explain the "monastic" quality of Anglicanism.

Given the importance of the patristic era in the perspective of the Caroline divines, it is noteworthy that retaining
Morning and Evening Prayer would have been no more
than most Christians, both monastic and non-monastic,
would have expected of themselves in the age of the Church
Fathers.[20] The fourth-century Egyptian monks had two main
synaxes during the day, just as the fourth-century cathedrals
had Morning and Evening Prayer attended by the laity as
well as the clergy. But Cranmer seems intuitively to have
understood something of the distinction between "monastic" and "cathedral" prayer,[21] having opted, to a significant
degree, for the "monastic". Or perhaps it is more accurate
to say that Cranmer's love of the Bible and of the patristic
readings of Scripture led him naturally into a more monastic understanding of the liturgical hours and the use of Scripture in worship. Just as the "monastic" understanding of
liturgical prayer in early monasticism emphasized listening
to and being formed by the words of Scripture, rather than
singing and speaking them primarily in an attitude of praise,
so too did Cranmer believe that the Bible was the living
Word of God and that if "his fellow countrymen could be
induced to read the word of God, or, if illiterate, to hear it

[19] Ibid., pp. 120–22.

[20] Ibid., pp. 52–53.

[21] Anton Baumstark's technical terms "cathedral prayer" and "monastic
prayer", articulated in his *Comparative Liturgy* (London: Mowbray, 1958),
pp. 111–29, are, as scholars recognize, fraught with difficulties. See Paul F.
Bradshaw, *Two Ways of Praying* (Nashville: Abingdon, 1995), pp. 13–14; Brian
Dunn, "Cathedral and Monastic Prayer: What Difference Does It Make?"
Worship 80, no. 1 (2006): 46; and Guiver, *Company of Voices*, p. 53. With that
caveat, however, and for want of agreed-upon terms that are any less prob-
lematic, I will use those terms in the present essay.

read, it would in course of time make its way into their hearts". In short, his ideal was that the liturgy should play its significant role in encouraging everyone to "heare, read, marke, learne, and inwardly digeste" [22] Holy Writ.

While Luther rejected the hours as an *officium* (work) and therefore unnecessary because of justification by faith, the BCP preserved the "monastic" quality of the hours.[23] Cranmer and the Caroline divines expected the people to be "monastic" in their liturgical outlook. For the most part, it caught on.[24]

This is not to suggest that the "cathedral" approach to liturgical prayer was not also present in Anglican churches, whether in cathedrals or parishes, or that the "monastic" approach has always been predominant in Anglican history. But an English tendency to be "balanced" or, as some might say, "restrained", along with the basic "monastic" spirituality built into the BCP, has prevented Matins and Evensong from becoming too heavily "cathedral". The monastic preference for listening to Scripture rather than merely using select portions of it in a ceremonially rich liturgy is demonstrated in the Caroline church's interest in writing, reading, and delivering sermons, an indication of the attentive interest on the part of seventeenth-century Anglicans in the meaning and value of the words of Scripture. And while the Carolines did not go as far as the Puritans would have liked in stripping their churches of ornament and their liturgies of ceremony, there was nonetheless a pronounced element of restraint and simplicity in seventeenth-century Anglicanism, as though the Carolines shied from anything purely "outwardlooking" or external, which the "cathedral" office can sometimes seem to be.

[22] Neill, *Anglicanism*, p. 54.
[23] Collect, Second Sunday in Advent, BCP (1549).
[24] Bradshaw, *Two Ways of Praying*, 39.

Now this balance is not merely English; it is Benedictine. The Rule of Saint Benedict breathes an air of balance, moderation, and discretion.[25] It does so, moreover, in the liturgical context[26] for the sake of cultivating a reflective, listening spirit of prayer more than emphasizing vocal expressions of intercessions and praise.

The Carolines also aimed at a balance between reason and emotion in their theology. They, like the fourteenth-century English mystics (Julian of Norwich, Walter Hilton, the anonymous author of *The Cloud of Unknowing*), eschewed both extremes: a theological straitjacket for the spirit and a sentimentality divorced from doctrine.[27] True piety with sound learning was the ideal. The more pastorally minded Carolines (Donne, Herbert, Taylor, Ken, Andrewes) can be as affectively drawn to the humanity of Jesus as was the charismatic Saint Bernard.[28] Yet sound learning tends to rule among the Carolines, in part because they drew much of their theological focus directly from the Church Fathers;

[25] Indeed, it is so deeply woven into Anglican spirituality that when religious life returned to the Church of England, an interesting phenomenon occurred. Whereas the historical "development" of Western monasticism has tended to run from contemplative to active, the first Anglican communities of the nineteenth century were forced to be active in order to justify themselves. They always maintained, however, as much of the monastic tradition as they could. In time, some of these communities have turned from external works altogether, devoting themselves more specifically to the contemplative life; see Mudge, "Monastic Spirituality", p. 512.

[26] The cellarer should "calmly" perform his duties (*RB* 31:17); the abbot should be "discerning and moderate" (*RB* 64:17); "all things are to be done with moderation" (*RB* 48:9); and so on. The numbers following the abbreviation *RB* refer to the chapter and verse numbers in *The Rule of St. Benedict: In Latin and English with Notes*, ed. Timothy Fry (Collegeville, Minn.: Liturgical Press, 1980).

[27] "Prayer should ... be short and pure" (*RB* 20:4). "In community ... prayer should always be brief" (*RB* 20:5).

[28] Another fourteenth-century English mystic, Richard Rolle, might be a bit too emotionally charged to be in quite the same company.

in other words, they hark back to the pre-Bernardine age, which meant jumping over, to some extent, the affectivity of Bernardine and post-Bernardine spirituality.[29] Even when the Anglican spiritual tradition has followed the Benedictine heritage through the prism of the Cistercian interpretation of the Rule, it has tended to identify more fully with the thoughtful William of Saint Thierry and the less austere Aelred of Rievaulx rather than with the more obviously charismatic and forceful Saint Bernard of Clairvaux.[30]

The seventeenth century was also an era of order in religious practice. This meant not only the order of the liturgical hours but also the order of other aspects of daily life in connection with prayer. Prayers were composed for everyday occasions: on waking, dressing, grace before meals, on starting a journey. This practice of prayers for the daily activities of life finds a counterpart in the Rule.[31] As the Rule strives to cultivate an habitual sense of the presence of God in alternating periods of prayer and work, so does the BCP.[32]

Much of the affective spirituality of the English seventeenth century was expressed as poetry, which channels affectivity in an ordered way. In considering how this quality relates to Benedictine monasticism, one cannot help thinking of Newman's assigning to Saint Benedict the badge of poetry as distinguished from Saint Dominic the scientific

[29] Martin Thornton, "The Caroline Divines and the Cambridge Platonists", in *The Study of Spirituality*, ed. Cheslyn Jones, Geoffrey Wainwright, and Edward Yarnold (New York: Oxford University Press, 1986), p. 432.

[30] Thornton, *English Spirituality*, p. 46.

[31] For example, prayers on changing the kitchen servers of the week (*RB* 35); prayers before or returning from a journey (*RB* 67). In addition to the prayers specifically prescribed by the *RB*, there have been periods in monastic history when, perhaps going beyond the bounds of moderation, nearly every activity of the day (dressing, washing, cooking, and so on) had its formalized prayers.

[32] Thornton, "Caroline Divines", p. 433.

and Saint Ignatius of Loyola the practical.[33] One thinks also of the primarily monastic influence behind the poetic liturgical literature of the Carolingian era.[34]

Reference to the creative, poetic use of language in liturgy brings us to another characteristic of Caroline spirituality: for the Carolines, language and piety were inseparable. Judging by their writing styles and their conspicuous lack of comment about the beauty of language, early monastics were not concerned about poetic language in their liturgy or in Scripture. The Carolingians, the Cistercians, the fourteenth-century English mystics, and the Carolines were all very interested in the beauty of language. I suspect that this difference has something to do with literacy. Common to oral cultures is the attribution of an almost magical, talismanic potency to the spoken word because of the fact that it is spoken, sounded, and hence power-driven.[35] Since illiteracy was significant among early monastics, the compelling force and power of Scripture must have been due—aside from the fact that it is God's Word—simply to hearing it spoken in the synaxes, whether from memory or read by the literate monks. In primarily literate contexts, however, where there is also an awareness of the importance of Scripture in daily reading and in the liturgy, the compelling force and power of Scripture—aside from the fact that it is God's Word—generally needs to be experienced in some way other than by listening. Rendering it in language that is compelling because of its beauty and rhythm was the answer. Regardless of how the language of the earlier versions of the BCP and the King James Bible

---

[33] John Henry Newman, "The Benedictine Schools", in *Essays and Sketches*, vol. 3 (New York: Longmans, Green, 1948), p. 236.

[34] Leclercq, *Love of Learning*, p. 236.

[35] Walter J. Ong, *Orality and Literacy: The Technologizing of the Word* (New York: Methuen, 1982), p. 32.

are received today, it obviously appealed to a spiritual yearning in the lives of the seventeenth-century English. The
Bible was read, and the Offices were prayed. The number
of editions of the Bible published after 1580, when books
were relatively inexpensive enough to be placed in the hands
of ordinary people, is astonishing.[36] The English Bible, moreover, written with a compelling mastery of the English
language, did more than anything to encourage literacy
among the seventeenth-century populace.[37]

Cranmer's use of language, given not only that it employed
the vernacular but also that it waxed powerful in rhythm
and cadence and beauty, was one way of achieving his desire
to involve all the people of the Church of England, both
clerical and lay, not as onlookers but as active participants
in its spiritual life. Cranmer expected more from the laity
than a passive, uncomprehending presence. He placed great
confidence in the laity; he expected a great deal from ordinary people.[38] We know that his effort to involve further
participation in the Eucharist by insisting that two or three
people receive Holy Communion with the presider met with
much resistance.[39] But the documentation of attendance at
daily Matins and Evensong attests to the fact that his expectations were not always and everywhere disappointed. While
involvement in the religious life on the part of the lower
socio-economic classes is difficult to ascertain, we do know
that the lay intelligentsia (Mary Astell,[40] Robert Boyle,
Margaret Godolphin, Mary Caning, Lady Ranelagh, to name

[36] Neill, *Anglicanism*, pp. 129–30.

[37] Thornton, "Caroline Divines", pp. 434–35.

[38] Neill, *Anglicanism*, p. 54.

[39] John N. Wall, "Anglican Spirituality: A Historical Introduction", in *Spiritual Traditions for the Contemporary Church*, ed. Robin Maas and Gabriel
O'Donnell (Nashville: Abingdon, 1990), p. 278.

[40] See Ruth Perry, *The Celebrated Mary Astell: An Early English Feminist*
(Chicago: University of Chicago Press, 1986).

but a few) certainly played a leading part in seventeenth-century religious life.[41] Similarly, the *RB* is designed for a predominantly non-clerical community.

Stability, one of the Benedictine vows,[42] is another quality held in common between Benedictine monasticism and Anglicanism. Both the BCP and Caroline spirituality, while not asking the same vow of the clergy and the laity, presupposed a stable community. Elements evocative of Benedictine stability include a common office, empirical guidance within the family, rubrics relating to residential qualifications for marriage and burial, and John Donne's emphasis on the Word being preached "in a settled church".[43]

For those who look upon liturgy from a particularly "rubrical" perspective, the following quality may be difficult to understand; this is fair enough since it is perhaps impossible to define. But it is, I believe, central to what makes "traditional" Anglican liturgical piety so distinct from liturgical expressions in the Catholic Church today, whether "traditional" or "progressive". The quality in question is recollection or what we might call a "homely" character. Cultivating a spirit of recollection is common to all spiritual traditions, but the Anglican approach seems particularly unassuming and takes no particular interest in the kinds of methods or stages that we find in other spiritual writers. Jeremy Taylor was one Anglican writer who set forth the basic appeal for contemplative recollection in his adage, "I would rather your prayer be often than long." [44] His words put us in mind of Benedict's instruction that "prayer should ... be short and pure",[45] as well as the whole spirit of the

---

[41] Thornton, *English Spirituality*, p. 241.
[42] For instance, *RB* 4:78, 58:9, and 60:9.
[43] Thornton, *English Spirituality*, p. 258.
[44] Ibid., p. 258.
[45] *RB* 20:4.

Rule. Both Caroline and Benedictine spirituality inculcate, moreover, a distinct strain of "homeliness", to use Julian of Norwich's term—a warm, tolerant, human devotion based on loving persuasion rather than fiery oratory. Anglicanism is more at home with the Benedictine image of the Church as a supportive family than with, for instance, the military image of the Jesuits. For this reason, Anglican liturgical piety, while eschewing liturgical lassitude, is also ill at ease with anything that resembles triumphalist, lock-step liturgical uniformity or grand emotional expression. It is noteworthy that the consciously triumphalist splendor of baroque architecture, a burnished-marble polemic in its own right for the establishment of religious and liturgical uniformity, has never gained a firm foothold in the Anglican ethos (notwithstanding the baroque splendor of Christopher Wren's Saint Paul's Cathedral in London). Similarly, in monasticism, both Benedictines and Cistercians did absorb baroque elements as monasticism flowed through the seventeenth century. Still, Benedict's language of moderation and his distinction between good zeal and the "wicked zeal of bitterness" [46] set up, at best, a constructive dissonance between monasticism and triumphalist grandeur.

Perspectives on private prayer and moral theology mark further similarities between the Anglican and Benedictine traditions. After Trent, the tendency in Catholicism was to separate moral and ascetical theology, which meant two distinct "sciences" of preparing souls for heaven emerged, the one occupied with the question of the legality or illegality of human acts, and the other concerned with spiritual progress and holiness. [47] While such a distinction is part of the contemporary Catholic landscape, Benedictine monasticism has

[46] *RB* 72:1.
[47] Thornton, *English Spirituality*, p. 241.

nonetheless always tended toward the notion that the conventual life of daily observances is in itself a means of spiritual direction and moral instruction.[48] Similarly, Caroline direction placed more emphasis on recollection in daily life than on particular techniques of formal prayer, and Caroline casuistry was not concerned with formal "self-examination" prior to sacramental confession, but with the practical art of making moral decisions during daily life, training the conscience to be used in habitual recollection.[49]

As to differences between the BCP and monasticism, the obvious difference is that the BCP does not ask for vows of obedience, stability, and conversion of life. The BCP and Caroline spirituality nonetheless fostered an approach to living the Christian life that encouraged Anglicans to live significant elements of these vows in their everyday lives, as in the observations made above concerning the distinctly Benedictine vow of stability.

Another difference is that the *RB* provides for the election of a superior from among the members of the monastic community. While Cranmer might have expected much from the laity, he and the English government had no intention of allowing the laity to vote on who would be their rectors, vicars, bishops, and so on.

Election, in a different sense, raises a major difference as well as a possible limitation inherent in Cranmer's vision. Ideally, men and women enter the monastic life because they freely elect to do so. They perceive in the monastic manner of life a spirituality to which they are called and that they freely elect as their own. Nevertheless, not everyone is at home with monastic spirituality. Not everyone,

---

[48] Jean Leclercq, "Spiritual Direction in the Benedictine Tradition", in *Traditions of Spiritual Guidance*, ed. Lavinia Byrne (Collegeville, Minn.: Liturgical Press, 1990), p. 28.

[49] Thornton, *English Spirituality*, pp. 240–41.

then, should expect to be at home with the monastic ethos
of the BCP. Cranmer, however, wanted an entire people
to fit into a certain spiritual mold. While the ethos of
seventeenth-century England might have been sufficiently
homogeneous and sufficiently "monastic" to sustain Caroline spirituality for a time, can we make the same assumptions today? It is noteworthy that a recent book on
Anglicanism, *The Study of Anglicanism*,[50] makes no reference to the monastic or Benedictine influences in Anglicanism, parting company—whether consciously or not—
from Bede, Thomas Mudge, and Martin Thornton. Has
contemporary Anglicanism left its monastic ethos behind?
If so, what is Anglicanism's ethos today? Although this is a
question we cannot answer here, it is certainly worth raising.

Possible Implications for the "Anglican Use"

The preceding section of this essay set forth some of the
important monastic qualities inherent in Anglicanism's identity. This identity is, I believe, the same "common identity" referred to in the 1980 Pastoral Provision for the
Anglican Use and expressed in the approved adaptation of
the BCP that resulted in the Book of Divine Worship
(BDW).[51] The Pastoral Provision therefore represents much

[50] See note 4 above.
[51] The 1980 Pastoral Provision of Pope John Paul II for the Anglican
Usage of the Roman Rite led to the adaptation of the BCP (in its 1928 and
1979 American Episcopal Church versions) for use by "Roman Catholics
coming from the Anglican tradition" (*Book of Divine Worship* [Mt. Pocono,
Penn.: Newman House, 2003], title page). The text of the Pastoral Provision can be found not only in Appendix B, but also—along with the history leading up to its signing on July 22, 1980—at Jack Barker, "The Pastoral
Provision for Roman Catholics in the U.S.A.", at http://www.
stmarythevirgin.org/jackbarker.htm.

breadth of spirit in the very fact that Rome has welcomed this "common identity" as one of its own liturgical expressions and theological perspectives. The implications both for ecumenism and for the enrichment of Catholic liturgical life are worth deeper reflection. Toward that end, I offer the following thoughts.

Of necessity, the aspect of the Pastoral Provision that has received much attention in the past three decades has been its role in welcoming converts from the Anglican Communion. This is because conversions indeed have taken place, and they have done so with all the attendant activity of a new foundation: ordinations, the creation of parishes, building of churches, approval and printing of the BDW, and so on. But now that the first generation of converts has achieved a sense of integration and establishment in the Catholic Church, perhaps we can step back and reflect on another implication of the Pastoral Provision: its ringing affirmation of Anglican liturgical spirituality and therefore a positive statement ecumenically. At the moment of this writing, ecumenical dialogue between Rome and Canterbury seems to be at a low point. The very fact, however, that Rome has approved the BDW represents a bright ray of hope in ecumenism, for this is nothing other than a profound intersection between the two traditions at the place that matters most to all of us: the liturgy. To draw from the Anglican poet's words about Little Gidding, Rome has affirmed again the Anglican tradition as a tradition "where prayer has been valid".[52] I propose that we give the Pastoral Provision its due as Rome's gracious "thank you" to countless generations of Anglicans through whom the Holy Spirit preserved and developed a rich and vibrant liturgical expression.

---

[52] T. S. Eliot, "Little Gidding", from *The Four Quartets*, in *T. S. Eliot: The Complete Poems and Plays 1909–1950* (New York: Harcourt, Brace and World, 1971), p. 139.

Another implication that follows from the comments made above is that the Anglican Use's common identity, when rightly understood and appreciated, might help the Catholic Church liturgically to breathe more freely, so to speak. Amid fears of liturgical "restorationism" on the one hand and suspicions of the "post–Vatican II generation" on the other, the Anglican Use is neither a restoration of pre–Vatican II liturgy nor a "Cranmerized" version of what now prevails in most English-speaking Roman-Rite parishes. It expresses a distinct liturgical identity, a "[form] of spiritual life", that, when properly understood, elaborates revealed truth in its own distinct way.[53]

As an example of the Anglican Use's distinct character, I limit myself to one final illustration. That Scripture "be understood of the people" was of vital importance to Cranmer and the Caroline divines, just as it is of vital importance to everyone who strives to live the monastic manner of life. This colors the way Scripture is read. While no one would claim that Anglican parishes always and everywhere maintain a monastic, quasi-*lectio*[54] sense of preparing and reading Scripture in the liturgy, it has been my experience that the entire ethos of the tradition nonetheless fosters an approach to reading Scripture liturgically that is quite distinct from the way one encounters it either in a "Tridentine" Mass or in almost any local parish's celebration of the

---

[53] Second Vatican Council, Decree on Ecumenism, *Unitatis redintegratio*, in *Vatican Council II: The Conciliar and Post Conciliar Documents*, study edition, ed. Austin Flannery (Collegeville, Minn.: Liturgical Press, 1992), sec. 4, p. 458.

[54] *Lectio divina* is the term used for the particularly monastic approach to sacred reading. The discussion by monastic authors of *ruminatio* (ruminating on Scripture) must have occurred to Cranmer when he wrote of Scripture as something the hearer or reader should "inwardly digeste". The literature on *lectio divina* is abundant. A good introduction for the uninitiated is Michael Casey, *Sacred Reading: The Ancient Art of* Lectio Divina (Liguori, Mo.: Liguori/ Triumph, 1995).

post–Vatican II Mass. Admittedly, I make nothing more than an anecdotal observation here. But to those "Roman Catholics coming from the Anglican tradition",[55] the way Scripture is read in the liturgy will say much, even if no more than subliminally, about just what our "common identity" is.

Lest the observations I have made in this essay portray the Anglican Use as a subversive innovation in the Catholic liturgical fold, we should recall that Anglicanism's common identity owes much to monasticism. No one will describe monasticism as a recent innovation in the life of the Church. Rather than constituting a radical innovation, the Anglican Use presents, I believe, an avenue by which the Holy Spirit can expand our liturgical scope by way of recovering one of the riches of the Church that has been pretty much hidden away, even from many monastic communities in recent centuries—and this would constitute another essay. To run the risk of a CliffsNotes view of liturgical history: monasticism rather too heavily dominated the entire Western Church's liturgical outlook in the Middle Ages. The rise of Scholasticism and the mendicant orders "put paid" to all of that, for no hegemony lasts forever. As noted earlier, however, England and Anglicanism took quite deeply to Benedictine monasticism to such an extent that Scholasticism did not make as great an impact. While it is not accurate to refer to Anglicanism's common identity as monastic *tout court*, it is so heavily redolent of the monastic approach to prayer in certain respects that it characterizes this very striking freshness that the Anglican Use carries into the Catholic liturgical context.

If, therefore, the Anglican Use poses a challenge to the status quo in the Catholic Church, it is not, I suspect, in

---

[55] *BDW*, title page.

the way that converts from the Episcopal Church are received into the Catholic fold. Instead, the challenge could well be that the Anglican Use jostles the givens of what has been, at least in the Catholic Church of the past century or so, a rather narrowly defined liturgical landscape. To put it another way, those who regard the Anglican Use liturgy as either a step on the way to restoring the Tridentine Mass or as an ethnic inculturation of the postconciliar Mass are not recognizing the "common identity" that lies at the basis of the Pastoral Provision. The Anglican Use is something altogether different: it is a liturgical reflection of an essentially monastic approach to theology and prayer. Perhaps a fuller appreciation of that difference can help to broaden the rather too restricted cycle of "Tridentine" versus postconciliar.

This language of "jostling the givens" will set off alarms in the minds of many. How different would this "jostling" be from the liturgical jolts and jerks, some might even say juggernauts, of the post–Vatican II years? I candidly admit that I do not have an answer to that question. But I can, at least, reiterate once more that the Anglican Use did not spring into being on a blank sheet of paper or in a liturgy committee. It has behind it a long tradition, stretching back further than the past several centuries of Anglicanism itself. As such, it cannot represent an excuse for the mere reactions, whether "conservative" or "progressive", that animated some of the experimental extremism and liturgical upheavals of recent decades. It presents, rather, an opportunity for a deeper, calmer reflection on the import of the following passage from the Decree on Ecumenism of the Second Vatican Council, *Unitatis redintegratio*:

> While preserving unity in essentials, let everyone in the
> Church, according to the office entrusted to him, preserve

a proper freedom in the various forms of spiritual life and discipline, in the variety of liturgical rites, and even in the theological elaborations of revealed truth. In all things let charity prevail. If they are true to this course of action, they will be giving ever richer expression to the authentic catholicity and apostolicity of the Church (no. 4).

Note that this passage in a document concerned with ecumenism applies not to the "separated brethren", but to "everyone *in* the Church" (emphasis added). The Anglican Use, I contend, is one among these varied "theological elaborations" of revealed truth that exist within the Church. As such, the Pastoral Provision calls for deeper reflection, not merely as a sort of statutory regulation for handling Episcopalian converts but as a sure sign that God, who knows us better than we know ourselves, never really lets us get away with a safe, narrowly defined status quo.

Brother John-Bede Pauley is a monk of Saint John's Abbey, Collegeville, Minnesota, an associate professor of music at St. John's University, Collegeville, and a former Episcopalian who was converted to Catholicism in 1986.

Chapter 11

The Anglican Use within the Western Liturgical Tradition

Importance and Ecumenical Relevance from the Perspective of Comparative Liturgy

Professor Hans-Jürgen Feulner, Th.D.

In the preface of the First Book of Common Prayer (1549) of King Edward VI, one reads:

> "And where heretofore, there hath been great diversitie in saying and synging in churches within this realme: some folowyng Salsbury use, some Hereford use, some the use of Banger, some of York, and some of Lincolne: Now from henceforth, all the whole realme shall have but one use." [1]

It is thus evident that at the time of the English Reformation there were at least five liturgical "Uses" or "diocesan usages" in the English church.[2] It is perhaps surprising that we have a variety of liturgical "Uses" (or "Rites") in the English church of the sixteenth century, and not only

---

Originally published in *Anglican Embers* 2, no. 12 (December 2009): 475–505. In memory of Fr. Eugene Beau Davis, SSC († Nov. 8, 2010).

[1] *The First and Second Prayer Books of Edward VI*, ed. Edward Charles S. Gibson, Everyman's Library, no. 448 (1964; London & New York, reprint 2008), p. 4.

[2] The term "Use" is often distinguished from that of "Rite".

the "Roman Catholic" Rite that one may expect to find everywhere in the West. In fact, we have always had a great variety of rites and liturgical usages—not only in the Christian East, but also in the Catholic Church. In order to understand the place and significance of the so-called Anglican Use among this variety of liturgical rites, diocesan usages, and mutual influences, a special method of Liturgical Studies will be employed. This method is not only instructive; it is also ecumenical per se.

Comparative Liturgy/Liturgiology— Vergleichende Liturgiewissenschaft

Let us begin by touching upon the method of Comparative Liturgiology (*Vergleichende Liturgiewissenschaft*)[3] that is attributed to the German scholar Anton Baumstark (1872–1948) and his immediate disciples Fritz Hamm (1901–1970) and Hieronymus Engberding (1899–1969).

The German Scholar Anton Baumstark

Anton Baumstark[4] was born into a well-educated Roman Catholic family in 1872. He began his academic career specializing in oriental studies, with a focus on Aramaic/

[3] See Fritz S. West, *Anton Baumstark's Comparative Liturgy in Its Intellectual Context* (Ann Arbor, Mich.: Ann Arbor University Microfilms International, 1988); West, *The Comparative Liturgy of Anton Baumstark*, Joint Liturgical Studies, no. 31 (Bramcote: Grove Books, 1995); *Acts of the International Congress: "Comparative Liturgy Fifty Years after Anton Baumstark (1872–1948)"; Rome, 25–29 September 1998*, ed. Robert F. Taft and Gabriele Winkler, Orientalia Christiana Analecta, no. 265 (Rome: Pontifical Oriental Institute, 2001).

[4] There are numerous short biographies of Baumstark in print: *Oriens Christianus* 37 (1953): 1–5; *Ephemerides Liturgicae* 63 (1949): 185–87; *Oxford Dictionary of the Christian Church* (Oxford: Oxford University Press, 1974), p. 144; *Lexikon für Theologie und Kirche*, vol. 2, 3rd ed. (Freiburg: Herder, 2006), pp. 94–95, etc.

Syriac materials. After university, he lived for five years in
Rome, where he redirected his scholarly endeavors. He
turned his energies toward the liturgy and literature of the
Church in the eastern Mediterranean, especially the non-
Byzantine East. He was co-founder and editor of *Oriens
Christianus*, a scholarly journal still in print today. Unable
to obtain a university appointment, he first taught classics
at a secondary school. He was married around this time to
a woman who was to bear him fourteen children, two of
whom died soon after birth. In this period, Baumstark wrote
his first standard work, *Die Geschichte der syrischen Literatur*
(*History of Syrian Literature*).[5] An especially important moment
in Baumstark's life was his relationship with the German
Abbey of Maria Laach. The Benedictine Abbot Ildefons Her-
wegen (1874–1946) encouraged the young scholar to also
turn his attention to the liturgies of the West, while providing Baumstark with a quiet place to work and opportunities to publish. Baumstark also served as editor of the
Jahrbuch für Liturgiewissenschaft. In 1921, he finally obtained
a university position, as *professor honorarius* for Early Christian Civilization at the University of Bonn. In addition to
his work in Bonn, he taught Semitic languages at Nijmegen
and Utrecht in the Netherlands, and later in Münster in
Germany as well. Because of his involvement in the National
Socialist Party of the Third Reich, Baumstark was removed
from the editorship of *Jahrbuch für Liturgiewissenschaft* and
retired early, in 1935, from his university position in Münster. He moved back to Bonn, where he died in 1948 at
the age of seventy-five.

Baumstark had a fecund mind and a productive pen. His
bibliography contains no less than 570 publications, both

[5] Anton Baumstark, *Geschichte der syrischen Literatur mit Ausschluß der christlich-palästinensischen Texte* (Bonn, 1922; reprint, Berlin: de Gruyter, 1968).

popular and scholarly, on a very wide variety of topics, including Judaism and influences on the Quran.[6]

The Method of Comparative Liturgiology

The nineteenth-century Anglican liturgical scholar John Mason Neale (1818–1866) seems to have coined both the English word "liturgiology" for the scientific study of liturgy, and the expression "Comparative Liturgy".[7] But Baumstark is the one who popularized and gave theoretical formulation to the method of *Vergleichende Liturgiewissenschaft* (Comparative Liturgiology), which has proven not only useful, but indispensable for the history of liturgy.[8] It has been demonstrated many times that the solution to some problems of liturgical history and interpretation is simply impossible without the methods of Comparative Liturgiology.[9]

Liturgy, in Baumstark's words, is a living activity, which can "never . . . be paralyzed into the rigour of an immobile dead formalism". By its very nature, liturgy is "subject . . . to a process of continuous evolution". The vocation of the historian of liturgy is "to investigate and describe the origins and variations of the changing forms of this enduring substance of eternal value" that is "the living heart of the Church".[10] This means the study of the evidence. And since

[6] Baumstark's bibliography has been published in complete form: Hans-Jürgen Feulner, "Bibliography of Anton Baumstark", in *Acts of the International Congress*, pp. 31–60.

[7] John Mason Neale, *Essays on Liturgiology and Church History* (London, 1863; reprint, New York: AMS Press, 1976), pp. 123–24.

[8] Anton Baumstark, *Vom geschichtlichen Werden der Liturgie*, Ecclesia Orans, no. 10 (Freiburg: Herder, 1923); Baumstark, *Comparative Liturgy*, rev. Eng. ed., Bernard Botte, trans. Frank L. Cross (London: Mowbray, 1958).

[9] See Robert F. Taft, "Anton Baumstark's Comparative Liturgy Revisited", in *Acts of the International Congress*, pp. 192–93.

[10] Baumstark, *Comparative Liturgy*, pp. 1–2.

the evidence presents similarities and differences, its study is comparative. If there were no differences, there would only be full correspondence, and nothing to compare or to explain. If there were no similarities, there would be no basis for a comparative method to begin with.

Hence in the early twentieth century, the comparative methodology was proven effective in studies of the Eastern liturgies, as a scientific approach to liturgical texts and structures. As mentioned above, Anton Baumstark did not limit his historico-liturgical research to the Eastern Rites, but studied the Western Latin liturgical traditions of the first millennium as well. He developed the beginnings of a Comparative Liturgiology, which he finally expounded in more detail in his *Liturgie Comparée* (*Comparative Liturgy*),[11] a work that first appeared in French. Baumstark was interested in the history of the liturgy, which presents itself to the liturgist as a product of growth, as something both given and enduring. The development of the liturgy lends itself well to Comparative Liturgiology, which investigates and identifies the major developmental trajectories of the liturgy and their principles. This is accomplished by a comparison and collation of the various Eastern and Western liturgical families. A Comparative Liturgiology seeks to take into account the wider historico-religious context, the Jewish liturgy, and the entire breadth of the liturgies of various Christian churches. Today, this wider perspective can be of particular ecumenical import.

Various approaches utilized in the past to Comparative Liturgiology developed the conviction that the separate rites are to be understood in their original languages; that the

---

[11] Anton Baumstark, *Liturgie Comparée. Principes et méthodes pour l'étude historique des liturgies chrétiennes*, rev. Bernard Botte, 3rd ed. (1939; Chevetogne: Éditions de Chevetogne, 1953).

separate *parts of a liturgical service* (so-called liturgical units[12])
and *structures* are to be compared to one another; and, finally,
that the historical change is to be analyzed in comparative
juxtaposition.

* * * * *

Division of the Eucharist into Liturgical Units and Subunits for Comparison

Parts of the Mass	Elements of the Eucharistic Part	Elements of the Eucharistic Prayer (Canon or Anaphora)	Elements of the Institution Narrative
		Opening Dialogue	
		Praefatio	
		Sanctus–Benedictus	
Opening	Preparation of the Altar	Oratio post Sanctus	Introduction
Liturgy of the Word	Offertory Prayers	Consecratory Epiclesis	Words over bread
Eucharistic Part	**Eucharistic Prayer**	**Institution Narrative**	**Words over wine**
Communion		Anamnesis + Oblation	**Acclamation**
Conclusion		Communion Epiclesis	
		Intercessions	
		Doxology	

[12] See also Robert F. Taft, "The Structural Analysis of Liturgical Units:
An Essay in Methodology", in *Worship* 52 (1978): 314–29; Taft, *Beyond*

Baumstark and those inspired by him sought to identify the basic principles, according to which the evolution of the liturgy could be grasped. These principles were sought in various ways: (1) through a comparative *structural* analysis of the liturgical texts; (2) through a comparative *textual* analysis on a *philological* basis; and (3) through a comparative *historical* study. Anton Baumstark and, especially, his above-mentioned students, Fritz Hamm and Hieronymus Engberding, worked on important developmental trends through a comparison and collation of the various liturgical families. They also formulated several basic "laws/principles" (*Gesetzmäßigkeiten*, in German) that serve to explain the development of the liturgy. These "laws", which are to be observed from the earliest forms of the liturgy until Late Antiquity, are also important for a proper understanding of later liturgical traditions.[13] Of course, these "laws/principles" of organic development of liturgy are limited to the liturgical families and rites in the first millennium until Late Antiquity or Early Middle Ages.[14]

East and West: Problems in Liturgical Understanding, 2nd ed. (Rome: Pontifical Oriental Institute, 1997), pp. 187–202.

[13] See for the methodology: Hans-Jürgen Feulner, *Die armenische Athanasius-Anaphora. Kritische Edition, Übersetzung und liturgievergleichender Kommentar*, Anaphorae Orientales, no. 1, Anaphorae Armeniacae, no. 1 (Rome: Pontifical Oriental Institute, 2001), pp. 63–67.

[14] What Baumstark called the "laws" of Comparative Liturgiology are not prior to nor a surrogate for the facts of liturgical history. Furthermore, "comparative liturgy is not concerned simply with the determination of facts" (Baumstark, *Comparative Liturgy*, p. 15), but with explaining them. What are these "laws"? These "laws" of organic development of liturgy are not comparable with physical or mathematical laws. The "laws" of Comparative Liturgiology are therefore better called "general norms" or "general principles" concerning the evolution of liturgy and liturgical "Rites" (in the sense of liturgical families or traditions, e.g., the Roman Rite, the Byzantine Rite). In German, one uses the word *Gesetzmäßigkeit* ("general norm" or "principle") as distinct from *Gesetz* ("law"); cf. Taft, "Anton Baumstark's Comparative Liturgy Revisited", pp. 196–97.

A modified method of Comparative Liturgiology, however, that also includes the different Protestant liturgies, must necessarily consider in its comparisons the substantial doctrinal and liturgical "rupture" from the sixteenth century onward, beyond those "*Gesetzmäßigkeiten*" (see below). Nevertheless, the impact of "laws" of liturgical development, which are still reflected in the nuclei of the Protestant liturgies (including the Anglican liturgical tradition), can be observed in the second millennium (up to our time) as well. We mainly follow Robert Taft's adaptation of the methodological reflections scattered throughout Baumstark's writings. Baumstark's principles, both those that were original to him and those first developed by his immediate disciples, cover distinct areas of liturgical history: (1) general principles concerning the evolution of liturgy and liturgical "rites"; (2) specific laws/principles regarding the evolution of liturgical texts and/or the evolution of liturgical structures and actions and their subsequent symbolization.

"Laws" or "Principles" of Liturgical Development[15]

General Principles

• *The evolution of liturgical rites moves from diversity to uniformity (not vice-versa).*

By this, Baumstark means that as time goes on, diverse local usages in a single area of liturgical diffusion solidify into a relatively homogeneous liturgical family or "rite", so that we have fewer diverse liturgical usages now than in the past. The divergent local forms of liturgical services were eventually

---

[15] Cf. for the following, especially, Taft, "Anton Baumstark's Comparative Liturgy Revisited", pp. 198–210; Feulner, *Die armenische Athanasius-Anaphora*, pp. 70–71.

brought together into regional liturgical families, which crystallized around the contemporary significant cultural and theological centers: Alexandria, Antioch, Rome, and Constantinople. Amongst these, it was Rome and Constantinople that were to exert the most lasting influence. But this overall evolution is countered by a retrograde movement. For as individual rites evolve toward ever greater internal unity, they also tend to diversify from one another by taking on local coloration through continued adaptation to the concrete circumstances of time and place. This "law" is a direct response to the former theory of the diversification of rites once propagated by Ferdinand Probst (1816–1899) of Tübingen.[16] According to Probst, the extant Rites of East and West evolved from a single primitive apostolic liturgical tradition. But Baumstark's insight remains valid: our present liturgical rites or families are the result of a process of synthesis, unification, and survival of the fittest. Today there is one Coptic Rite where there was once throughout Egypt a multiplicity of variant local usages. And the Byzantine Rite by the tenth/eleventh century had replaced or absorbed the local usages in Asia Minor.

• *Liturgical development proceeds from simplicity to increasing enrichment.*

Originally simple liturgical rituals become more and more complex by additions and restructurings. This "law" is very important for the form and redaction criticism of liturgical texts in order to look for the urtext of a liturgical formula by text-comparative methods.

---

[16] Ferdinand Probst, *Liturgie der ersten drei christlichen Jahrhunderte* (Tübingen, 1870); Probst, *Sakramente und Sakramentalien in den ersten drei christlichen Jahrhunderten* (Tübingen, 1872); Probst, *Liturgie des vierten Jahrhunderts und deren Reform* (Münster, 1893).

• *The development of liturgy is but a series of individual developments.*

The history of the liturgy consists not in one, progressive, unilinear growth of entire rituals as homogeneous single units, but via distinct developments of their individual components. From this "law" follows that, for the knowledge of the history of a liturgical ritual, we have to patiently examine all of its component parts. By "liturgical unit", Baumstark seems to mean a complete ritual—the ritual of Baptism, the Marriage ritual, etc. Research, however, has verified that neither texts nor structures evolve—at least not always nor necessarily—homogeneously as integral units. Larger textual units like the Eucharistic Prayer can comprise several subunits—Opening Dialogue, Preface, Sanctus, Oratio post Sanctus, Epiclesis, Institution Narrative, Anamnesis, Oblation, Intercessions—each of which can have its own form and redaction criticism independent of the rest. The same is true of individual structural units: they can have a life of their own, often independent of what is developing (or not) in the rest of the ritual.

• *Free and improvised prayers develop to formulaic prayers.*

A fixed prayer formulary was often preceded by a more ancient oral tradition. A classical example is the liturgical texts of the so-called Apostolic Tradition (*Traditio Apostolica*) of the early third century attributed to Hippolytus of Rome.

• *Liturgical relationships*

Through a comparison of separate Rites with one another, it is possible to establish important liturgical connections or relationships, such as

- between the Rite of the city of Rome and the Latin liturgy of North Africa, as well as between the Rite of the city of Rome and that of the Alexandrian liturgical family;
- between the Old Gallican, Old Spanish (and Celtic) Rites on the one hand, and the West-Syrian liturgical family on the other;
- between the Maronite Rite and the Syro-Mesopotamian ("Nestorian") Rite of the East-Syrian type;
- between the Armenian Rite and Jerusalem, as well as the liturgical usages of Persarmenia and Syria;
- between the West-Syrian liturgical family and the Alexandrian liturgical family.

Specific Laws

- *The older a text is, the less it is influenced by the Bible.*

A literal dependence on Scripture generally signals more recent liturgical texts. The classic instance is the Institution Narrative, which earlier anaphoras (Eucharistic Prayers) never cite verbatim from one of its New Testament redactions.

- *The more recent a text is, the more symmetrical it is.*

Stylistic smoothness usually betrays a later composition or an earlier one subjected to later polishing. This tendency to symmetry is anterior to the later influence of the biblical text, for in some cases an earlier symmetry is destroyed in a still later period by the growing influence of biblical language on liturgical texts (e.g., the Institution Narrative or Epiclesis of Eastern anaphoras).

• *The later it is, the more liturgical prose becomes charged with doctrinal elements.*

The dogmatic decisions of the ecumenical councils and other synods have influenced the liturgical texts by doctrinal elements. The Anaphora of Saint Chrysostom, for instance, is a clear development from the greater simplicity of its urtext, the so-called Anaphora of the Apostles, and is heavily freighted with doctrinal additions that are the fruit of anti-Arianism. Similar processes at work in the evolution of other oriental anaphoras have been shown by liturgists. The "law" of the insertion of doctrinal elements is particularly valuable for dating texts *ante quem non*, since certain doctrinal emphases did not enter a text until they had become an issue in the life of the Church.

• *Older usage is preserved in the more solemn liturgical seasons.*[17]

This "law" affirms that more solemn liturgical seasons, like Lent, tend to maintain older liturgical usages, which may have given way at other times under the insertion of new rituals. We still have the unique full prostration of the priest in front of the altar on Good Friday or the clearing of the altar after the Mass of the Last Supper on Holy Thursday: older general usages that have disappeared at the end of Antiquity might be preserved only in a more solemn liturgical season.

• *Originally utilitarian liturgical actions later will be symbolized.*

Certain actions that are purely utilitarian by nature may receive a symbolic meaning either from their function in the liturgy

[17] See Anton Baumstark, "Das Gesetz der Erhaltung des Alten in liturgisch hochwertiger Zeit", *Jahrbuch für Liturgiewissenschaft* 7 (1927): 1–23.

as such or from factors in the liturgical texts that accompany them. Liturgical vestments and liturgical vessels that no longer serve their original purposes find a new rationale for their continued existence via a process of symbolization. This classical method of Comparative Liturgiology has already shown in a fascinating manner the abundance of liturgical traditions not only in the Christian East, but also in the West. There is a great variety of liturgical rites and uses, sometimes brought together in regional "liturgical families". Because of the radical break of the Reformation in both theology and liturgical practice, Protestant liturgies do not lend themselves well to the classical method of Comparative Liturgiology. A modified methodology, however, may demonstrate mutual influences and relationships in regard to the Protestant liturgies as well.[18]

The Catholic "Anglican Use" within the Western Liturgical Tradition

As we said above, it is evident that at the time of the English Reformation there were at least five "Uses" or "diocesan usages" in the English church. These English Uses had as their basis the Old Gallican–Roman Rite and may be considered local adaptations and modifications of it. The differences consisted of proper ceremonial and additional texts according to the particular Use. These five "Uses" in England were associated with the major bishops' sees of England, especially those of Salisbury (Sarum)

---

[18] For an application of a modified methodology in regard to the Anglican liturgical tradition, see Hans-Jürgen Feulner, *Das "Anglikanische Ordinale". Eine liturgiegeschichtliche und liturgietheologische Studie*, vol 1, *Von den altenglischen Pontifikalien zum Ordinale von 1550/52* (Neuried: Ars Una, 1997), passim.

and York, geographically representing the north and south of England.[19]

Liturgical Rites and Uses in Medieval Europe[20]

The Celtic Rite

According to our present-day knowledge, it seems fair to assert along with Frank E. Warren[21] and William Maskell[22] that the more ancient liturgy used in England before the time of Saint Augustine of Canterbury was the so-called Celtic liturgy. According to the studies of Comparative Liturgiology, the Celtic liturgy seems to have been influenced by the liturgies of Milan, Rome, Gaul, and also from the West-Syrian liturgical family. In fact, there was little that was properly Celtic and did not depend in some way on the ancient Roman, Ambrosian, and Old Gallican Rites. The form of the eucharistic liturgy was basically that of the Old Gallican Rite.[23]

The Old Gallican–Roman Rite

The arrival of Saint Augustine of Canterbury around the year 597 led to a change in the liturgy of the Church in England. Augustine wrote to Pope Gregory the Great asking him which liturgy should be followed in England: the Old Gallican Rite or the Roman liturgy. Gregory's response

---

[19] See Alan F. Detscher, *The Evolution of the Rite for the Ordination of Priests in the Protestant Episcopal Church in the United States of America* (Rome: Pont. Athenaeum Anselmi, 1981), p. 10.

[20] See, especially, Feulner, *Das "Anglikanische Ordinale"*, pp. 9–15.

[21] See Frank E. Warren, *Liturgy and Ritual of the Celtic Church* (Oxford: Clarendon Press, 1881).

[22] See William Maskell, *The Ancient Liturgy of the Church of England* (Oxford, 1882).

[23] Ibid. pp. liv–lvi.

was that "he might himself choose either; or select the liturgy which he thought most suitable from the various forms in the Catholic Church, provided only that he had regard to the circumstances and prejudices of the country and the glory of God".[24]

As a result, the Old Gallican-style liturgy of England was combined with the Roman liturgy to yield a hybrid rite, namely, the Old Gallican–Roman Rite. This process of adaptation and mixture of the Rites to yield a new form possessing characteristics of both also took place on the Continent, and the mixed sacramentaries of the eighth century attest to such an enterprise.[25]

The Diocesan Usages in England

The manner in which various liturgical practices were adopted and adapted varied from diocese to diocese and resulted in the various Uses of the English church. A rather thorough study of the English Uses has been made by Archdale A. King in his *Liturgies of the Past*.[26] It is important to note that the responsibility for the ordering of the liturgy was in the hands of the local bishop, and so it is not surprising that it was in individual dioceses that the Uses of England developed.

• *The Sarum Use*

The most famous and probably most important of the five English Uses was that of Sarum (or Salisbury, as it is now

---

[24] Ibid. pp. lvii–lviii.
[25] See Detscher, *Evolution*, pp. 11–12.
[26] Archdale A. King, *Liturgies of the Past* (London: Bruce Publishing, 1959).

called). The formation of this Use is attributed to Osmund, the eleventh-century Bishop of the Diocese of Salisbury/ Sarum. However, it is more probable that Richard Poore, who held the office of dean (1197–1215) and later bishop (1217–1228), was more instrumental than Osmund in the formation of the Use of Sarum, and, in fact, he is the first to employ the term "Sarum Use".[27] The Sarum Use was practiced throughout southern England (even in the See of Canterbury) and in other parts of Great Britain, e.g., Ireland.[28] Its influence was extended over a period of several hundred years, although it was not accepted over local customs without some resistance.

• *The Other Uses in England*

In regard to the four other Uses, there is little that can be said. Their practice was more or less confined to the dioceses for which they are named, or at least to those dioceses nearby. The Uses of Lincoln and Bangor were not as popular as those of York and Hereford.[29] Unfortunately, we do not possess many liturgical books of these former Uses, and we do not even have any extant copies of the Lincoln Missal.[30]

Thus, at the time of the Reformation in England, there was no absolute uniformity of liturgical practice. The liturgical forms in use were basically Roman, or, rather, Old Gallican–Roman, but there were many local variations of them according to the particular Use of the area. The Sarum Use was by far the most common. It was the one that the

[27] See Walter H. Frere, *The Use of Sarum*, vol. 1: *The Sarum Customs* [...] (Cambridge, 1898), p. xix.
[28] See Maskell, *Ancient Liturgy*, p. lxv.
[29] Ibid.
[30] Ibid., note 3.

architect of the English liturgical reform, Archbishop Thomas
Cranmer (1489–1556),[31] was probably most familiar with,
since it was the Use of his Archiepiscopal See of Canterbury.

Uses/Usages of Dioceses and Religious/Monastic Orders outside England

Incidentally, history witnesses to the same phenomenon on
the European mainland: many dioceses, especially in Germany, had their own "diocesan usages" until well into the
eighteenth and nineteenth centuries. For example, Cologne
adopted the Roman Rite in 1791, and Münster only in 1865.
Also, Lyon in France, Ravenna, and other cities in Italy
had their own "diocesan usages". Still today, the Diocese of
Braga in north Portugal has its own "diocesan usage". Con-
versely, the Ambrosian Rite of the Church of Milan is to
be seen as a separate, independent "Rite", and not only as
a local particularity within the framework of the Roman
Rite. The same is to be said about the Old Spanish ("Mozarabic") Rite in Toledo, Spain. Moreover, many religious communities or orders had their own liturgical traditions within
the framework of the Roman Rite, for example, the
Dominicans, the Carmelites, the Cistercians, and the Pre-
monstratensians. Today, only the Carthusians still practice a
rich liturgical life of their own. The Council of Trent had
in fact allowed all "special Rites" (of dioceses and religious
orders) that were then older than two hundred years to be
retained. The Sarum Use would have also fallen under this
category.

---

[31] See Diarmaid MacCulloch, *Thomas Cranmer: A Life* (New Haven, Conn.:
Yale University Press, 1996).

The English Reformation and Its Liturgical Books

The First Book of Common Prayer, 1549

The Reformation of the sixteenth century was rooted partly in the spread of printing, and in England the availability of liturgical books not only exhibited the progress of the Reformation but actually stimulated it. The English vernacular "Great Bible" (1540) had a fundamental role in this, being itself both the instrument of reform and the indispensable accompaniment of the reformed liturgical services. After the break between the Church of England under King Henry VIII (reigned 1509–1547) and the Roman Church, there was a gradual change both in theology[32] and liturgical practice. Ultimately, under Henry VIII's successor, Edward VI (reigned 1547–1553), the liturgical books were totally revised. Four liturgy-related books should be mentioned: The Litany (1544)[33] and The King's Primer (1545),[34] both during Henry VIII, and the Book of Homilies (1547)[35] and The Order of the Communion (1548),[36] both under

---

[32] *Articles about Religion* (aka *Ten Articles*, 1536); *The Bishops' Book* (aka *Institution of a Christian Man*, 1537); *The King's Book* (also known as *A Necessary Doctrine and Erudition for any Christian Man*, 1543). Cf. Feulner, *Das "Anglikanische Ordinale"*, pp. 135–55; Geoffrey J. Cuming, *A History of Anglican Liturgy*, 2nd ed. (London: Macmillan, 1982), pp. 32–35.

[33] William Maskell, *Monumenta Ritualia Ecclesiae Anglicanae*, vol. 2, 2nd ed. (Oxford, 1882), pp. 196–201. Cf. Cuming, *History of Anglican Liturgy*, pp. 35–38.

[34] *The Primer set forth by the King's Majesty and his Clergy* (1545).

[35] See Feulner, *Das "Anglikanische Ordinale"*, p. 157, note 5; Cuming, *History of Anglican Liturgy*, p. 39.

[36] See Henry A. Wilson, ed., *The Order of the Communion, 1548: A Facsimile of the British Museum Copy C.25.f.15*, Henry Bradshaw Society, no. 34, (London, 1908). The version of the *Order* is mainly derived from Martin Bucer's work in Cologne, resulting in the *Einfaltiges Bedencken*, a church order published by authority of Archbishop Hermann von Wied in 1543 and translated in 1547 into Latin as *Simplex ac pia deliberatio* (cf. Geoffrey J. Cuming, *The Godly Order: Texts and Studies Relating to the Book of Common Prayer*, Alcuin Club Collection, no. 65 [London: SPCK, 1983], pp. 68–90). See also Feul-

Edward VI. But the first liturgical book to provide a complete and distinct range of services in English was the 1549 Book of Common Prayer, and its authorization put an end to the use of the Latin services.

The main architect of the First Book of Common Prayer[37] was Archbishop Thomas Cranmer. It became obvious in the later days of the reign of Henry VIII that there would be no radical changes in the externals of the Church of England. However, after the death of Henry and the accession of his young son, Edward VI, Thomas Cranmer was able to implement his plans for a liturgical reform. The First Book of Common Prayer, published in March 1549, was intended to replace the liturgical books hitherto in use:[38] the Missal (for the Mass), the Breviary (for the Daily Office), the Manual (for occasional services: Baptism, Marriage, Funeral, etc.), the Processional (for processions), and, to a minor extent, the Pontifical (for the services appropriate to a bishop: Confirmation, Ordination, Consecration of Churches and Altars, etc.). The only service from the Pontifical that found its way into the Prayer Book was Confirmation (that was also in the Manual). After the fall of Lord Protector Edward Seymour (1506–1552), Duke of Somerset, there was a rumor that the Book of Common Prayer would be withdrawn. In order to protect the book, the Privy Council under John Dudley (1504–1553), Earl of

---

ner, *Das "Anglikanische Ordinale"*, pp. 166–68; Cuming, *History of Anglican Liturgy*, pp. 40–44.

[37] *The Book of Common Prayer and Administration of the Sacraments, and Other Rites and Ceremonies of the Church: After the Use of the Church of England* (1549). See also Thaddäus A. Schnitker, *The Church's Worship: The 1979 American Book of Common Prayer in a Historical Perspective*, Europäische Hochschulschriften Series 23, Theology 351 (Frankfurt: Peter Lang Publishing, 1989), pp. 15–25.

[38] See Henry B. Swete and Arthur J. Maclean, *Church Services and Service-Books before the Reformation* (London: SPCK, 1930).

Warwick, issued an order for the calling in of all the Latin service books so that they could be defaced and destroyed. However, since the Ordination rites had not yet been published, the Pontificals were exempt from this requirement. In 1550, the new Ordination rites were published in the so-called Ordinal.[39]

The figure behind the liturgical reform was the abovementioned Archbishop Thomas Cranmer.[40] It was to him that the bulk of the task of revision fell, and it was his theological concepts that are given expression in the revised rites. Although Cranmer collected and used liturgical material from many sources, including Protestant ones,[41] the First Prayer Book was still quite conservative. The Communion Service of the 1549 Prayer Book maintained the format of distinct rites of Consecration and Communion, which had been introduced in the 1548 Order of Communion; but with the Latin Rite of the Mass (chiefly following the structure of Sarum Use),[42] translated into English. The Ordinal, however, followed mainly the pattern of the Latin draft text of the German Protestant Martin Bucer

---

[39] *The Form and Manner of Making and Consecrating of Archbishops, Bishops, Priests, and Deacons* (1550). See Frank E. Brightman, *The English Rite: Being a Synopsis of the Sources and Revisions of the Book of Common Prayer*, vol. 2 (Farnborough: Gregg, 1970), pp. 928–1017.

[40] See Edward C. Ratcliff, "The Liturgical Work of Archbishop Cranmer", *Journal of Ecclesiastical History* 7 (1956): 189–203; Jasper Ridley, *Thomas Cranmer* (Oxford: Clarendon Press, 1962).

[41] Cranmer borrowed much from German sources, particularly from works commissioned by Hermann von Wied, Archbishop of Cologne, and also from Andreas Osiander and the Church Orders of Brandenburg and Nuremberg. Many phrases are characteristic of the German reformer Martin Bucer, or of the Italian Peter Vermigli.

[42] See Brightman, *English Rite*, 2:638–720; Colin Buchanan, ed., *Eucharistic Liturgies of Edward VI: A Text for Students*, Grove Liturgical Study, no. 34 (Bramcote: Grove Books, 1983), pp. 7–20; Cuming, *History of Anglican Liturgy*, pp. 51–59.

(Butzer, 1491–1551)[43] from Strasbourg with only secondary additions from the Sarum Pontifical. The true main emphases of Cranmer's text are the public prayer of the Church and the imposition of hands. This could be clearly shown by way of a modified Comparative Liturgiology with additional theological implications.[44]

Martin Bucer, who had come to Cambridge in 1549, was asked by Thomas Cranmer to give his views on the rites and ceremonies of the First Prayer Book. In his *Censura (Critical Examination)*[45] of 1551, Bucer gave his assessment, commended what ought to be retained, proposed amendments, and pointed out what ought to be abolished.[46] As regards the Eucharistic Prayer, he preferred that the epiclesis over the gifts be changed to an invocation over the persons who receive Communion. Here again the method of Comparative Liturgiology can help to determine clearly the influences from Bucer's *Censura* and other sources on the Second Prayer Book.

The Second Book of Common Prayer, 1552

The First Book of Common Prayer and the Ordinal were both destined to have a very short life. They were to be revised within a few years of their publication as the more

---

[43] See C. Hope, *Martin Bucer and the English Reformation* (Oxford: Blackwell, 1946); Herbert Vogt, *Martin Bucer und die Kirche von England* (dissertation; Münster, 1966).

[44] Cf. Feulner, *Das "Anglikanische Ordinale"*, pp. 157–221.

[45] M. Buceri, *Scripta Anglicana fere omnia* [...], ed. by C. Hubert (Basel, 1577), pp. 456–503. See M. Bucer, *Censura super Libro Sacrorum*, in Edward C. Whitaker, ed., *Martin Bucer and the Book of Common Prayer*, Alcuin Club Collection, no. 55 (Great Wakering: Mayhew-McCrimmon, 1974), pp. 10–173.

[46] See Vogt, *Bucer und die Kirche von England*, pp. 96–100.

Protestant (Calvinistic) element of the English Reformation gained more control in the church and state.[47]
After the "Second Act of Uniformity of Common Prayer and Administration of the Sacraments",[48] the revised Second Book of Common Prayer was published in 1552, including the ordination rites.[49] Cranmer recognized that the 1549 rite of Communion had been susceptible to conservative misinterpretation. Consequently, in 1552 he thoroughly integrated Consecration and Communion into a single rite.[50] This new order comes close to an essentially Zwinglian idea of the Eucharist.[51] In the Baptism service, the exorcism, the anointing, and other elements were omitted.[52] More drastic was the renewal of the Burial service and of the Ordination rites. Cranmer's work of simplification and revision was also applied to the Daily Offices, which were to become Morning and Evening Prayer, and which he hoped would also serve as a daily form of prayer to be used by the laity. This simplification was anticipated, which a comparative methodology could prove, by the work of Cardinal Francis Quiñones (1482–1540), a Spanish Franciscan, in his abortive revision of the Roman Breviary published in 1537.[53] The radical liturgical and theological breaks of the 1552

---

[47] Cf. Feulner, *Das "Anglikanische Ordinale"*, pp. 223–26; Cuming, *History of Anglican Liturgy*, pp. 70–74; Schnitker, *Church's Worship*, pp. 25–29.

[48] 5&6 Edw. 6, c. 1. Cf. Henry Gee and William J. Hardy, eds., *Documents Illustrative of English Church History* (1910; reprint, New York, 1966), no. 71, pp. 369–72.

[49] *The Book of Common Prayer and Administration of the Sacraments, and Other Rites and Ceremonies in the Church of England* (1552).

[50] Cf. Brightman, *English Rite* 2:639–721; Buchanan, *Eucharistic Liturgies*, pp. 21–33.

[51] Cf. Cuming, *History of Anglican Liturgy*, pp. 77–81.

[52] Cf. ibid., pp. 81–83.

[53] *Breviarium Romanum a Francisco Cardinali Quignonio editum*, ed. John W. Legg (Cambridge, 1888); *The Second Recension of the Quignon Breviary*, ed. John W. Legg, Henry Bradshaw Society, nos. 35 and 42 (London, 1908, 1912).

Prayer Book with the past are evident, and one might consider the change in the title of the book not unreasonable in view of the alterations: "*The Book of Common Prayer . . . Ceremonies of the Church:* After the Use of *the Church of England*" (1549) became "*The Book of Common Prayer . . . Ceremonies in the Church of England*" (1552).

The 1559 and 1662 Prayer Books

In July 1553, Queen Mary (1553–1558) restored the "old" religion by replacing the 1552 Second Book of Common Prayer with the former Latin service books.[54] Under Queen Elizabeth I (1559–1603), however, the 1552 Prayer Book was reintroduced in June 1559,[55] scarcely altered, in order to represent a swing again in a more Catholic direction.[56]

[54] 1 Mar., stat. 2, c. 2 (see Gee and Hardy, *Documents*, no. 73, pp. 377–80). See also Schnitker, *Church's Worship*, pp. 29–30.

[55] 1 Eliz. 1, c. 2 (see Gee and Hardy, *Documents*, no. 80, pp. 458–67).

[56] The 1559 Book of Common Prayer altered the 1552 Prayer Book in four respects: (1) The litany no longer petitioned deliverance "from the tyranny of the Bishop of Rome, and all his detestable enormities" (Brightman, *English Rite*, 1:177). (2) Whereas in the 1549 edition the words of administration of the Body of Christ had been "The body of our Lord Jesus Christ which was given for thee, preserve thy body and soul unto everlasting life" and the words of administration of the Blood reading accordingly, they had been changed in the 1552 book to "Take and eat this, in remembrance that Christ died for thee, and feed on him in thy heart by faith, with thanksgiving"; the delivery of the cup had been accompanied with the words: "Drink this in remembrance that Christ's blood was shed for thee, and be thankful." The two sentences for the administration of bread and wine were now, in the 1559 Book, linked together (Brightman, *English Rite*, 2:700–701). (3) The so-called Black Rubric, kneeling at the reception, was suppressed (Brightman, *English Rite*, 1:clxx, 721). (4) And the ornaments' rubric before Morning and Evening Prayer essentially repeated the provisions of the Uniformity Act, without the saving clause of a further possible amendment (Brightman, *English Rite*, 2:127). See also John E. Booty, ed., *The Book of Common Prayer 1559: The Elizabethan Prayer Book*, Folger Documents of Tudor and Stuart

In 1557, the Scots Protestant lords had adopted the English Prayer Book of 1552, for Reformed worship in Scotland. However, when John Knox (1510–1572) returned to Scotland in 1559, he continued to use *The Form of Prayers and Ministration of the Sacraments*[57] he had created for the English exiles in Geneva, and in 1564, this supplanted the Book of Common Prayer under the title of the Book of Common Order.[58] The first Prayer Book introduced in Scotland was that of 1637, but it was never even put into use. However, after the "Glorious Revolution" of 1688, which overthrew James II and brought William and Mary to the throne, the Church of Scotland was delivered firmly into the hands of the Presbyterians, leaving those who preferred Anglican forms with no home. These formed the Scottish Episcopal Church and began to take as their Prayer Book the old 1637 Scottish Book of Common Prayer.[59] It was reprinted several times in the 1700s, and by the mid- to late eighteenth century forms based on this book were in common use in the Scottish Episcopal Church. So when Samuel Seabury came in 1784 to the Scottish church to be ordained the first American bishop, he was urged to take these Scottish forms as the basis for the American Episcopal (Anglican) liturgy. He did, and as a result this book can be seen as a direct ancestor

---

Civilization, no. 22 (Charlottesville: University Press of Virginia, 1976); Schnitker, *Church's Worship*, pp. 31–37.

[57] John Knox, *The Form of Prayers and Ministration of the Sacraments, etc.* [. . .] (1556), ed. William D. Maxwell, *The Liturgical Portions of the Genevan Service Book*, 2nd ed. (London: Faith Press, 1965).

[58] See Cuming, *History of Anglican Liturgy*, pp. 88–89.

[59] The book is basically a moderate revision of the then current Prayer Book: the Prayer Book of 1559, as revised in 1604. There were a large number of changes, but the vast majority of them are quite minor. See Gordon Donaldson, *The Making of the Scottish Prayer Book of 1637* (Edinburgh: University Press, 1954); Francis Procter and Walter H. Fere, *The Book of Common Prayer*, 3rd ed. (London: SPCK, 1965), pp. 143–51.

of the 1790 American Book of Common Prayer—particularly with regards to the Communion Service.

The 1662 Book of Common Prayer of the Church of England was printed only two years after the restoration of the monarchy.[60] In reply to the "Presbyterian Exceptions",[61] some six hundred changes were made to the book of 1559, mostly minor, giving the Puritans little of what they wanted (except the so-called Black Rubric from 1552, which had been omitted in 1559 and was restored in 1662), but implementing rather more conservative changes (an attempt to restore the Offertory; after Communion the unused but consecrated bread and wine were to be reverently consumed in church). It was this edition that was to be the "official" Book of Common Prayer during the growth of the British Empire and, as a result, has had a great influence on the national Prayer Books of Anglican provinces worldwide.[62]

Further Revisions (and the 1928 Prayer Books)

By the nineteenth century, pressures on the 1662 Prayer Book had increased, connected with the Oxford Movement

[60] *The Book of Common Prayer and Administration of the Sacraments, and Other Rites and Ceremonies of the Church, according to the Use of the Church of England, together with the Psalter or Psalms of David, pointed as they are to be sung or said in churches: And the Form and Manner of Making, Ordaining and Consecrating Bishops, Priests, and Deacons* (1662). See Schnitker, *Church's Worship*, pp. 43–47.

[61] *The Grand Debate Between the Most Reverend Bishops, and the Presbyterian Divines, Appointed by His Sacred Majesty, as Commissioners for the Review and Alteration of the Book of Common Prayer, &c., Being an Exact Account of their whole Proceedings. The most perfect copy* (London, 1661). See Edward Cardwell, *A History of Conferences and Other Proceedings: Connected with the Revision of the Book of Common Prayer from the Year 1558 to the Year 1690*, 3rd ed. (Oxford, 1849), pp. 303–63; Edward C. Ratcliff, *The Savoy Conference and the Revision of the Book of Common Prayer*, in *From Uniformity to Unity 1662–1962*, ed. Geoffrey F. Nuttall and Owen Chadwick (London: SPCK, 1962), pp. 89–148.

[62] See Cuming, *History of Anglican Liturgy*, pp. 116–27.

in England. The use of elements of the Roman Rite (including the use of candles, liturgical vestments, and incense) had become widespread (and was known as "Ritualism"). Following a Royal Commission report in 1906, work began on a new edition of the English 1662 Prayer Book. In 1927, this proposed, more conservative Prayer Book was finished, but finally rejected by the Parliament for the second time, after some alterations, in 1928.[63]

The Episcopal Church in the United States separated itself from the Church of England in 1789. Its Prayer Book, published in 1790, had as its sources the English 1662 Book of Common Prayer and the 1637 Scottish Book of Common Prayer that Bishop Seabury of Connecticut had brought over, following his consecration in Aberdeen in 1784. Further revisions of the American Prayer Book of 1790 occurred in 1892 and 1928,[64] in which minor changes were made, removing, for instance, some of Cranmer's exhortations and introducing prayers for the dead. In 1979 a more substantial revision was made.[65]

---

[63] See ibid., pp. 165–90.

[64] *The Book of Common Prayer and Administration of the Sacraments and Other Rites and Ceremonies of the Church according to the use of the Protestant Episcopal Church in the United States of America Together with the Psalter or Psalms of David* (New York: J. Pott & Company, 1929). See Schnitker, *Church's Worship*, pp. 49ff.

[65] *The Book of Common Prayer and Administration of the Sacraments and Other Rites and Ceremonies of the Church Together with The Psalter or Psalms of David according to the use of the Episcopal Church* (New York: Seabury Press, 1979). For a description of the revision of the 1979 American Prayer Book, see Schnitker, *Church's Worship*, pp. 105ff.

Some Perspectives for the Future:
What is to be done and how can the method of
Comparative Liturgiology be useful?

Comparative Liturgiology and Ecumenism

As shown above, a modified Comparative Liturgiology that deals not only with liturgical "laws/principles" but also with the comparison of liturgical units and subunits within their historico-liturgical and theological context can also uncover valuable insights regarding the mutual influences of Western liturgical traditions, including the Protestant liturgies. Indeed, the historico-critical method of a Comparative Liturgiology concerns not only the past, but ultimately the proper understanding of the present. Moreover, historico-critical liturgical studies can more easily recognize both convergent and divergent developments in various liturgies, as well as their causes. An understanding of other liturgies and of the motivation behind their changes results in a better understanding of one's own liturgy. At the same time, such a Comparative Liturgiology is also truly *ecumenical*, shedding light on the genuine wealth of local traditions in the West (and East). It can also elucidate how these various Western traditions can have their legitimate place within the Catholic Church, including of course the "Anglican Use", as it was temporarily and officially approved by Rome in 2003 in the Book of Divine Worship for the use of different personal parishes in the USA.[66]

New Ecumenical and Pastoral Challenges in the USA

Now, however, we are faced with more far-reaching developments and challenges of the Anglican community, especially

---

[66] The original text of the Book of Divine Worship was first approved in 1987; it was printed with ecclesiastical approbation in 2003.

(albeit not only) in the USA. In this regard, we can generally distinguish three major groupings in the USA:[67]

    (A)   the personal, Catholic, "Anglican Use" parishes according to the Pastoral Provision;

    (B)   constant appeals for union from individual bishops, priests, faithful, and even from entire parishes of the Episcopal Church in the USA;

    (C)   the Anglican Church in America (ACA) as part of the Traditional Anglican Communion (TAC).

A. The Pastoral Provision

The Pastoral Provision created in June 1980 by the Holy See allows for some exceptions to the regular practice of the Latin Rite of the Roman Catholic Church in the USA. First, it allows diocesan bishops to establish personal (Catholic) "common identity" parishes (commonly known as the "Anglican Use"[68] parishes), which use a liturgy adapted from the Anglican liturgy. Second, it allows married, former Episcopal ministers to enter the Catholic Church and then to become priests. This is an exception to the general rule requiring Latin-Rite Catholic priests to be celibate.[69]

---

[67] Here we must limit ourselves to the USA, while keeping in mind that there are also many other various Anglican groups and communities outside the USA.

[68] Interestingly, the phrase "Anglican Use" does not occur in the official documents promulgating the Pastoral Provision; these documents instead refer to "common identity" parishes.

[69] Document outlining the Pastoral Provision issued by the Congregation for the Doctrine of the Faith (July 22, 1980), Prot. N. 66/77 (see http://www.atonementonline.com/resource001.html).

Along with the re-ordination[70] of married Episcopal ministers, the Pastoral Provision of 1980 permitted the establishment of "Anglican Use" parishes in the USA and created a special missal using liturgical elements from the Anglican tradition. This special liturgy was subsequently approved in 1987 by the Congregation for Divine Worship and the Discipline of the Sacraments and the Committee for the Liturgy of the national US Conference of Catholic Bishops (USCCB). As a result, the Book of Divine Worship of 2003[71] mainly contains elements of the 1928 and 1979 versions of the American Book of Common Prayer as well as the 1973 Roman Missal. Before a working version of the Book of Divine Worship was adopted for trial/interim use in 1984, the first Anglican Use parishes in the USA continued using the so-called Anglican Missal (see below).

Anglican Use parishes are rare and found only in certain dioceses of the USA. Any Anglican parish seeking to join the Roman Catholic Church and become an "Anglican Use" parish must have the permission of the local Catholic bishop. Some Anglican parishes in Canada and the UK have applied to become "Anglican Use", but unfortunately

---

[70] The "absolute" re-ordination of former Anglican ministers is required because of the Apostolic Letter *Apostolicae curae* of Pope Leo XIII in 1896 (DS 3315–19). See also the "Doctrinal Commentary on the Concluding Formula of the *Professio Fidei*" of the Congregation for the Doctrine of the Faith (June 29, 1998), no. 11: "With regard to those truths connected to revelation by historical necessity and which are to be held definitively, but are not able to be declared as divinely revealed, the following examples can be given: . . . the declaration of Pope Leo XIII in the Apostolic Letter *Apostolicae Curae* on the invalidity of Anglican ordinations" (*L'Osservatore Romano* [Weekly Edition in English; July 15, 1998], pp. 3–4; Latin original text in: *Acta Apostolicae Sedis* 90 (1998): 550–51).

[71] *The Book of Divine Worship: Being Elements of the Book of Common Prayer Revised and Adapted According to the Roman Rite For Use by Roman Catholics Coming From the Anglican Tradition* (Mt. Pocono, Penn.: Newman House Press, 2003).

have been refused permission. Hence, since 1987 (or rather 2003), the few personal "Anglican Use" parishes (according to the Pastoral Provision) in the USA officially have been using the Book of Divine Worship, which—next to the Eucharist—also includes the Daily Office and several other sacramental liturgical services, for example, Baptism, Marriage, and Burial of the Dead. In view of the possibility that the Holy See may see fit to modify the canonical organization or configuration of these parishes, perhaps with a juridical structure similar to an apostolic administration or personal prelature,[72] it may be worth considering the development of further liturgical services, including Anointing of the Sick, Confession, the pontifical rites for Confirmation and Ordination, as well rites for the Consecration of Churches and Altars. It has furthermore become clear after many years of liturgical experience that the heretofore developed liturgical services of the Book of Divine Worship need to be revised and supplemented as appropriate. This is necessary in order more strongly to give expression—in the spirit of Comparative Liturgiology—to the specific Anglican heritage and liturgical legacy found in the 1549/[1662]/ 1928 Books of Common Prayer and other sources, of course with the necessary adaptations to bring worship according to the Anglican Use into fuller conformity with the Catholic liturgical tradition (*lex credendi, lex orandi*: loosely translatable as "the law of believing is the law of praying").[73]

---

[72] A personal prelature, however, is an association of clerics only (see cann. 294–97 of the *Codex Iuris Canonici/1983*)! See also the doctoral thesis of Monsignor James M. Sheehan at the Pontificia Università della Santa Croce in Rome: "A New Canonical Configuration for the 'Pastoral Provision' for Former Episcopalians in the United States of America?" (Rome, 2009).

[73] According to Prosper of Aquitaine: *legem credendi lex statuat supplicandi*. See also W. Taylor Stevenson, "*Lex Orandi–Lex Credendi*", in *The Study of Anglicanism*, ed. Stephen Sykes and John Booty (London: SPCK, 1988), pp. 174–88.

B. Requests from Episcopalians

Individual converts or entire parishes of the Episcopal Church in the USA must either—in the best case—take the rather difficult path via the Pastoral Provision and request the opening of their own "Anglican Use" parishes, or join an available one. In the worst case, the vast majority of such converts liturgically and canonically enters regular Roman Catholic parishes, a path most often taken outside the USA (and even in the USA). This is due to the fact that the Book of Divine Worship is for the moment valid only in the USA, since it was composed on order of the USCCB and in cooperation with the Congregation for Divine Worship in Rome.

In the meantime, there are also parishes and even entire dioceses that are leaving the Episcopal Church in the USA to join the jurisdiction of other Anglican provinces in South America or Africa or recently created their own church (e.g., the Anglican Church in North America [ACNA]).[74] But we need not include this movement in our considerations.

C. The Traditional Anglican Communion

The Traditional Anglican Communion (TAC) is an international communion of churches in the "Continuing" Anglican Movement independent of the Anglican Communion and the Archbishop of Canterbury. The TAC was formed in 1991 after a congress of Anglican bishops, priests, and lay people. Today, the federation or union of the TAC consists of fifteen church bodies,[75] among them the Anglican Church

---

[74] See the ACNA website, http://www.theacna.org.

[75] *Africa*: Anglican Church in Southern Africa, Traditional Rite; Church of Umzi Wase Tiyopia; Continuing Anglican Church in Zambia. *America*: Anglican Church in America; Anglican Catholic Church of Canada; Missionary

in America (ACA).[76] The current primate (since 2002) is Archbishop John Hepworth of the Anglican Catholic Church in Australia. For the most part, the TAC upholds a Catholic interpretation of the Thirty-Nine Articles (of 1563),[77] and most parishioners of the member churches can be described as traditional Anglo-Catholics in their theology and liturgical practice. The liturgical services are not celebrated according to the more recent national Books of Common Prayer, but mainly according to the Anglican Missal of 1921 (usually in more recent editions, and in some cases according to the conservative 1928 American Book of Common Prayer), which partially reflects, in a broader sense, the liturgical usage in England before the Reformation (Sarum Use).

In October 2007, in a Plenary Session in Portsmouth (England), the bishops of the TAC recognized the *Catechism of the Catholic Church* (*CCC*) and asked the Holy See for full, corporate, and sacramental (comm)union. Negotiations are still being conducted. Of course, there are considerable problems regarding celibacy, since most of the priests and bishops of the TAC are married. But these problems may somehow find a canonical solution.

The ACA is a "continuing" Anglican church body and the US branch of the TAC. The ACA was created in 1991 following extensive negotiations between the Anglican Catholic Church (ACC) and the American Episcopal Church (AEC, a "continuing" church body not to be confused with the

---

Diocese of Central America; Missionary Diocese of Puerto Rico. *Asia*: Anglican Church of India; Orthodox Church of Pakistan; Nippon Kirisuto Sei Ko Kai; The Church Missionary Society (CMS). *Australia*: Anglican Catholic Church in Australia; Church of Torres Strait. *Europe*: Traditional Anglican Church (England); Church of Ireland, Traditional Rite.

[76] Diocese of the Northeast; Diocese of the Eastern United States; Diocese of the Missouri Valley; Diocese of the West.

[77] But some member churches reject the Thirty-Nine Articles altogether.

Episcopal Church in the USA). The ACA has accepted most of the teachings of the Roman Catholic Church that have been traditionally rejected by Anglicans. The ACA claims roughly a hundred parishes with a membership of around fifty-two hundred.

Some Concluding Remarks and Proposals

With the aid of a modified (not the classical) Comparative Liturgiology, which is not only limited to "laws/principles" of organic development, but also comprises the comparison and the mutual influences of different Rites and liturgical Uses (and their component liturgical units), we could notice a huge variety of different liturgical Rites and Uses in East *and West*. The Catholic Church also includes many Eastern Rites, such as the Melkite Rite, the Maronite Rite, the Syrian-Catholic Rite, the Coptic-Catholic Rite, the Chaldean Rite, the Armenian-Catholic Rite, and some more. And even the Latin Rite is a liturgical family that includes the widely practiced and most common Roman Rite in addition to—yet today—the Ambrosian Rite of Milan, the Old Spanish ("Mozarabic") Rite in parts of Spain, the Zaire Use in some parts of Africa, the diocesan usage of Braga in north Portugal, the Use of the Carthusian monastic order, as well as other liturgical Uses and forms.

From the point of view of a modified Comparative Liturgiology, we can also define the "Anglican Use" as a particular liturgical form of worship within the Western liturgical tradition of the Catholic Church. In a broader sense, the Anglican Use partially derived from the pre-Reformation Sarum Use in England with later liturgical changes, additions, and omissions over the following centuries. An expanded and modified Anglican Use within the Catholic Church would be a true and fruitful liturgical enrichment.

If in the future Rome would grant a canonical and hence
also a liturgical solution for these current and prospective
Anglican and Episcopalian converts (including those from
the TAC and other jurisdictions), then the Church will be
automatically faced with the urgent necessity of providing
one single common liturgical *ordo* for all three of the above-
mentioned groupings, as well as obligatory liturgical books.
This *ordo*, in the sense of an Anglican Use (less probably an
"Anglican-Catholic Rite"),[78] would have to be worked out
on the basis of the Book of Divine Worship (as the "official" liturgical book already approved by the Church), but
with consideration of other liturgical books, especially the
American Missal and the English Missal, together with the
other sacramental rites of that tradition, including the 1549
and 1928 Books of Common Prayer. It may be worth examining also the liturgical books of the so-called Western
Orthodox Rite (of the Antiochian Orthodox Patriarchate),
which includes an adaptation of the Anglican liturgy.[79] The

[78] The Holy See surely won't establish an Anglican-Catholic Patriarchate
in the sense of a *sui juris* church like the Eastern Catholic patriarchates because
there is no historical (and liturgical) basis for this in the West.

[79] The Liturgy of Saint Tikhon (based on the 1928 American Prayer Book
and the Anglican Missal, altered by removing the *filioque* from the text of the
Nicene Creed, and including prayers for the dead, and strengthening the
epiclesis within the Eucharistic Prayer, and by adding the pre-Communion
prayers from the Byzantine Rite) and the Liturgy of Saint Gregory (version
of the Roman Tridentine Mass that has been altered to remove the *filioque*
and inserting a Byzantine epiclesis). See *Western Rite Service Book: Saint Andrew
Service Book; The Administration of the Sacraments and Other Rites and Ceremonies
according to the Western Rite Usage of the Antiochian Orthodox Christian Archdiocese
of North America*, 3rd ed. (2005); *The Book of Common Prayer: The Administration of the Sacraments and Other Rites and Ceremonies of the Church in the English
Parochial Tradition, according to the Orthodox Catholic Usage—Together with the
Psalter, or Psalms of David* (Glendale, Colo.: Andrewes Lancelot Press, 2009).
See also B.J. Andersen, *An Anglican Liturgy in the Orthodox Church: The Origins and Development of the Antiochian Orthodox Liturgy of Saint Tikhon* (M.Div.
diss.; Crestwood, N.Y.: Saint Vladimir's Seminary, 2005).

method of Comparative Liturgiology could be especially helpful here, identifying the specific Anglican elements and integrating them into organic and reasonable unity within the Western tradition.

Some Notes on the Anglican Missal, English Missal, and American Missal[80]

The Anglican Missal (even in the American edition)[81] frequently reflects its intention of reuniting those parts of the liturgy that were lost during the English Reformation with the English 1662 Book of Common Prayer. Its view, as presented by its creator, the Society of Saints Peter and Paul, was to consider the Reformation an "accident of history", and thus its goal was to re-create, insofar as possible, the pre-Reformation Mass in English, while retaining those parts of Cranmer's liturgy mandated for use in the Book of Common Prayer, which remains by the act of Parliament *the* legally official liturgical norm for the Church of England.

The English Missal[82] was not very different. In it, one finds a collection of choices for the Ordinary and Canon.

[80] I am indebted to Reverend Canon Father Eugene Beau Davis (d. November 8, 2010) and Reverend Father Christopher Kelley (Saint Mary of the Angels Anglican Church, Hollywood, Calif.) for their important information for this section.

[81] The first edition of the Anglican Missal was published in London by the Society of Saints Peter and Paul in 1921; the first American edition appeared in 1943, published by the Frank Gavin Liturgical Foundation of Mount Sinai, Long Island, N.Y., and in 1947 a revised edition was published (reprinted in 1961); the publication rights were given (or sold) to the Anglican Parishes Association in the 1970s, which reprinted the 1947 edition.

[82] The English Missal was first published in London by W. Knott and Son in 1912 and went through five editions, two of which include the revised Roman Catholic Holy Week of 1958, as well as one American edition that conforms to the American 1928 Book of Common Prayer (and was completely exhausted by the early sixties); the English Missal was reprinted by

There are both Latin and English texts to the Tridentine Mass, and versions of the Eucharistic Prayer of the 1549 and 1662 Books of Common Prayer. As a rule, if the Tridentine Collects and other prayers differed from the Book of Common Prayer, the Roman norm was retained.

The American Missal[83] was, as the name implies, created in order to present the "Western" Rite, a term devised by Anglo-Catholics to conceal their clear intent of regaining and fostering all that was lost and suppressed from the "Roman Rite". In any event, its objective was to present the fullness of the ancient pre-Reformation rite in specific conformance to the 1928 American Book of Common Prayer that is often at variance with the English Book of Common Prayer. Each national Book of Common Prayer varies in some ways from every other national edition. Other differences in the American Missal concern the rubrics, which are presented for the celebrant alone, while the Anglican Missal includes those for all three ordained ministers. In the American Missal, the others are described in its General Instructions. The American Missal has an additional benefit of including a large number of Collects from national Books of Common Prayer around the world. And it includes the Book of Common Prayer Ordinary and Canon *exactly* as they appear in the 1928 Prayer Book, without other interpolations from any other source.

Canterbury Press, Norwich, England, in 2001, but regrettably with rubrics printed in black, rendering text and rubric indistinguishably.

[83] The American Missal was originally published in 1931 by Morehouse Publishing Company (Milwaukee, Wis.); a revised edition was undertaken and published by Father Earle Hewitt Maddux, SSJE, in 1951 and printed by the Society of Saint John the Evangelist (SSJE) (Cambridge, Mass.); it was reprinted in 1988 with permission of SSJE by All Saints Press (Macon, Ga.), which no longer exists.

And so, what needs to be done?

1. The Holy See should organize a committee of competent liturgists from the abovementioned *three* main groupings (Anglican Use parishes, TAC, and other former Anglicans from the Episcopal Church in the USA), so as to collect and sort collectively all the liturgical services of the various groups, already now, in order to present ideas and liturgical suggestions for *one* revised and modified Book of Divine Worship,[84] so as to engage in discussion and arrive at a common liturgical proposal that would not contradict the received Catholic faith (cf. *lex credendi—lex orandi*).

Rome cannot allow *three or more* different Anglican Uses for each Anglican group or community that seeks

---

[84] Besides the desirability of retaining any particular "Anglican" elements or contriving a book that would be more appealing to prospective Anglican converts from TAC or elsewhere, the Book of Divine Worship, which was hastily assembled, needs to be corrected by all means. Some obvious errors need mending; omissions and ambiguities need fixing just to make the liturgical book suitable for delivering a robust program of Catholic eucharistic worship; some essential Catholic elements are missing at the Holy Mass (like the Rite of Sprinkling Holy Water ["Asperges" and "Vidi Aquam"]); and some Propers are lacking (for the Immaculate Conception and All Souls' Day, among others). Moreover, there are problems with the incongruities and dissonances of the regrettable mingling of diverse liturgical idioms: (1) The disharmony between Rite I (in traditional Prayer Book English) and Rite II (in contemporary language), and (2) the even more conspicuous collision of the elements imported from the ICEL (International Commission on English in the Liturgy) translation of the post–Vatican II Roman Missal/ Sacramentary (1973) in the Offertory Prayers and Prayers over the Gifts. Rite I and Rite II do not have their own integrity. The Book of Divine Worship is skewed to Rite II language, even though most all of the "Anglican Use" parishes use Rite I normatively. And the ICEL translations inserted in the text of the Mass are obviously incompatible with the hieratic liturgical English used elsewhere. The author of this article is going to prepare a more detailed study for a prospective revision of the Book of Divine Worship, to be published in 2012/2013 (including all the below-mentioned liturgical books).

union with the Holy See, for understandable liturgical and ecclesiological reasons. And surely the Holy See may not give special permission for other Anglican Uses according to the American Missal or Anglican Missal or English Missal, nor for an Anglican Use according to the countless different national Prayer Books such as the American Prayer Books of 1928 or 1979, all in addition to the already existing Anglican Use according to the 2003 Book of Divine Worship. A committee of competent liturgists of the different directions/ groups of former Anglicans should think about *one* combined Anglican Use/Rite, maybe with only one or two alternative formulae for the Eucharist at the most. The template for revision could be the already officially approved Book of Divine Worship, but with more liturgical elements from the Anglican and American Missals, the 1549/1928 Prayer Books, the Anglican Service Book,[85] the Western Orthodox Rite, and other sources, including the missing rituals (e.g., Anointing of the Sick, Confession, Marriage, Confirmation, etc.).[86] Relevant liturgical studies need to be conducted as soon as possible.[87]

---

[85] The Anglican Service Book (4th ed., 2007) is a traditional-language version of the 1979 American Book of Common Prayer, enriched by having adapted other sources such as the Anglican Missal, the Sarum Missal, and the Book of Occasional Services (2003).

[86] See, for example, the very interesting proposals published in *The Anglican Use Sacramentary*, ed. C. David Burt, vols. 1 and 2 (Mansfield, Mass., 2007); Burt, ed., *The Anglican Use Gradual*, 2n ed. (Mansfield, Mass., 2006); Burt, ed., *The Anglican Use Office*, (Mansfield, Mass., 2007).

[87] See also the important remarks in footnote 84 above. Other essential texts are the following: The Sarum Missal in English (1868; 2004); The English Missal (1933; 1958; 2001); The Anglican Breviary (1955; repr. 1998); The English Office Book (1956; 2006); The Monastic Breviary: Matins (1961); The People's Anglican Missal in the American Edition (1961); Missale Romanum (1962); The Monastic Diurnal (1963); Missale Romanum–Roman

A distinction must thereby be made between "sacramental" and "non-sacramental" liturgical services. The "non-sacramental" services can be adapted in respect to the local customs or needs of a parish or religious community/order (especially the Daily Office). The "sacramental" services (Eucharist, Baptism, Anointing of the Sick, Confession), however, need to be more or less uniform (only with a few alternative formulae). One should also keep in mind the possibility of "inculturation" mentioned at Vatican II in its Constitution on the Sacred Liturgy *Sacrosanctum Concilium (SC)*,[88] that is, the adaptation of liturgical rituals to local and supralocal customs—in this case, to the Anglican heritage.

All these complex considerations should finally be extended to the other Anglican groups (outside the USA and also beyond the TAC) interested in full (comm)union with the Holy See. It is clear that only Rome can make a final decision about a further modified Anglican Use and its liturgical books.

2. Additional work is needed on all the rites that have heretofore not been included in the Book of Divine

---

Missal (interim editions, 1964/1966); Graduale Sacrosanctae Romanae Ecclesiae de Tempore and de Sanctis (1974); The Anglican Service Book (1991); The Old Sarum Missal (1998); The English Ritual (2002); Altar Missal According to the Use of The Anglican Catholic Church of Canada (2010), etc.

[88] "Provisions shall also be made, when revising the liturgical books, for legitimate variations and adaptations to different groups, regions, and peoples, especially in mission lands, provided that the substantial unity of the Roman rite is preserved; and this should be borne in mind when drawing up the rites and devising rubrics" (*SC*, no. 38). "Within the limits set by the typical editions of the liturgical books, it shall be for the competent territorial ecclesiastical authority mentioned in Art. 22, 2, to specify adaptations, especially in the case of the administration of the sacraments, the sacramentals, processions, liturgical language, sacred music, and the arts, but according to the fundamental norms laid down in this Constitution" (*SC*, no. 39).

Worship (Confession, Confirmation, Consecration of Churches and Altars, etc.).

3. The Calendar, together with Temporal and Sanctoral Propers, needs correcting and amending. The Book of Divine Worship lacks Propers for the Solemnity of the Immaculate Conception, All Soul's Day, and the Feast of the Immaculate Heart, among others. In addition, it would be highly desirable to provide Propers for particular feasts.

4. As church songs are also part of liturgy in general, there is a need to think about a new, or at least renewed, Hymnal.

5. Liturgical education should also be provided for priests sometime in the future. Perhaps a "Liturgical Institute" could be founded for the study of pastoral-liturgical questions and for continuing formation and training of priests and lay people.

Comparative Liturgiology has clearly demonstrated not only the existence, but also the importance and ecumenical relevance of different liturgical families, Rites, and Uses in East and West. These are a genuine and necessary enrichment of the Church. A modified and renewed Catholic Anglican Use within the Western liturgical tradition would be a valuable benefit for the Catholic Church. This would also have a signal effect not only for different Anglican groups worldwide seeking union with Rome because of different issues, but possibly even for other Protestant groups. For this reason, it is worth every effort to find them a liturgical home, preserving their liturgical heritage as much as possible and enabling full communion with the Holy See.

A worldwide Anglican Use within the Latin Rite would also be a pastoral-liturgical benefit for the Roman Catholic parishes, in the sense of a fruitful influence for a new *ars celebrandi* (art of celebrating liturgy) concerning liturgical vestments, liturgical music, liturgical symbols, etc.

By way of conclusion, it should be stressed that the above considerations are not inspired by proselytism. That is to say, they are not influenced by any "Conversion-Ecumenism" that intends to proselytize Anglicans and other Protestants. It was rather the intention of this inquiry to provide these fellow Christians with a liturgy within the Catholic Church, when the other prerequisites for unity are met. There is doubtlessly yet a long and difficult path ahead, but one shall believe—and certainly pray—that a beneficial solution will ultimately be found.[89]

Hans-Jürgen Feulner is a university professor of Liturgical Studies and Sacramental Theology at the Catholic Faculty of the University of Vienna, Austria. He is a member of the North American Academy of Liturgy, the Societas Liturgica, and other international associations. His numerous publications on the different liturgical Rites of East and West according to the method of Comparative Liturgiology also include a multivolume study on the Anglican Ordinal, of which volume I, *Das "Anglikanische Ordinale" (The "Anglican Ordinal"*, 1997), has been published in German and is to be continued.

[89] I would like to thank Doctor Vassa Larin (University of Vienna, Austria) and Professor Clinton A. Brand, Ph.D. (University of Saint Thomas, Houston, Texas) for their critical review and correction of my English text. —In the meantime, the Holy Father published the Apostolic Constitution "Anglicanorum Coetibus" (Nov. 4, 2009) granting the erection of Personal Ordinariates for former Anglicans, and an international commission of liturgists has been set up by the Congregation for the Doctrine of the Faith (in cooperation with the Congregation for Divine Worship) to work on liturgical issues of the forthcoming ordinariates.

A PETITION OF THE PRO-DIOCESE OF SAINT AUGUSTINE OF CANTERBURY TO THE SCDF

Most Holy Father,

We the representatives of the Pro-Diocese of St. Augustine of Canterbury whose names are hereto subscribed, being of diverse nationalities and races, yet as one in our desire to return to our holy mother, the Catholic and Apostolic Church, and sharing a common debt to those portions of the Anglican Tradition that have remained loyal to the teachings of the Catholic Church, with a humble yet hopeful heart submit this petition to the Chair of Peter.

We pray and beseech your Holiness to receive and accept us into the Roman Catholic Church, for we are sheep not having a shepherd and would return to the care of that Holy Apostle singularly commissioned by the Divine Lord to feed his sheep.

To this end we dare to pray that Your Holiness may cause to be undertaken those steps which will lead to the elimination of every defect which may exist in our priestly orders; to our being granted the oversight, direction, and governance of a Catholic bishop, to the determination of that polity and use that would be ours to follow in obedience to and in union with the Holy See; and to the removal of all doubt which may be found to exist in regard to our understanding of and fidelity to the fullness of Catholic doctrine, discipline and worship.

We tender in return the unfeigned allegiance of our whole hearts and minds and souls, offering with that allegiance the Anglican patrimony that has been ours in so far as it is compatible with, acceptable to and an enhancement of Catholic teaching and worship. We offer also our firm conviction that many others of that Anglican Tradition are ready also to return to Peter once the pastoral care of the Chief of the Apostles has been manifest in restoring to his bosom his prodigal Anglican sons and daughters.

We humbly beseech our Lady, the Ever-Blessed Mother of the Church, to lay our prayer before the throne of her Divine Son in Heaven, even as we are bold to lay that same petition before the throne of Peter here on earth.

In witness whereof we have set our signatures on the Solemnity of All Saints being the first day of November, in the one thousand nine hundred and seventy ninth year of our Lord and in the second year of the pontificate of Your Holiness.

The Reverend Canon Albert J. duBois
The Reverend John D. Barker
The Reverend Harold Buckley
The Reverend Leslie Hamlett
The Reverend William Turner St. John Brown
The Reverend Clark A. Tea
The Reverend Burket Kniveton
Dr. Theodore Lee McEvoy
Mr. Brian George Minto

SACRA CONGREGATIO PRO
DOCTRINA FIDEI

Roma, July 22, 1980
Prot. N. 66/77
(Enclosure)

His Excellency
The Most Reverend John R. QUINN
Archbishop of San Francisco
President, N.C.C.B.

Your Excellency,

The Congregation for the Doctrine of the Faith, in its Ordinary Session of June 18, 1980, has taken the following decisions in regard to the Episcopalians who seek reconciliation with and entrance into the Catholic Church.

I. General Decisions:

1. The admission of these persons, even in a group, should be considered the reconciliation of individual persons, as described in the Decree on Ecumenism

"Redintegratio Unitatis", no. 4, of the Second Vatican Council.

2. It will be appropriate to formulate a statute or "pastoral provision" which provides for a "common identity" for the group.

II. Elements of the "Common Identity":

1. Structures: The preference expressed by the majority of the Episcopal Conference for the insertion of these reconciled Episcopalians into the diocesan structures under the jurisdiction of local Ordinaries is recognized. Nevertheless, the possibility of some other type of structure as provided for by canonical dispositions, and as suited to the needs of the group, is not excluded.

2. Liturgy: The group may retain certain elements of the Anglican Liturgy; these are to be determined by a Commission of the Congregation set up for this purpose. Use of these elements will be reserved to the former members of the Anglican Communion. Should a former Anglican priest celebrate public liturgy outside this group, he will be required to adopt the common Roman Rite.

3. Discipline: (a) To married Episcopalian priests who may be ordained Catholic priests, the following stipulations will apply: they may not become bishops; and they may not remarry in case of widowhood. (b) Future candidates for the priesthood must follow the discipline of celibacy. (c) Special care must be taken on the pastoral level to avoid any misunderstanding regarding the Church's discipline of celibacy.

III. Steps required for admission to full communion:

1. Theological-catechetical preparation is to be provided according to need.

2. A profession of faith (with appropriate additions to address the points on which there is divergence of teaching between the Anglican Communion and the Catholic Church) is to be made personally by all (ministers and faithful) as a "conditio sine qua non".

3. Reordination of the Episcopalian clergy, even those who are married, shall be allowed in accord with the customary practice, after the examination of each individual case by the Congregation for the Doctrine of the Faith.

IV. The statute or "pastoral provision" will not be definitive, but rather will be granted "ad tempus non determinatum".

V. Particulars regarding the execution of the decision:

1. The contents of the statute or "pastoral provision" are to be determined with the agreement of the Episcopal Conference. In what concerns the liturgical aspects of the statute, the Congregation for the Sacraments and Divine Worship will be asked for its accord. The Congregation for the Doctrine of the Faith will keep informed of any developments both the Secretariat for Promoting Christian Unity and the Congregation for the Oriental Churches (the latter in view of the possible influence on the particular dispositions for

ecclesiastical celibacy among Eastern-rite priests in the United States).

2. A Catholic ecclesiastical Delegate, preferably a Bishop, should be designated, with the approval of the Episcopal Conference, as the responsible person to oversee the practical applications of the decisions here reported and to deal with the Congregation for the Doctrine of the Faith in what pertains to this question.

3. These decisions should be implemented with all deliberate speed in view of the waiting period already undergone by the Episcopalians who have presented this request. These decisions were approved by His Holiness Pope John Paul II in the audience granted to the undersigned Cardinal Prefect of the Congregation on June 20, 1980.

The complexity of the above decisions, Your Excellency, recommends early contact between yourself and the Congregation in order to discuss the details and procedures for their implementation. Given your knowledge of the matter, it would seem ideal that, even after your term as President of the Episcopal Conference has expired, you might remain as Bishop-Delegate (cf.V,2) responsible for overseeing the admission of these persons into full communion with the Catholic Church. Permit me to express the hope that, if convenient for you, you will contact the Congregation for the purpose of initiating the necessary discussion of this question during your stay in Rome to participate in the 1980 Synod of Bishops.

Finally, I am enclosing a letter which I would be grateful to you for forwarding, after you have taken note of its contents, to Father John Barker of the Pro-Diocese of St. Augustine of Canterbury, informing him that their petition has been accepted in principle. Since you will be in the best position to know what publicity may be deemed unavoidable or suitable, I would like to leave in your hands the manner and timing of any communication about the fact or nature of the decisions here reported. I am sure you will have already noted in the decisions as reported a concern for the sensitive areas of ecumenism and celibacy.

You will no doubt want to inform Bishops Law and Lessard of the above mentioned decisions, since they were so closely involved in the negotiations during various phases. Since the group in question involves a certain number of English clergy and faithful, the Congregation will undertake to give the necessary information to the hierarchy of England and Wales.

With every best wish for Your Excellency, I remain.

Sincerely yours in Christ,

sig//Franjo Card. Seper, Pref.

APOSTOLIC CONSTITUTION
ANGLICANORUM COETIBUS

PROVIDING FOR PERSONAL ORDINARIATES FOR ANGLICANS ENTERING INTO FULL COMMUNION WITH THE CATHOLIC CHURCH

In recent times the Holy Spirit has moved groups of Anglicans to petition repeatedly and insistently to be received into full Catholic communion individually as well as corporately. The Apostolic See has responded favourably to such petitions. Indeed, the successor of Peter, mandated by the Lord Jesus to guarantee the unity of the episcopate and to preside over and safeguard the universal communion of all the Churches,[1] could not fail to make available the means necessary to bring this holy desire to realization.

The Church, a people gathered into the unity of the Father, the Son and the Holy Spirit,[2] was instituted by our Lord Jesus Christ, as "a sacrament—a sign and instrument,

---

[1] Cf. Second Vatican Council, Dogmatic Constitution *Lumen gentium*, no. 23; Congregation for the Doctrine of the Faith, Letter *Communionis notio*, nos. 12, 13.

[2] Cf. Dogmatic Constitution *Lumen gentium*, no. 4; Decree *Unitatis redintegratio*, no. 2.

that is, of communion with God and of unity among all people." [3] Every division among the baptized in Jesus Christ wounds that which the Church is and that for which the Church exists; in fact, "such division openly contradicts the will of Christ, scandalizes the world, and damages that most holy cause, the preaching the Gospel to every creature." [4] Precisely for this reason, before shedding his blood for the salvation of the world, the Lord Jesus prayed to the Father for the unity of his disciples. [5]

It is the Holy Spirit, the principle of unity, which establishes the Church as a communion. [6] He is the principle of the unity of the faithful in the teaching of the Apostles, in the breaking of the bread and in prayer. [7] The Church, however, analogous to the mystery of the Incarnate Word, is not only an invisible spiritual communion, but is also visible; [8] in fact, "the society structured with hierarchical organs and the Mystical Body of Christ, the visible society and the spiritual community, the earthly Church and the Church endowed with heavenly riches, are not to be thought of as two realities. On the contrary, they form one complex reality formed from a two-fold element, human and divine." [9] The communion of the baptized in the teaching of the Apostles and in the breaking of the eucharistic bread is visibly manifested in the bonds of the profession of the faith in its entirety, of the celebration of all of the sacraments instituted by Christ, and of the governance of the

---

[3] Dogmatic Constitution *Lumen gentium*, no. 1.

[4] Decree *Unitatis redintegratio*, no. 1.

[5] Cf. Jn 17:20–21; Decree *Unitatis redintegratio*, no. 2.

[6] Cf. Dogmatic Constitution *Lumen gentium*, no. 13.

[7] Cf. ibid; Acts 2:42.

[8] Cf. Dogmatic Constitution *Lumen gentium*, no. 8; Letter *Communionis notio*, no. 4.

[9] Dogmatic Constitution *Lumen gentium*, no. 8.

College of Bishops united with its head, the Roman Pontiff.[10]

This single Church of Christ, which we profess in the Creed as one, holy, catholic and apostolic "subsists in the Catholic Church, which is governed by the successor of Peter and by the Bishops in communion with him. Nevertheless, many elements of sanctification and of truth are found outside her visible confines. Since these are gifts properly belonging to the Church of Christ, they are forces impelling towards Catholic unity."[11]

In the light of these ecclesiological principles, this Apostolic Constitution provides the general normative structure for regulating the institution and life of Personal Ordinariates for those Anglican faithful who desire to enter into the full communion of the Catholic Church in a corporate manner. This Constitution is completed by Complementary Norms issued by the Apostolic See.

I. §1 Personal Ordinariates for Anglicans entering into full communion with the Catholic Church are erected by the Congregation for the Doctrine of the Faith within the confines of the territorial boundaries of a particular Conference of Bishops in consultation with that same Conference.

§2 Within the territory of a particular Conference of Bishops, one or more Ordinariates may be erected as needed.

---

[10] Cf. CIC [Codex Iuris Canonici], can. 205; Dogmatic Constitution *Lumen gentium*, nos. 13, 14, 21, 22; Decree *Unitatis redintegratio*, nos. 2, 3, 4, 15, 20; Decree *Christus Dominus*, no. 4; Decree *Ad gentes*, no. 22.

[11] Dogmatic Constitution *Lumen gentium*, no. 8.

§3 Each Ordinariate possesses public juridic personality by the law itself (ipso iure); it is juridically comparable to a diocese.[12]

§4 The Ordinariate is composed of lay faithful, clerics and members of Institutes of Consecrated Life and Societies of Apostolic Life, originally belonging to the Anglican Communion and now in full communion with the Catholic Church, or those who receive the Sacraments of Initiation within the jurisdiction of the Ordinariate.

§5 The *Catechism of the Catholic Church* is the authoritative expression of the Catholic faith professed by members of the Ordinariate.

II. The Personal Ordinariate is governed according to the norms of universal law and the present Apostolic Constitution and is subject to the Congregation for the Doctrine of the Faith, and the other Dicasteries of the Roman Curia in accordance with their competencies. It is also governed by the Complementary Norms as well as any other specific Norms given for each Ordinariate.

III. Without excluding liturgical celebrations according to the Roman Rite, the Ordinariate has the faculty to celebrate the Holy Eucharist and the other Sacraments, the Liturgy of the Hours and other liturgical celebrations according to the liturgical books proper to the Anglican tradition, which have been approved by the Holy See, so as to maintain the liturgical, spiritual and pastoral traditions of the Anglican Communion within the Catholic Church, as a precious gift

---

[12] Cf. John Paul II, Apostolic Constitution *Spirituali militium curae* (April 21, 1986), I § 1.

nourishing the faith of the members of the Ordinariate and as a treasure to be shared.

IV. A Personal Ordinariate is entrusted to the pastoral care of an Ordinary appointed by the Roman Pontiff.

V. The power (*potestas*) of the Ordinary is:

a. *ordinary*: connected by the law itself to the office entrusted to him by the Roman Pontiff, for both the internal forum and external forum;

b. *vicarious*: exercised in the name of the Roman Pontiff;

c. *personal*: exercised over all who belong to the Ordinariate;

This power is *to be exercised jointly* with that of the local Diocesan Bishop, in those cases provided for in the Complementary Norms.

VI.   §1. Those who ministered as Anglican deacons, priests, or bishops, and who fulfil the requisites established by canon law[13] and are not impeded by irregularities or other impediments[14] may be accepted by the Ordinary as candidates for Holy Orders in the Catholic Church. In the case of married ministers, the norms established in the Encyclical Letter of Pope Paul VI *Sacerdotalis coelibatus*, n. 42[15] and in the Statement *In June*[16] are to be observed. Unmarried ministers must

[13] Cf. CIC, cann. 1026–32.
[14] Cf. CIC, cann. 1040–49.
[15] Cf. *AAS* 59 (1967): 674.
[16] Cf. Congregation for the Doctrine of the Faith, *Statement of 1 April 1981*, in *Enchiridion Vaticanum* 7: 1213.

submit to the norm of clerical celibacy of CIC can. 277, §1.

§2. The Ordinary, in full observance of the discipline of celibate clergy in the Latin Church, as a rule (*pro regula*) will admit only celibate men to the order of presbyter. He may also petition the Roman Pontiff, as a derogation from can. 277, §1, for the admission of married men to the order of presbyter on a case by case basis, according to objective criteria approved by the Holy See.

§3. Incardination of clerics will be regulated according to the norms of canon law.

§4. Priests incardinated into an Ordinariate, who constitute the presbyterate of the Ordinariate, are also to cultivate bonds of unity with the presbyterate of the Diocese in which they exercise their ministry. They should promote common pastoral and charitable initiatives and activities, which can be the object of agreements between the Ordinary and the local Diocesan Bishop.

§5. Candidates for Holy Orders in an Ordinariate should be prepared alongside other seminarians, especially in the areas of doctrinal and pastoral formation. In order to address the particular needs of seminarians of the Ordinariate and formation in Anglican patrimony, the Ordinary may also establish seminary programs or houses of formation which would relate to existing Catholic faculties of theology.

VII. The Ordinary, with the approval of the Holy See, can erect new Institutes of Consecrated Life and Societies of Apostolic Life, with the right to call their members to Holy Orders, according to the norms of canon law. Institutes of Consecrated Life originating in the Anglican Communion and entering into full communion with the Catholic Church may also be placed under his jurisdiction by mutual consent.

VIII. §1. The Ordinary, according to the norm of law, after having heard the opinion of the Diocesan Bishop of the place, may erect, with the consent of the Holy See, personal parishes for the faithful who belong to the Ordinariate.

§2. Pastors of the Ordinariate enjoy all the rights and are held to all the obligations established in the Code of Canon Law and, in cases established by the Complementary Norms, such rights and obligations are to be exercised in mutual pastoral assistance together with the pastors of the local Diocese where the personal parish of the Ordinariate has been established.

IX. Both the lay faithful as well as members of Institutes of Consecrated Life and Societies of Apostolic Life, originally part of the Anglican Communion, who wish to enter the Personal Ordinariate, must manifest this desire in writing.

X. §1. The Ordinary is aided in his governance by a Governing Council with its own statutes approved by the Ordinary and confirmed by the Holy See.[17]

---

[17] Cf. CIC, cann. 495–502.

§2. The Governing Council, presided over by the Ordinary, is composed of at least six priests. It exercises the functions specified in the Code of Canon Law for the Presbyteral Council and the College of Consultors, as well as those areas specified in the Complementary Norms.

§3. The Ordinary is to establish a Finance Council according to the norms established by the Code of Canon Law which will exercise the duties specified therein.[18]

§4. In order to provide for the consultation of the faithful, a Pastoral Council is to be constituted in the Ordinariate.[19]

XI. Every five years the Ordinary is required to come to Rome for an *ad limina Apostolorum* visit and present to the Roman Pontiff, through the Congregation for the Doctrine of the Faith and in consultation with the Congregation for Bishops and the Congregation for the Evangelization of Peoples, a report on the status of the Ordinariate.

XII. For judicial cases, the competent tribunal is that of the Diocese in which one of the parties is domiciled, unless the Ordinariate has constituted its own tribunal, in which case the tribunal of second instance is the one designated by the Ordinariate and approved by the Holy See. In both cases, the different titles of competence established by the Code of Canon Law are to be taken into account.[20]

[18] Cf. CIC, cann. 492–94.
[19] Cf. CIC, can. 511.
[20] Cf. CIC, cann. 1410–14 and 1673.

XIII. The Decree establishing an Ordinariate will
determine the location of the See and, if appropriate, the principal church.

We desire that our dispositions and norms be valid and effective now and in the future, notwithstanding, should it be
necessary, the Apostolic Constitutions and ordinances issued
by our predecessors, or any other prescriptions, even those
requiring special mention or derogation.

*Given in Rome, at St. Peter's, on November 4, 2009, the Memo-
rial of St. Charles Borromeo.*

BENEDICTUS PP. XVI

INDEX

243